Lovett's Lights on REVELATION

ABOUT THE AUTHOR

DR. C. S. LOVETT

Dr. Lovett is the president of **Personal Christianity Chapel,** a fundamental, evangelical interdenominational ministry. For the past 41 years he has had but one objective—**preparing Christians for the second coming of Christ!** This book is one of over 40 of his works designed to help believers **prepare for His appearing.**

Dr. Lovett's decision to serve the Lord resulted in the loss of a sizable personal fortune. He is well equipped for the job the Lord has given him. A graduate of American Baptist Seminary of the West, he holds the **M.A.** and **M.Div.** degrees conferred *Magna Cum Laude.* He has also completed graduate work in psychology at Los Angeles State College and holds a **Ph.D.** in counseling from the Louisiana Christian University.

A retired Air Force Chaplain (Lt. Colonel), he has been married to Marjorie for 50 years and has two grown daughters dedicated to the Lord.

Lovett's Lights on REVELATION

by C. S. Lovett

M.A., M.Div., Ph.D.

President of Personal Christianity

author of:

Dealing With The Devil
Witnessing Made Easy
Latest Word On The Last Days
"Help Lord—The Devil Wants Me Fat!"
Longing To Be Loved

published by:

PERSONAL CHRISTIANITY

Box 549

Baldwin Park, California 91706-0549

ISBN 0-938-148-44-3
1992 edition

PRINTED IN THE UNITED STATES OF AMERICA

"WHO HAS ALL THE TRUTH?"

Many books have been written on the Revelation by honest, scholarly men all expressing different opinions. That's because the Revelation abounds with mysteries and symbols and men handle them within their own frames of reference. Add to that our differing backgrounds, prejudices and education and it's no wonder there are such wide ranges of opinion. For this reason, no one should categorically say he has the final word. Yet, an author can honestly say, *"This is how the Lord has led me to understand the Revelation."*

In this book, I am setting forth what I feel the Lord has given me. Will I be wrong on some points? Probably. And my views may change some as the Lord gives me more light. If you disagree with me on certain things, ask the Holy Spirit to counsel me. I've determined not to allow prejudices to keep me from being responsive to Him.

Aware that none of us completely sheds his predisposition to long held ideas, some of my leanings are bound to show up. Even if the Holy Spirit were to give us *perfect insight* into these mysteries, we'd quickly corrupt them with our imperfect minds and fallen natures. It is to God's glory that He can get anything approaching the truth through His servants...but somehow He does, praise His name. For that reason I ask the Holy Spirit to escort you through this book, pointing out those things that will profit you most.

C.S. Lovett

WHAT YOU'LL FIND AS YOU READ

The truths of this book are exposed in 3 ways.

1. REPHRASED TEXT. "Lovett's Lights" is NOT a translation. It is a paraphrase. Where two or three words are needed to bring forward the meaning from the original language, a paraphrase gives one that liberty. You cannot do that with a strict translation. With translators restricted to English equivalents for the Greek, they often find NO WAY to express what the Holy Spirit is trying to say, because the Greek language is far more flexible than English. A paraphrase allows you to use as many words as necessary to make the meaning clear.

2. THE LIGHTS. After every few verses of text, you will come upon a paragraph set in different type face, indented and identified with the LAMP symbol. These are the "LIGHTS." Their purpose is to reveal in as few words as possible the hidden meanings and show how they relate to other great truths of the Bible. Background information such as customs of the time and the way certain words were used in Bible times, are included where they provide a key to interpretation.

3. QUESTIONS AND STATEMENTS. You will encounter questions and statements scattered strategically throughout the book. These are intended to keep the author's burden in view. This helps you evaluate what you are reading in the light of what the author seeks to communicate.

See the old man contemplating? That's the apostle John. He's on an island, well actually it is a Roman penal colony for political prisoners. It was while a prisoner on this Island of Patmos that John wrote the Revelation. How he got there and why is a unique working of the Lord. Understanding this, should help you understand the book.

It was a time of trouble for the 90 year old apostle. According to most scholars, John was banished to the Island of Patmos toward the end of the reign of Domitian. Domitian Caesar died A.D. 97 and his reign was every bit as brutal as that of Nero. The church suffered terribly under this emperor.

It is recorded that whenever Domitian would come into a public place, he had the heralds announce him as *"Our Lord and God Domitian!"* Every year, during his reign, citizens of the empire had to appear before public officials, burn incense to the emperor while confessing,

"Caesar is Lord." Anyone refusing to do so, was regarded as an enemy and immediately became a political prisoner.

The dedicated Christians of course, refused to do this. History reports they would say, *"Jesus is Lord and there is no other."* This cost them the loss of their property and civil rights, and more often than not, their lives. When it was John's turn to burn incense and make his confession, he refused, and it earned him a prepaid trip to the Island of Patmos. This rocky, barren island 40 miles off the coast of Asia Minor was roughly 10 miles long and 6 miles wide.

ALL EARLIER REVELATION WAS INCOMPLETE

"I will come again! I shall return!"

Those are probably the most comforting words of the Lord Jesus.

BUT WHEN? The answer to that question has puzzled believers down through the ages. With the years starting to roll by and no sign of Jesus' return, the early saints were scratching their heads. The Lord had spelled out the signs by which they could know the time of His return was getting close. But it wasn't enough.

Something more was needed. The prophetic details supplied by the Old Testament were far from complete. What was needed was some sort of overview that would tie up the prophetic package; something that would give a detailed picture of the last days.

Sixty years after the Lord ascended to heaven, He got in touch with John and revealed to him the missing pieces of the prophecy puzzle. On the Island of Patmos, the Lord had John all to Himself, something that might have been impossible otherwise. By means of visions and angels, Jesus told him what to write. Once the work was finished, the book of Revelation was ready for God's people.

BUT THE VISIONS CREATED A PROBLEM

The island guards knew John was writing. And John knew the soldiers would be looking for subversive ideas in his writings. Anything he wanted to send to the churches on the mainland was sure to be inspected. To speak openly against the Roman government or write about its destruction, would be regarded as seditious. He didn't dare express his thoughts in plain language. This meant everything had to be in code. At the same time, the code would have to be familiar to the believers.

John wrote down what was given to him, but he clothed the truths in the symbols of Daniel, Ezekiel, and Zechariah. Would that work? Sure. Those prophets themselves had written under similar circumstances and John's readers knew their codes. This way, when the Roman soldiers examined his writings, they made no sense to them. They viewed them as the writings of a madman. Their attitude was, *"If anyone wants to read this nonsense, let them."* That's how John was able to get his book off the island and to the churches on the mainland.

Even though the letter is addressed directly to 7 specific churches in Asia, we'll find that collectively, those seven churches represent the whole church as it has moved down through the centuries. What's more the truths are presented in such a way that the churches of every succeeding generation can feel the words were written for their time. Interestingly enough, the conditions that existed in those 7 churches can be found in many churches today. Yet, we must be careful to note that John mentions things that can only be applied to the generation on earth at the time of Jesus' return.

Inasmuch as John wrote his book in code, we have to accommodate ourselves to symbolic language. A good way to do that would be to read the books of Daniel, Ezekiel and Zechariah, to get some feel for the symbolism. John writes as did those prophets, so don't let it bother you when he uses animals and stars to represent people, or oceans to represent nations. Just understand it is all in code which will become clear as we move through the chapters. If you'll adopt this attitude, we'll have some fun making our way through the mysteries of...the Revelation!

READ THIS TO GET STARTED

"Sam, if you're going to tackle THE REVELATION, you need a strategy. And if you don't have one, get one. Otherwise you'll find yourself in a mess."

That was the counsel given by an old friend and teacher upon learning I was about to take up the Revelation. I knew what he meant. When you behold the sea of books written on the Revelation, you ask yourself, *"Why another?"* Believe me, I wouldn't consider it were it not for the Holy Spirit's insistence. A Bible teacher for forty years, I resisted the idea until His urging was so strong I had to yield. Besides, I did have a strategy in mind.

My strategy is based on two assumptions:

FIRST ASSUMPTION

God has marked out a 7000 year time frame for the human story. That is, from Genesis through the Revelation, 7000 years are allotted for man on the earth. Of those 7000 years, 4000 passed during the Old Testament period. 2000 years were designated for the church age, making a total of 6000 years. That last 1000 years are the millennium, the time of Jesus' personal reign over the earth.

THE BIBLICAL ACCOUNT OF MAN'S TESTING

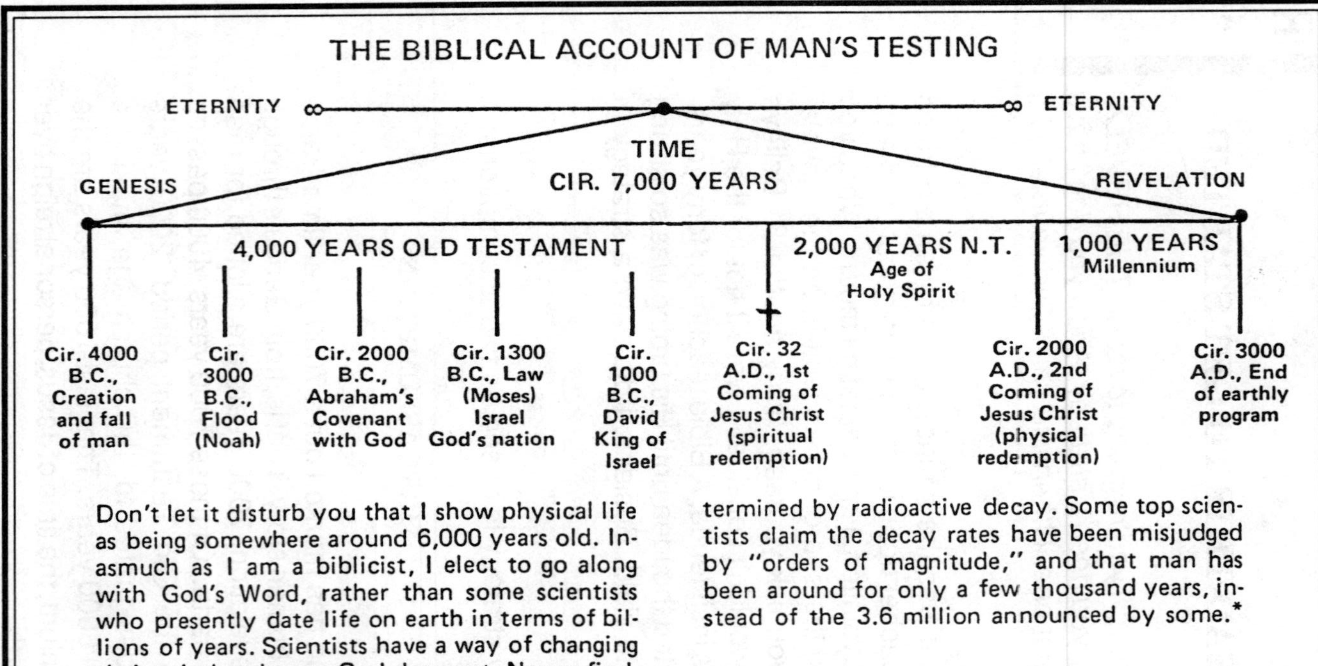

Don't let it disturb you that I show physical life as being somewhere around 6,000 years old. Inasmuch as I am a biblicist, I elect to go along with God's Word, rather than some scientists who presently date life on earth in terms of billions of years. Scientists have a way of changing their minds, whereas God does not. Newer findings are beginning to challenge those dates determined by radioactive decay. Some top scientists claim the decay rates have been misjudged by "orders of magnitude," and that man has been around for only a few thousand years, instead of the 3.6 million announced by some.*

*Dr. Robert Gentry, *Popular Science,* Nov. 1969

ETERNITY

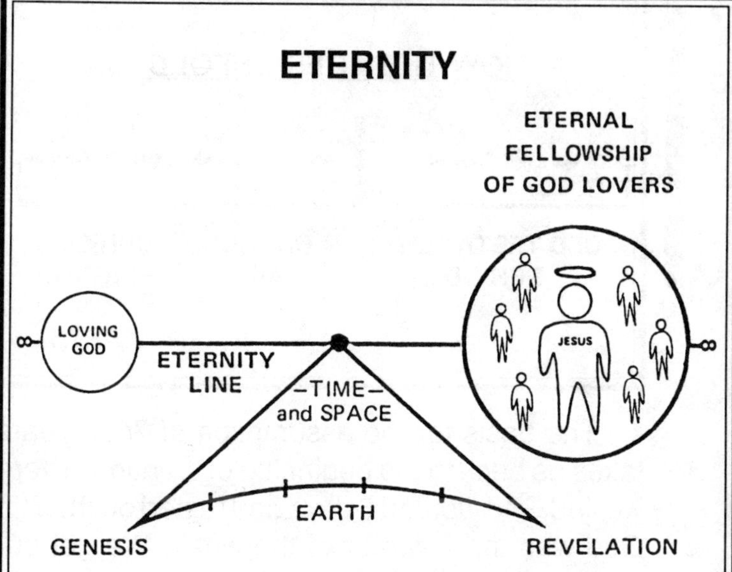

GOD'S EARTHLY PROGRAM

Behold again the drawing of God's eternal purpose. It holds the key to many verses. God has only one plan, eternal fellowship with those who love Him. Everything He does is consistent with that plan. God is NOT a loner. He wants people. He needs people. Why? What's the point of being a lover with no one to love? The purpose of **program earth** is to supply God with friends for eternity. Those who love Him are destined for that eternal fellowship. Those who don't are separated from Him eternally. The fact that God has already seen the "earthly movie," permits Him to make His choices in eternity. However, when He announces those choices to us before they happen, we are tempted to judge Him as being arbitrary. But it really isn't so. His choices are all governed by His eternal purpose, not by personal whim. He wishes He could have every man, but it is obvious the God-rejectors just don't FIT the plan. That's why Jacob was selected over Esau.

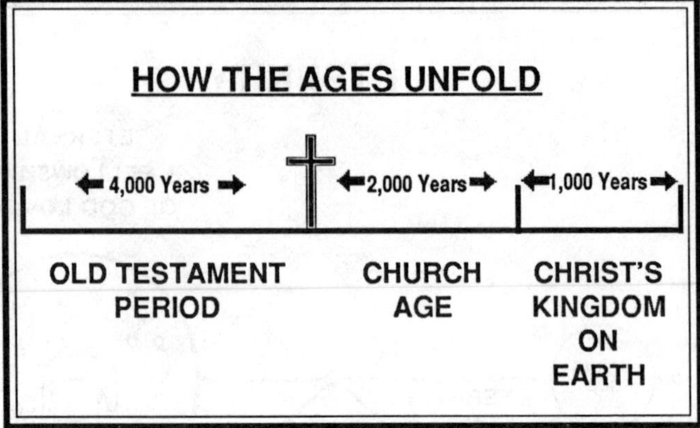

The basis for the assumption of 7000 years takes us back to the beginning of creation. There we find God worked 6 days and rested on the 7th. God was the inventor of the week. We get our days and months and years from the movements of heavenly bodies, but the week is *God's own idea.* In giving us the 7 day week, He also gave us the outline of the human story. Letting each day of the seven represent a 1000 years of time for man on the earth, we come up with a total of 7000 years. Scholars have attempted to establish this as a fact, but to me it remains an assumption. However, we can draw an inference from something the apostle Peter said:

> **"Beloved be not ignorant of this one thing, that one day with the Lord is as a thousand years, and a thousand years as one day" (2 Pet.3:8).**

On the basis of this assumption, some astonishing things must take place before the 6000 years end. We are in the final decade of those 6000 years right now—*if our calendars coincide at all with God's calendar—and we may be way off on that.* The one book of the Bible that reveals the most about the furious events due to occur near the end of this decade, if our assumption is correct, is the Revelation.

SECOND ASSUMPTION

John's Revelation is rooted in the book of Daniel. Around 530 B.C., Daniel saw the end-time events in visions and was instructed to write them down. But he didn't understand them, so he asked the angel speaking to him, *"My Lord, what will be the outcome of these things?"*

The angel replied,

> **"Go your way Daniel, for the words are to be kept secret and sealed until the time of the end" (Dan 12:9).**

Thus the exciting details were sealed until such a time as God would choose to reveal them. It was to the apostle John that God elected to remove the seals and reveal what was in Daniel's book. He commanded John to write down what he saw, the same as He commanded Daniel. So the Revelation exposes what Daniel was instructed to seal up a little over 2500 years ago.

NOTE: If you did not read the preface which explains how God got John on the Island of Patmos and why, then I should repeat that the Revelation is written in code. The code consists of SYMBOLISMS found in the books of Daniel, Ezekiel and Zechariah, which means we have to accommodate ourselves to symbolic language. If you'll scan Daniel, Ezekiel and Zechariah, you'll get some feeling for the symbolism. Without an idea of what they mean, you will be

baffled when John uses animals and stars to represent people, and oceans to represent nations. As we move through the chapters, I'll point out the codes. They will become clear as we move along.

NOT A NICE BOOK

The Revelation is not a very nice book. It's a book of judgments. There's not a smile in it. Why? *God is fed up.* His angry feelings are spread all over the pages of this book. What's more, He's not the only one who's upset. The devil is angry too. The world is obviously in for a rough time when both God and the devil are angry. The Revelation is addressed primarily to those about to endure the wrath of the antichrist, those living during the time of the beast and the Great Tribulation.

It opens with the Lord Jesus ordering John to write down *everything* he sees and send it to seven specific churches on the mainland. That is instructive, for the question is often raised as to how much tribulation the church will be called upon to endure before the Lord Jesus returns. When we realize *everything* in the book was written for those believers, we realize the answer is at hand, and that will become quite clear as we proceed through the book.

The Lord also gives John some personal words, memos actually, for each of the seven churches. He wants these included in John's book. While the memos are addressed to *churches* in general, the challenge to overcome is addressed to *individuals.* They are not promises to churches, they are challenges to believers.

"But what have these memos to do with us?"

Imagine you have gone to a house that is listed for sale, but when you get there you find it locked and no one around. What do you do? You go around the outside and look in the windows. In this way you get an idea of what the whole house is like.

In the same way, we will look at the church through the 7 memos dictated by the Lord and get an idea of what the whole church will be like when the Lord is ready to bring judgment on the world. As you read, don't try to separate the churches from the rest of the Revelation. It is a testimony to the genius of God that everything in the book is for those 7 churches...and for us. The entire work is a single volume.

KEYS THAT UNLOCK THE REVELATION

As you cannot enter a locked house without the key, neither can one unlock the mysteries of the Revelation without the keys. I'm going to give you 3 that I use for unlocking the book.

KEY #1. The difference between the Great Tribulation and God's wrath. These are two separate and different things. The Great Tribulation consists of Satan's wrath, the wrath of antichrist and the wrath of the beast. *The Day of the Lord* is God's wrath. While the church will go through the Great Tribulation, it will not suffer the wrath of God. The Lord Jesus bore God's wrath for us at Calvary.

KEY # 2. The 7 seals cover the whole book. Apart from the introductory vision of Christ and His memos to the 7 churches, as well as the prelude to opening the scroll in Chapters 4 & 5, everything revealed to John is laid bare with the breaking of the 7 seals. When the seventh seal is broken, 7 trumpets are before us. Ah, but that *doesn't remove* them from the 7th seal. THEY ARE THE 7TH SEAL. When we get to the 7th trumpet many things happen that also belong to the 7th seal, including the rapture, the pouring out of the 7 bowls of God's wrath and the return of the Lord. <u>It is important to understand that the 7th seal *totally unveils* the future</u>.

KEY #3. An old man is writing this book. While he gives us the full story, he interrupts himself from time to time, as different ideas occur to him. He'll be moving along in the narrative when it strikes him to go back and clear up something. As a result, we encounter a number of interruptions. Some commentators call them parentheses, but a number of them are clearly flashbacks. We'll encounter at least five such interruptions as we proceed through the book.

These keys will serve you well as you proceed through the book, particularly from Chapter 6 on. You can rely on them. They will unlock mystery after mystery for you. The Lord Jesus wants you to understand this book, because it will help you become serious about living for Him *and dying for Him*.

THE SIMPLEST OUTLINE OF THE BOOK

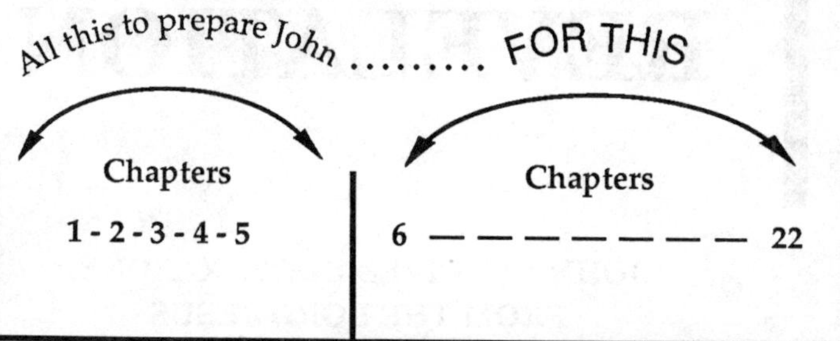

Here is the simplest outline of the book. The book opens with John beholding a vision of the Lord Jesus in which the Lord instructs him to write down what he sees and send it to 7 churches on the mainland. What he is going to see is so mind-boggling that he has to be prepared for it. Therefore the first 5 chapters of the book prepare John for what is going to be revealed to him. The remaining Chapters 6 to 22 contain the revelation he has been prepared to receive. Obviously this is an oversimplification, but it helps greatly to understand these two main divisions of the book.

REVELATION

JOHN RECEIVES INSTRUCTIONS FROM THE LORD JESUS

1 **1. This is the revelation of Jesus Christ, which God gave Him that He might show His servants those things which must soon come to pass. And He sent His angel to make it known to His servant John. 2. In reporting what he saw, John bears witness to the word of God and the testimony of Jesus.**

REVELATION. The revelation which God gave to Jesus to pass on to John, is a "movie," a movie God has already seen. In fact, the whole human story, the story of man on the earth, has been played out from first to last, in the mind of God. And He gave Jesus a video cassette of the last days. That video is this book, called "The Revelation." The hero of this video is the Lord Jesus Himself. The grand event is Jesus' return to the earth—as a MAN. He left this earth a DISGRACED man, but He'll be returning to earth as a GLORIFIED man. Even at this moment, the Lord Jesus is..."The *MAN* Christ Jesus"

(1 Tim. 2:5). We will see that Jesus, though now glorified, is still in the *role* of the Son. And He will continue in this role until the human story is completed and eternity begins for the family of God in heaven.

SHOW. But how did Jesus arrange for John to see the video? We glance ahead to verse 10 for the answer. There John tells us he was "in the spirit on the Lord's day." Being "in the spirit," suggests something similar to what the apostle Paul experienced when he was "caught up" to the third heaven and saw things that were inexpressible (2 Cor. 12:2). By way of visions, John found himself in the realm of the spirit able to behold scenes yet to take place. That's the beauty of a heavenly video. John's mind became a television screen on which the Lord Jesus played the video. What John saw, he was told to write down and send to the 7 churches on the mainland. As the video played through his mind (via visions), a double challenge confronted him. Not only must he explain his visions in the language of his day (not our day), but he had to get his manuscript past the guards and off the island. This required him to use the code of the Old Testament prophets. But that was OK, since his readers were familiar with the Old Testament writings. This accounts for the strangeness of the book. Anyone trying to read it today, *without knowing the code,* finds it strange, almost senseless.

COMMENT: John doesn't use the word VISION here, but later on he will. Throughout the book, John will be shown many things all of which will come to him by way of visions. Normally men behold things via the eye gate. That is, the eyes pick up patches of light and dark and send them to the brain as electrical impulses. Similarly sounds strike the eardrum and those impulses travel to the brain. The brain, which is a computer, translates all these impulses into images and then displays them on the imagination screen. This is how we all see. But God is not locked into our clumsy process. He can send images directly to the screen of the mind. When He does, we call it a vision. A vision is no less real than if we had actually studied the event with our eyes. You and I cannot distinguish between data that arrives in our minds via the 5 senses and that which God imparts directly.

SOON COME TO PASS. This is the last prophecy of the word of God, the last word from heaven. Yet even this last word doesn't tell us everything. We won't hear any more from heaven until a trumpet blast shatters the silence of 2000 years. When that happens, the archangel's voice will announce the arrival of the Lord. That's the next word we're going hear from heaven, the voice of the archangel. John says it will come to pass SOON. But how should we understand this? Certainly not in the sense of a clock. More likely he means in the sense of the next event—God's judgments and wrath. They are soon in *sequence*, but not soon *in time*.

3. Blessed is the one who reads aloud the words of this prophecy and all who hear the words and take them to heart, because the time is really close.

BLESSED. Three kinds of people are mentioned here with blessing for all three. Not too many could read in those days. Those who could, would be blessed if they read the words aloud to those who couldn't. Those who couldn't read were blessed simply by hearing the words. This was because of the comfort it brought to learn that Jesus was still alive and in control of things. Then there were those who heard and understood what John was saying and purposed to be overcomers just to please the Lord. Obviously the greater blessing is theirs.

4. Thus John, in writing to the seven churches in the province of Asia, says grace and peace be yours, from Him Who is and was and Who is yet to come, and from the seven spirits before the throne; 5. and from Jesus Christ, the faithful witness, the first born of the risen dead and the ruler of the kings of the earth. Having proved His love for us by cleansing us from our sins with His own blood, 6. He has made us a royal family of priests to serve His God and Father. To Him be the glory and power forever. Amen.

SEVEN CHURCHES. The 7 churches of Asia were all located in Asia Minor, the western half of modern Turkey, with the church at Ephesus serving as the home church. John was likely arrested at Ephesus where, as the last apostle, he served as the principal leader of the church. We are not to suppose his letter is by any means limited to these seven churches, but rather see them as representative of the total church as it moved from John's day to ours. Because his message is prophetic, it may be more for us than it was was for them. That only seven churches are named is consistent with the rest of the Lord's sevens in this book. The seven spirits also send their greetings to the churches. Who are they? If angels, they are no doubt connected with the 7 churches. With the 7 churches about to be challenged by what lies ahead, these are probably the same 7 angels involved in the judgments of God (8:2). To suggest the 7 spirits represent a sevenfold work of the Holy Spirit doesn't harmonize with sending greetings to the churches. What's more, the Spirit's work is more than sevenfold.

FROM JESUS CHRIST. While John is the messenger, it is Jesus' message. The Lord Jesus is described as the *faithful witness.* Thus we can expect Him to be totally honest in revealing what is about to come upon the church. *Firstborn* refers to His rank and supreme place in the church. *Ruler of kings,* proclaims His authority and sovereignty. Those due to suffer for Him in the dark days ahead, will be comforted by the fact that He is alive and in control. Surely those words comforted the frustrated apostle cooling his heels on that barren island.

FAMILY. God is a family man. While the church is pictured in scripture as a

1.) body, Eph. 1:22,23.

2.) a building, 1 Pet. 2:5.
3.) a bride, 2 Cor. 11:2
4.) a city, Rev. 21:2
5.) a family, Eph. 3:15

the one thing God desires more than anything else, is fellowship with His own family (1 John 1:3). The real purpose of Jesus' sacrifice was to secure for God an eternal family. By His blood, the Lord redeemed a bride for Himself and a family for His Father. Without a family, God is incomplete. There is no point in owning all of heaven without someone to share it with. Obviously then, Jesus' work remains unfinished until the whole family has been gathered unto God.

7. Behold! He comes with clouds and every eye will see Him, including those who pierced Him; and His coming will bring tremendous grief to all the peoples of the earth. So it will be. Amen.

BEHOLD. The word "*behold*" may seem old fashioned to some, but it fits this event beautifully. The whole world will behold Jesus when He returns with "*ALL of His saints*" (1 Thess. 3:13). His coming will be like *lightning* flashing from East to West, dazzling, even blinding against a darkened sky (Matt. 24:27; Luke 21:27). There will be clouds, but a closer look reveals the CLOUD IS A CROWD. The sign of the Son of Man is a cloud, a cloud of people (Matt. 24:30). This cloud can be identified with the cloud of witnesses in Heb. 12:1. Morning, noon and night, around the globe people will see Him in the sky! (Luke 17:34-36; Matt. 24:40,41). Everyone on earth will see Him, for He's going to be in the sky for a time, days even, perhaps weeks. You and I won't behold Him from the earth for we'll be with Him in the sky, caught off the earth to join Him in the "twinkling of an eye!" at the last trumpet (1 Cor. 15:52). The moment the last trumpet sounds, we're out of here.

GRIEF. The bulk of mankind has no interest in Jesus. It's as He said . . . *"Narrow is the way that leads to life and FEW there be that find it"* (Matt. 7:14). The world was happy to see Jesus go and will be sick at the sight of His return. They have happily sung "Joy to the World," every Christmas until now, but His appearance in the sky will generate worldwide grief and groaning and wailing. This will be especially true of those who pierced Him (the Jews), when they realize they crucified their own Messiah. With judgment already falling, the sight of Jesus in the sky announces even worse judgment for those who reject Him. The kings of the earth will frantically assemble at Armageddon to resist His return, determined to "*head Him off at the pass*" (Rev.16:13,14,16; 19:15). The slaughter will be astonishing (Rev. 14:20). But nothing can prevent it from happening. That is the force of *"So it will be."*

8. "I am the Alpha and the Omega," says the Lord God, "Who is, Who was, and Who is yet to come, the Almighty!"

ALPHA AND OMEGA. It's almost as if the Lord Jesus interrupts John to speak for Himself—and what a claim He makes! In effect He is saying, "I am Jehovah of the Old Testament! The God of Abraham, Isaac and Jacob." Thus He proclaims Himself to be the eternal God, the Almighty! (This is the El Shaddai of the Old Testament). At the same time, He calls Himself the Alpha and Omega (the first and last letters of the Greek alphabet), meaning: He is the beginning and the end. Ah, but eternity has NO beginning or ending, no Alpha nor Omega. In eternity there is no such thing as is and was and is yet to come. Only TIME can have past, present and future tenses. Thus He is saying, "I am the eternal God operating inside time and space —as a MAN!"

9. I John, your brother and a partaker with you in the suffering and kingdom and perseverance which are in Jesus, was on the island that is called Patmos. I was there because I had preached God's word and the truth about Jesus.

PARTAKER. John writes to the 7 churches as one familiar with their suffering. He is experiencing the same things himself. Under the emperor Domitian, believers faced grinding persecution and tribulation. John is saying, *"We're all in the same boat. But the boat isn't all that bad, because we're also in the kingdom through our faith in Jesus. We all have the same blessed future*

<u>*awaiting us, therefore we can endure to the end no matter how tough it gets."*</u> Early church leaders tell us John was arrested because the authorities felt his preaching was seditious. They banished him to this island in an attempt to hinder the growth of the church. Obviously, however, his exile was part of God's plan that he might receive this wonderful revelation of the future.

10. I found myself in the spirit on the Lord's day. And I heard a voice behind me like that of a loud, clear trumpet call. 11. The voice said to me, "Write on a scroll all that you see and send it to the seven churches in Asia: to Ephesus, to Smyrna, to Pergamum, to Thyatira, to Sardis, to Philadelphia, and to Laodicea."

IN THE SPIRIT. John was enjoying the presence of the Lord in a way normal for believers, when something happened. He was carried forward by the Holy Spirit some 1900 years into the future to behold the terrible judgments of the *"Day of the Lord."* This is what he was told to write down. Thus he introduces us to the <u>central theme</u> of his book...THE DAY OF THE LORD! He is *not* saying he was filled with the Spirit on a Sunday morning. He was enabled by the Spirit to see end-time events unfold before his eyes. Satan did this with Jesus. He took Him to a high place and *"showed Him all the kingdoms of the world in a moment of time"* (Luke 4:5). If Satan could do that with Jesus, then Jesus could certainly show John the last days of man on the earth. This is why the "Day of the Lord," is the theme of the book.

NOTE: It's true Sunday was picked by the early church as the day of worship. After all, the Lord rose on Sunday. His first meetings with His disciples were on Sunday. And Pentecost, the birthday of the church, occurred on Sunday. But it wasn't called the "Lord's day"—till a later time. The setting aside of one day a week was common practice in the Roman Empire. They did it to honor the emperor by marking the day he ascended his throne. They called it—"the Lord's day." John's use of the term is based on the Roman custom. When he says, "the Lord's day," he is looking forward to the day when Jesus is enthroned as the "King of kings. "

A VOICE. John doesn't recognize the voice he hears. That's to be expected, for when he turns around, he will be staring into the eyes of the glorified Christ. He will be stunned and overwhelmed by what he sees. Yet, John was somewhat prepared for this. He saw the Lord transfigured atop the mount when Moses and Elijah appeared there with Him (Matt. 17:2). Apparently the transfiguration scene, as glorious as it was, is here overshadowed by the glory confronting the old apostle. It is the voice of the King of kings commanding him to write down all that he sees and send it to the seven churches. We will be meeting each of those churches in the next two chapters.

WHAT DID JOHN DO WHEN HE HEARD THE VOICE?

12. I turned around to see whose voice was speaking to me; and as I turned, I saw seven lampstands of gold. 13. In the midst of these

golden stands, I beheld a person like a son of man. He was clothed in a robe that came to His feet and was girded about His chest with a golden sash. 14. His hair was as white as wool, snow-white wool and His eyes blazed like fire. 15. His feet were like bronze still glowing after being in a furnace, and His voice was like the roar of a great waterfall. 16. In His right hand were seven stars and from His mouth came a sharp two-edged sword. His face was like the sun when it shines at full brilliance.

I SAW. On hearing this great voice behind him, John turns about to see a human being, a MAN. The MAN is standing encircled by seven golden lampstands. From verse 20 we learn these lampstands represent the seven churches due to receive this book. But the MAN in the midst is <u>*"like a son of man."*</u> Here we need the code. For this we turn to the Old Testament where the prophet Daniel was given a similar vision: *"I saw in the night visions, and behold, with the clouds of heaven, there came one like a son of man"* (Dan. 7:13-14). The same "son of man" Daniel saw, was now in front of John. But John has never seen a man like this man;

a man whose face matched the brilliance of the sun; a man whose face blinded Saul on the Damascus Road.This is Jesus appearing in the glory that was His before His incarnation (John 17:5).

THE MAN. John reels at the sight of this man. He doesn't recognize Him, obviously. His long robe, made of fine twined linen and intricately embroidered, indicated royalty, while the sash that gathered His robe was made of interwoven gold. The whiteness of His hair is significant, but again we need the code to see why. In Daniel 7:9 the "Ancient of Days," (clearly God Himself) is described as having hair *"white as snow."* That description in Daniel is now transferred to the exalted Christ. But look at Jesus' eyes. This is not the meek, humble, gentle Jesus who preached the gospel of peace. These eyes blaze with anger. His feet, visible just below His long robe confirm this. Those feet will tread the wine press of the fury of God's wrath, and they still glow from their time in the furnace of His suffering. And His voice, far from being soothing and comforting, is a roar that shakes the earth, heralding judgment on all who hate Him. This is someone who is enraged.

STARS AND SWORD. It would be hard for anyone to believe this Man and the lowly Carpenter/Rabbi of Galilee were the same. We're seeing a picture of a Lord who is fed up with rebellious man. Yes, and even with trifling, lukewarm Christians. God is patient—patience personified—but there's a limit to how much He'll take. We're seeing the other side of Jesus. This is the indignant, outraged, furious Christ ready to deal with man on the earth. And will His dealing include the church? Absolutely. That's why the next 2 chapters are in the book of Revelation. *"Judgment must begin with the house of God"* (1 Pet. 4:17). That is also why the churches are addressed (and warned) before the Lord moves on to anything else. He has some strong words for the churches. That's what the "*sword*" is all about. While the two-edged sword was the most effective weapon of the day, Jesus is not talking about swords, but about *WORDS.* God's most effective weapon is His word. He speaks and light appears. He speaks anything and it's done. He does all things *"By the word of His power"* (Heb.1:3). Nothing can resist that power. If He chooses, He can speak and the armies of His enemies will slaughter each other. This is likely what happens when the armies of the beast march against Jerusalem.

HOW DID JOHN RESPOND TO THIS REVELATION OF JESUS?

17. When I saw Him, I fell at His feet as though dead. But He graciously laid His right hand on me and said, "Don't be afraid, I am the First and the Last, 18. and I am the living One. I was dead, but now, as you can see, I am alive for evermore. And beyond that, I hold the keys of death and Hades."

FELL AS THOUGH DEAD. The sight is overwhelming. The voice is overwhelming. The apostle Paul probably fell off his horse when he encountered the brightness of Jesus and found himself on the ground. Now John lies crumpled at His feet, *something that didn't happen at the transfiguration.* Ezekiel fell (Ezek.1:28), so did Daniel (Dan. 8:17). No wonder men will beg the mountains to fall on them and hide them *"from the face of Him Who sits on the throne!"* (Rev. 6:16). When they see Jesus in the sky, God's anger against sinful man will reach its climax. It is showing in His eyes and His voice in this revelation. After all, He is a "consuming fire" (Heb.12:29).

COMMENT: In spite of His visible anger, the Lord moderates His fury to comfort His prostrate servant. Placing His right hand on John, He speaks words the apostle had heard before...*"Fear not."* That sounds familiar. Jesus assures John He is the same One he walked with for those three and one half years, the One Who had died, but is now alive. That should do it. The *"one whom Jesus loved"* now realizes he has nothing to fear from this awesome figure, Who is none other than his own dear Savior and friend.

WILL THE LORD EXPLAIN THE LAMPSTANDS AND STARS?

19. "Write down therefore, what you see—that is, what is occurring right now, and what will take place hereafter. 20. As for the meaning of the seven stars which you saw in my right hand and the seven golden lampstands: the seven stars are the angels of the seven churches, and the seven lamps are the seven churches themselves."

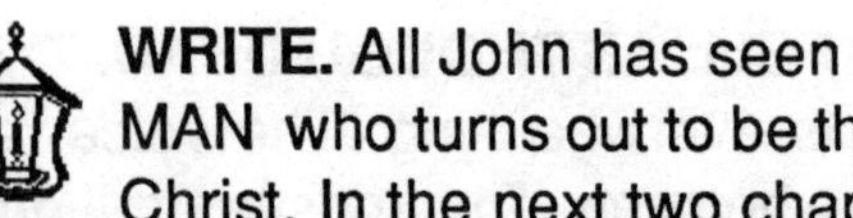

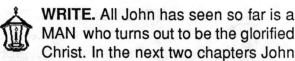

WRITE. All John has seen so far is a MAN who turns out to be the glorified Christ. In the next two chapters John will be given specific words for the churches. He will write separate letters to each of the churches, charging the pastors to see that they are read to the congregations. Now that we have seen the Lord's angry mood, we might well wonder what He'll say to those seven churches. It may not be all that nice. As noted before, this is not a nice book. But praise God we have it. When you have laid hold of it, you'll realize you have been given a chance to prepare yourself for what lies ahead. With the right preparation, you will be able to *"endure to the end"* (Matt. 24:13).

THE CHURCHES

The next two chapters contain the challenges John was to send to the seven churches. Some authors devote a third or more of their commentaries to discussions on the seven churches, developing all kinds of lessons and background information. With such an abundance of material available, I'm reluctant to add any more. Consequently, I will be brief in discussing the messages. True they are referred to as letters, but in reality they are short challenges.

This could lead someone to ask,

"Why would the Lord include messages to churches in a book filled with judgments? And why start the book with these messages to the churches?"

The Revised English Version gives the apostle Peter's answer:

"*The time has come for the judgment to begin: it is beginning with God's own household. And if it is starting with us, how will it end for those who refuse to obey the gospel of God?*" (1 Pet. 4:17)

It is the way of the Lord to deal with His own before sending judgment on others. Why these messages to the churches? To warn them. To give them time to "clean up their act." He wants them ready for the testings ahead and these challenges are meant to impress upon them the need for patient endurance in the coming persecutions.

ABOUT THOSE SEVEN CHURCHES

Two are really good, and two are really bad. Three are a mix of good and bad. They line up like this:

1. **EPHESUS:** the first named, had lots of good works to its credit. It was sound doctrinally, but had cooled toward Jesus, having forsaken *intimacy* with Him. It was working FOR Him, rather than WITH Him.

2. **SMYRNA:** was a good church. So good, in fact, the Lord had not one complaint against it. But that's to be expected, since it was severely persecuted. *Persecution* always refines God's people. However, they still need counsel concerning the greater persecutions yet to come.

3. **PERGAMUM:** called Pergamus in the KJV, this church, while faithful to Jesus, *compromised* its convictions. Eager to get along in this world, it compromised with evil for the sake of comfort and survival.

4. **THYATIRA:** a busy church, doing a lot for Jesus. Actually she was growing. But she *tolerated false teaching* in her midst; a teacher who taught that sexual immorality and idolatry for business reasons was covered by grace. This church is severly reprimanded.

5. **SARDIS:** is a rich church, a phony church, a bad church. It pretends to be spiritual, but is *deader than a doornail.* It is deeply involved in paganistic practices. The Lord has nothing good to say about it. However, some in the church are genuine. A small remnant is walking with Jesus and will be OK as long as they remain overcomers.

6. **PHILADELPHIA:** like Smyrna, is a good church receiving praise from the Lord. Since this church has *stood firm under testing*, the Lord promises to keep this church from the dreadful hour of God's wrath due to come upon the world.

7. **LAODICEA:** the other really bad church. It's *lukewarmness* makes the Lord want to throw up. A wealthy, smug church, it felt it could handle things without any help from the Lord. Blind to its sick condition, the Lord tells them to get on track or get out!

We find all seven of these churches today, with each church a window for us to look through and get a picture of the universal church; a church headed for rough times. Eager to prepare His church for tribulation, the Lord tells His people what they must become in order to be ready—*overcomers.*

REVELATION 2

MESSAGES TO THE SEVEN CHURCHES

As the head of the church, the Lord has every right to tell His people what is wrong with them and what they should do about it. And the more so, when He knows their weaknesses will cripple them when they encounter the severe persecutions ahead. It is a kindness to alert them to their faults while they still have time to overcome them. As overcomers, they will be able to endure the awful tribulations coming their way. In effect, the Lord is putting them on notice that they must be ready for what is coming or they won't survive.

EPHESUS: A sound, successful church with a serious fault.

Ephesus was the mother church of the other churches in Asia Minor. It was the largest city of the province through which all traffic heading East from Greece, Rome, Italy and Spain passed. On his third missionary journey, the apostle Paul established a seminary in Ephesus, teaching there for more than two years. From this school, trainees fanned out all over the province to start other churches. With this city such a mix of religion, idolatry and immorality, it was tough to maintain doctrinal purity. What's more, the church was plagued with those claiming to be apostles. After building a following, these false teachers would exploit their followers for personal advantage. Observe that each message is marked with some identifying feature of the glorified Christ as He appeared to John.

2 **1. “To the angel of the church at Ephesus write: The One Who holds the seven stars in His right hand and walks among the seven golden lampstands, says this to you: 2. I know all that you are doing, your hard work and your perseverance. I know you cannot tolerate wicked men and you have put to the test those who claim to be apostles, but are not, and you have found them to be false. 3. Not only that, you have persevered. And all these hardships you have had to endure for My name have not left you weary.”**

STARS. Note how the Lord identifies Himself with the seven stars and the lampstands. He is asserting His right to speak bluntly. Ephesus was one place where it would be hard to maintain biblical and personal purity. It was the trade center and market place of that part of the world. What's more, its temple to the sex goddess Artemis (Diana) was one of the seven wonders of the world. Satan had plenty to use in luring Christians into idolatry and immorality, but the Ephesian church resisted it all. This church separated itself from the world, truly a praiseworthy church, on the surface at least.

4. “But, there is one charge I make against you: that wonderful love you had at the first, you have now lost. 5. Consider how far you have fallen—and repent! Go back to the way your were. If you don't, I will come and remove your lampstand from its place. 6. Yet, you have this to your credit: you hate the detestable ways of the Nicolaitans, even as I do.”

ONE CHARGE. Until the Lord states His charge, one would think this church was perfect. But there is a major flaw. Equating being busy and successful with spirituality, they substituted works for love. Instead of working WITH the Lord, they were working FOR the Lord, leaving Jesus out. This is a serious accusation. Christianity is essentially a fellowship. The Lord *needs intimacy* with His people and it hurts when a "successful" church excludes Him. The Lord won't ignore this. He promises to put them "out of business" if they don't repent of this.

NICOLAITANS. After a stinging accusation of this church's sin, the Lord adds a comforting word of praise. He says, in effect, *"At least you hate the Nicolaitans as much as I do."* We're going to meet these Nicolaitans again in the Pergamum and Thyatira churches. The Nicolaitans professed to know Jesus, but taught that believers had a right to participate in immoral heathen practices. With the blood of Christ covering all sin, they preached lawlessness as a proper way of life. The Lord hates that teaching and applauds the vigorous stand the leaders of the Ephesian church had taken against it.

7. "You who have ears, listen to the message the Spirit has for the churches! To him who overcomes, I will give the right to eat of the tree of life that stands in the garden of God!"

EARS. Notice how each message ends with an exhortation to listen for the voice of the Spirit. The messages to the churches were written on the pages of a book, but a book is *outside the believer.* By itself, it is powerless. The message must be accompanied by the witness of the Spirit, which is Christ's own Spirit dwelling within the believer. It is the Spirit's task to validate what we hear and read. He speaks that witness *to our hearts.* To overcome, means to listen to (heed) the voice of the Spirit and do what He says. The right to eat of "the tree of life" symbolizes our entrance into that fellowship with God that existed before sin came into the world via the garden of Eden.

SMYRNA: A suffering church with no faults.

As the number one city of Asia, Smryna was absolutely loyal to Rome. Located 35 miles North of Ephesus, it was the first to build a temple to Rome. Its citizens joyfully proclaimed ..."Caesar is Lord!" Here was a city ready to smash the church out of existence. With rich trade flowing through its natural port on the Aegean sea, lots of Jews lived there. Caught between the popular loyalty to Rome and the hostile Jewish population, it was hard for believers to live the Christian life. Polycarp, A.D. 135, the most famous martyr of the early church fathers, was burned alive here for his refusal to acknowledge Caesar as Lord. It was viewed as treason to refuse the emperor this honor and execution was the usual sentence.

8. "To the angel at the church of Smyrna write: These are the words of the First and the Last, Who was dead and came to life again: 9. I know how hard pressed you are, and how

poor, but the truth is you are rich. I also know how you have been slandered by those who say they are Jews, but are not. What they really are is a synagogue of Satan."

HARD PRESSED. Note again how the Lord identifies Himself by taking some feature of the initial description in Chapter One. He selects "was dead and came to life again," because the Smyrnan Christians were facing death themselves. Later He will say that faithfulness unto death earns a special reward (14:13). As He rose never to die again, so will they. Aware these believers are being slandered by an extremely hostile Jewish population, the Lord denies such Jews are for real. He sees them as servants of Satan, doing the devil's work in Smyrna. Subjected to violence and poverty, the Smyrnans were economically destitute, but ever so rich spiritually.

10. "Do not be afraid of the sufferings that are to come upon you. Be advised the devil is going to put some of you in prison to test your faith there. For ten days you will be sorely tried, but be faithful even to the point of death and I will give you the crown of life."

TEN DAYS. Jesus advises the Smyrnan Christians that a time of intense suffering lies ahead. They needed to know this, so when they see it coming, they will understand it is part of God's plan for them. Prison in Smyrna usually meant death. The Lord uses the symbolic term "*ten days,*" to indicate the period of suffering will be short, but very crushing. Yet they are to continue to stand up for Jesus even though it leads to death. They must be prepared to die. The Lord will reward such faithfulness with the crown of life (actually a victor's crown, a wreath). This crown translates into a nice position in Christ's kingdom.

11. "You who have ears, listen to what the Spirit says to the churches. He who overcomes cannot be harmed by the second death."

SECOND DEATH. Here again we have a closing exhortation. The Holy Spirit confirms what the Smyrnans have just read. Even if they die for Jesus, there is no way they could end up in the lake of fire, "which is the second death" (Rev. 20:14). Satan might whisper, *"Once you're dead, who knows where you might end up? It's too late to do anything then."* But the Holy Spirit counters that notion from within saying, "*THERE IS NO WAY THAT DEATH CAN TOUCH AN OVERCOMER.*" As the church enters the period of judgments described by John later in this book, the Spirit's witness will be critical. It is urgent that believers get used to hearing and recognizing the voice of the Spirit. Then, when the "*ten days*" come upon us and our Bibles are confiscated, we'll still enjoy Spirit to spirit communication with the Lord. Don't forget, these messages apply as much to us as they did to the Smyrnans, perhaps even more.

PERGAMUM: A faithful church, but loaded with false teachers.

If Satan wanted an area headquarters, Pergamum would be the place. Located 65 miles North of Smyrna and 15 miles in from the coast, it was the capital of the province, a city completely dedicated to religion. With temples to honor a number of deities, as well as being the seat of emperor worship, it was a notorious center of wickedness. There was also a huge altar, one that resembled a giant throne and which was dedicated to Zeus, chief of the Greek gods. This may have occasioned Jesus' words... *"Where Satan has set up his throne."* Vested with the power of life and death, the magistrates could execute at will. Though constantly facing the Roman sword, this church nonetheless stood firm. Antipas, one of their number, had previously met such a death. Jesus' sharp two-edged sword stands in contrast to the Roman sword.

12. "To the angel of the church at Pergamum write: The One Who has the sharp two-edged sword says this: 13. I know very well where you live. It's where Satan sits enthroned and yet you are true to My name. You did not deny your faith in Me, even in the days of Antipas, my faithful witness, who was put to death there in your city, where Satan has set up his throne."

SATAN. Did you think Satan was somehow cast into the "lake of fire?" Not yet. That awaits him. For now he is quite free, though within certain limits imposed on him by God. He is allowed to move about as the *"prince of the power of the air"* (Eph.2:2). As a spirit being, the devil has no body, so there is no way he could use an actual building. Yet when he finds a city or center of immorality, all he has to do is set up shop in the hearts of those who prefer evil to righteousness and he has a substantial stronghold of evil. With the devil dealing in lies, the most effective weapon against him is the truth. But when a church compromises the truth, its power is gone and all sorts of trouble can develop in its midst.

14. "Even so, I still must find fault with you. You have some in your fellowship who hold to the teachings of Balaam. It was Balaam who showed Balak how to lure the people of Israel into sin by eating food sacrificed to idols and to commit immoral acts. 15. What's more, you also have those who hold to the teachings of the Nicolaitans. 16.You must repent of this or I will come to you quickly and war against them with the sword of My mouth."

BALAAM. The sword has never been a threat to the church. Christianity *thrives* on ill-treatment. During the persecutions of the early centuries the gospel spread like wildfire. But Satan discovered that internal attacks by false teachers were a far greater weapon. So while the church at Pergamum had safely endured physical persecution, it had fallen into Satan's trap by tolerating false teachers within its ranks. Back in Balaam's day, the prophet counseled the Midianite women to mix with the Israelites. The Midianite women seduced the Israelite men and the nation became corrupt. God sent a terrible plague upon her. Also at Pergamum, Nicolaitans (false teachers) tolerated in the fellowship caused the church to be permissive with regard to immorality and idolatry. The fact that the church did not stand against such teachers, provoked the Lord to anger.

SWORD. Observe that Pergamum's fault was the opposite of that at Ephesus. At Ephesus the truth was defended vigorously. But at Pergamum, the church was *INDIFFERENT* to the error infecting the fellowship. It was compromising with the lax standards of the outside world. The Lord warns that He will come and fight against those involved in this error with the "sword" of His mouth. We know what that sword is—His word (Heb. 4:12). With the church headed for judgment, and those judgments destined to be severe, those refusing to repent will find themselves on the receiving end of those judgments.

17. "You who have ears, listen to what the Spirit says to the churches. He who overcomes, I will feed with the hidden manna. I will also give him a white stone and on it will be a new name, known only to him who receives it."

MANNA / STONE. The Lord holds out great rewards to overcomers. He provided manna (a miracle food) for the Israelites during their wilderness wanderings. Manna here could refer to God's provision for His overcomers during that period when no man can buy or sell unless he bears the mark of the beast. Some divine provision will be needed unless the Lord means for all to perish. The overcomer will receive a "white stone" with "a new name" written on it. You and I were named by our parents, but that name applies only to the earthly family. When we're born again into God's family, He has the right to give us a new name, possibly a *nick name or pet name* that would bespeak family intimacy. Jesus' words here are intended to encourage the Pergamum Christians to act like beloved children of God and get rid of the false teachers.

THYATIRA: A church with a list of good works, but tolerating evil.

The least important of the seven cities, Thyatira is located roughly 40 miles Southeast of Pergamum. The church of this city gets the longest letter. Until now, all the cities mentioned have been important, but this obscure city was not important to Rome. Because of this, it was not dominated by emperor worship. However, there was little job security for believers, because each of the guilds had gods of their own and Christians refusing to get involved in their pagan feasts and sexual practices found it tough to keep their jobs. The Lord's focus on this church deals with a problem that exists in many churches today—*sex and food.*

18. "To the angel of the church at Thyatira
write: The Son of God is speaking this mesage to you, the One whose eyes blaze like fire and whose feet are like glowing bronze. 19. I know
all about your good deeds; your love, your faith, your generosity and your perseverance; indeed, right now you're doing more than you did at first."

SON OF GOD. For the first time in this book, we find the Lord Jesus referring to Himself as the Son of God. To this small, rather obscure church, the Lord speaks the longest of His messages to the seven churches. We know He is dead serious, for He selects the features of blazing eyes and glowing feet as His identifiers. Those eyes penetrate deeply into the evils of this church and His feet are ready to stamp judgment upon the evil doers. There were a lot of pressures on this church, but some were enduring them and remaining faithful to Jesus. The Lord acknowledges the good qualities of this church, before He brings His charge against her.

20. "However, I must make this charge against you: you tolerate that woman Jezebel, who claims to have the gift of prophecy and misleads My servants with her teaching. She lures them into sexual immorality and the eating of food sacrificed to idols."

JEZEBEL. Apparently there was a woman in the church who claimed to be a prophetess. No one really knows who she was, but she was called Jezebel, because she influenced believers in much the same way as did the Jezebel of the Old Testament. She claimed God was giving her messages for the church and lured many believers into adopting her evil life style. Her teachings were the same as those plaguing the church at Pergamum—idolatry and immorality. Exploiting the power of her personality and falsely claimed inspiration, she got members of the church to go along with the pagan practices of the city. Some of these were vile, but she argued powerfully, *"Why starve, when a little compromise, which is covered by Jesus' blood, could make life a lot easier for you?"* That must have made sense to those struggling to feed their families, since many were being denied a living because of their faith.

21. "I have given her time to repent of her immorality, but she refuses to abandon her immoral ways. 22. So I will throw her on a bed of suffering and pain and make those who commit adultery with her suffer intense tribulation unless they renounce her immoral ways. 23. I will kill all of her children outright, so that all of the churches will know that I am the One Who searches the hearts and minds of people and that I am going to give each of you what his deeds deserve."

BED. Remember, this is the Son of God exposing Jezebel's evil. He has given her time to repent, but since that has not happened, He's going to play rough. He is casting her and her followers onto a bed of suffering. We may assume this refers to *the Great Tribulation* God is sending on all who refuse to repent. When this happens all will realize that while we might fool ourselves, we can't fool Him. He knows us better than we know ourselves. He reads people's hearts, judging their motives. Those involved with Jezebel, even the Jezebels of today, face a bitter end. It will be clear that those *blazing* *eyes* see precisely what every person deserves. This will be very plain in that day.

24. "But as for the rest of you in Thyatira, those of you who do not go along with her teachings, and have not gotten involved in what she calls the deep secrets of Satan—I am not going to impose any further burden on you; 25. other than to say this: hang on to what you have until I come."

HANG ON. Things were really rough for Christians in Thyatira, worse than with the other churches. So bad, in fact, a believer was forced to compromise his convictions to hang on to a job. Apparently the Lord felt the Thyatiran believers had their hands full clinging to the truth and at the same time surviving in a place where Satan wielded such power. In Jezebel, the devil had a powerful agent working for him. Her charismatic charm likely made her popular with the pagans who controlled the jobs. This gave her considerable leverage in winning followers. With such power in her hands, those who stood firm and resisted her, were doing as well as could be expected.

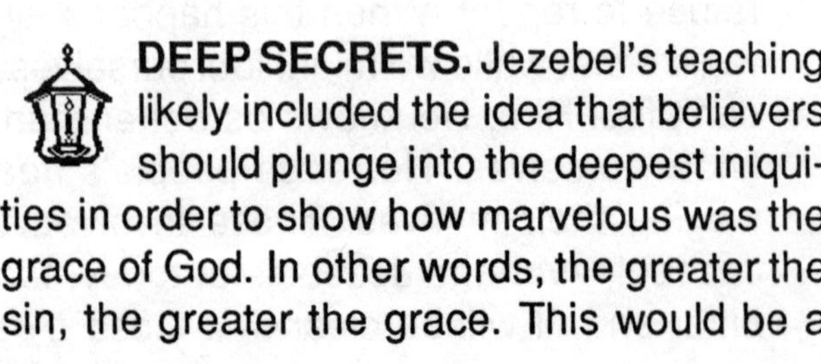

DEEP SECRETS. Jezebel's teaching likely included the idea that believers should plunge into the deepest iniquities in order to show how marvelous was the grace of God. In other words, the greater the sin, the greater the grace. This would be a flesh-pleasing idea. Besides, it would permit her followers to participate in the pagan feasts as well as the immoral acts associated with the worship of Artemis. Thyatira was well known for its magnificent temple to Artemis (a sex goddess) with its temple prostitutes. Jezebel may have suggested that the whole city of Thyatira could be won to Christ by presenting a more liberal gospel. It was against this very thing that the apostle Paul wrote...*"What then? Shall we sin because we're not under the law, but under grace? God forbid"* (Rom. 6:15).

26. "To him who overcomes, that is who perseveres in doing My will to the very end, I will give authority over the nations. 27. He will rule them with a rod of iron, smashing them to pieces like pottery. He will exercise the same authority which I have received from My Father 28. and I will give him the morning star."

OVERCOMER. Some feel that simply believing in Jesus makes one an overcomer in the sense that Jesus means here. Believing in Jesus does give one victory over hell, but that is not the overcoming referred to in these messages. This overcoming has to do with triumphing over temptation, persecution and self, by obedience and perseverance. This kind of overcoming means a readiness to die rather than give up the fight. Real overcomers are like salmon fighting their way upstream, leaping waterfalls and bruising rapids, allowing nothing to keep them from their objective. That's the kind of overcomer Jesus is talking about. His rewards are for that sort of overcomer, Christians determined to cross the finish line running as hard as they can. No rewards are held out to casual Christians, those who settle down in the world, content to live for themselves and their families. Their comforts and good times are about all the reward they can expect.

I WILL GIVE. The Lord offers two specifics to overcomers: 1.) authority over the nations and 2.) the morning star. This thrusts the timing into the millennium. As joint heirs with Him, believers will share in His absolute power over the nations (Rom. 8:17). There will be many different jobs in the kingdom, ranging from maintenance workers to ambassadors. With most Christians more interested in this life, than in reigning with the Lord, the best jobs will go to those proving their faithfulness by their works and sacrifices. The "morning star," considered the brightest in the heavens, refers to those who will be the "stars" of Jesus' kingdom. Just as we have luminaries in the movie world and the sports world, so will there be the luminaries of Christ. But these ranks (stars) will not be handed out arbitrarily, they must be earned (Mark 10:40).

29. "You who have ears, listen to what the Spirit says to the churches."

LISTEN. When Jesus says listen, He means with the hearing of obedience. James agrees: *"Be ye doers of the word and not hearers only, deceiving your own selves"* (Ja.1:22). What the Lord is saying to the churches, He means for them to take to heart and act on it. With God, *"To obey is better than sacrifice"* (1 Sam. 15:22). With terrible storms of judgment coming our way, the wise Christian will build his life on obedience, rather than on seeking the comforts and delights of this world. Jesus' last words of the Sermon on the Mount stressed what men are to do with His words. To build your life on a rock, you must heed what Jesus says and DO IT. Otherwise your house won't stand the fierce blasts of the Great Tribulation (Matt. 7:24-28).

REVELATION 3

MESSAGES TO THE LAST THREE CHURCHES

The Lord is telling each of the seven churches what He sees in them and what is needed to get ready for the awful judgments coming on the world. Those willing to take a stand for Jesus and try to overcome their faults, will not only find themselves ready for the coming trials, but unbelievable rewards await them. Thus the challenge to each person in every church is...OVERCOME!

SARDIS: A dead church that could live should it wake up in time.

Once a great city, Sardis fell twice to its enemies because of its carelessness and lethargy. Now the church of that city, located 30 miles South of Thyatira, has fallen into the same pattern. Wealthy and spiritually lazy, it has abandoned its vigilance to become apathetic and lethargic. There is no persecution, no hostility from the Jews, and none of the opposition that plagued the other churches. Without the trials on which Christianity thrives, the spiritual life oozed out of this church. So the Lord pronounces it dead. Today's Christians, given wealth, health and time to enjoy the pleasures of the world, come to the same end. Christianity thrives on suffering and sacrifice, not on ease, comforts and good times.

3 **1. "To the angel of the church at Sardis write: These are the words of the One holding the seven spirits of God and the seven stars: I know all that you are doing; I know you have a reputation for**

being alive, but you are dead. 2. Wake up! Revitalize what you still have! Put some strength into it, because it will die if you don't. You see, I have not found any of your work complete in the sight of My God. 3. Remember, therefore, the teaching you received; act on it and repent! If you don't wake up, I'll come upon you like a thief, and you will not know the moment of My arrival."

REVITALIZE. This church had meetings. The scriptures were preached and the people sang praises to God, but that didn't immunize them from the world. Dead churches often do those things. While the church *appeared* to be alive, there was no spiritual fire. They went through the motions of a church, but they were not involved with the Holy Spirit. But all is not lost. If they'll pick up on the teachings they received, and get serious with the Lord, the Holy Spirit will revitalize them. As long as a person is alive, he can repent and be quickened. The One holding the seven spirits of God will always quicken those willing to repent. But He will also see to it that those refusing to repent suffer the coming wrath—the wrath poured out when Jesus returns. We must assume the unrepentent in this church are unsaved.

MY GOD. When the Lord says..."My God," it reminds us that He is still the "man Christ Jesus" (1 Tim. 2:5). He is not returning as GOD, but in the *role* of the Son. He is a MAN and He is coming back as a MAN, in fact, as a King over other kings and Lord over other lords...a very human experience. Having departed this world as a disgraced rabbi, the Lord is returning in great power and glory (Matt. 25:31). Since He is returning as an *heir,* the millennial kingdom is His inheritance and we will be "joint heirs with Him" (Rom. 8:17). The kingdom is Jesus' reward for His faithfulness as an obedient Son. He is inheriting the throne of "His father David" (Luke 1:32).

4. "But what I have found is this: you have a few people there in Sardis who have not defiled their clothes. They shall keep Me company, dressed in white, for they deserve it. 5. He who overcomes shall be clothed in similar white garments and I will never blot his name out of the book of life. To the contrary, I will publicly announce his name in the presence of My Father and His angels. 6. You who have ears, listen to what the Spirit is saying to the churches."

WHITE. Sardis was as immoral as any of the other towns. It appears many in this dead church became involved in the pagan sexual practices, which in turn caused them to become cold and indifferent to spiritual truth. Consequently they were no longer able to respond to God's word. Yet, there were a few among them who loved Jesus and shuddered at the thought of dishonoring Him by participating in the evils of that day. These people were *alive* and kept their garments of righteousness untarnished. This doesn't mean they never sinned, but that they never lost their desire to please the Lord in what they *did* and *said* and *thought*. Such people the Lord desires as companions and will see to it that they are near Him forever.

BOOK OF LIFE. God keeps books. We will see them opened at the great white throne judgment (Rev. 20:11, 12). In the book of life are recorded the names of all true believers, or the family of God. This book was prepared *before* the foundation of the world (Rev. 17:8). God in His foreknowledge has already seen the human story enacted from beginning to end. This is why, *"The Lord knoweth them that are His"* (2 Tim. 2:19). Some have suggested God doesn't really know His own and therefore when certain ones refuse to repent, He erases their names from His book. It doesn't fit God's character to enter names only to find He has made mistakes. Such a view challenges God's foreknowledge. When Jesus says He will not blot out a believer's name, it simply means a true Christian is secure in his salvation. And that's great to know when tribulation fires besiege you and Satan is tormenting you with doubts.

OVERCOMES. Not only does Jesus promise never to blot out the name of a single Christian, but He goes to the opposite extreme, declaring the believer's name before all of heaven. In another place, the Lord says *"He is not ashamed to call them brethren"* (Heb. 2:11). A further promise assures overcomers they will be clothed in white. Throughout the Bible, white garments represent the righteousness of God imparted to the saints. As partakers of the divine nature, believers are as righteous as God (2 Cor. 5:21). Therefore white clothing is an apt term for heavenly attire. However, we are not to understand that the overcomer is always triumphant. He may have lots of failures, yet he is a real overcomer if he consistently tries to please the Lord with his life. *"With God: trying is winning."* Anyone having a problem with this, should focus on what the Spirit says to the churches about overcomers.

PHILADELPHIA: An obedient church that will not see the wrath of God.

Philadelphia, located some 30 miles Southeast of Sardis, was the city of "brotherly love." But this name was not inspired by Christian love. The king of Pergamum, who sponsored the founding of this *missionary city,* did so out of love for his older brother... hence *Philadelphia.* It was a missionary city built on the border of an area that was as yet untouched by Greek culture. The purpose was to spread the Greek language and customs into regions as yet untouched by Greek influence. The emperor's approval for this amounted to an "open door." While the church in this city was not under real pressure, it was still faithful and obedient.

7. "To the angel of the church at Philadelphia write: These are the words of the Holy One, the True One, Who wears the key of David, so that when He opens a door, no one can shut it

and when He shuts a door, no one can open it. 8. I know what you're trying to do for Me there and I also know that in spite of your little strength you have been true to My word and have not denied My name. So look! I have placed an open door before you which no one can shut."

KEY. The Lord does not use an identifier from the first chapter this time. He prefers to identify Himself as the "Holy One of Israel." He also identifies Himself as the "True One," in contrast to the rulers of the Jewish synagogue who falsely pretended to bear the authority of David's house. They said they had the WAY to God, the key to heaven. We shouldn't think of the key in the ordinary sense, but rather as an insignia (like a Phi Beta Kappa key), that identifies Jesus as the one with absolute control over who enters the kingdom and who doesn't. The church at Philadelphia was quite small, shy on good teachers and was weak. The Jewish community, on the other hand, was strong and hostile and had undoubtedly excommunicated the members of the Philadelphian assembly. But they are not to worry, because Jesus has placed before them an open door into the *HEAVENLY KINGDOM* and no one can shut it. These words of assurance are a reward for their faithfulness to His word.

9. "As for those in Satan's synagogue, those liars who falsely claim to be Jews and are not, watch how I deal with them. I will make them come and bow in reverence at your feet and

acknowledge that you are the ones I have loved. 10. Because you have obeyed My command to stand firm patiently, I will also keep you from the hour of trial that is soon to fall upon the whole world to test those who dwell upon the earth."

JEWS. We are now at the heart of the Philadelphian struggle, the conflict between the church and the synagogue. The Jews believed their ancestry made them the real people of God and that the Christians were the phonies. But Jesus says, *"No, the Jews are the phonies, they have no open door into the kingdom such as you have. In spite of their claims, they are no different than the pagans."* While the Jews may one day be the preeminent nation (since God keeps His promises), they will have no SPIRITUAL RANK, no standing with God at all. To the contrary, they will come and bow at the believers' feet and acknowledge that they were wrong and that those who trusted in Jesus were right and that the Christians are the real "seed of Abraham" (Gal. 3:29). It will be the Jew's ultimate humiliation to bow and admit that the church is the true Israel of God once Jesus assumes His throne.

HOUR OF TRIAL. Many commentators do not distinguish between the Great Tribulation and the wrath of God. Yet clearly, the hour of trial is NOT the Great Tribulation, but the *wrath of God.* The purpose of the book of Revelation is to prepare believers for the tribulation, not wrath. In these messages, the churches are urged to stand firm in the face of the coming tribulation. God's wrath, an entirely different matter, is HIS FURY poured out on an unbelieving world (2 Thess. 1:7,8). The only reason for the rapture of the church is to remove God's people from the earth before God's wrath is poured out. Believers are not *"children of wrath"* (Eph. 2:3), neither are they *"appointed unto wrath"* (1 Thess. 5:9). Paul says we will be *"delivered from the wrath to come"* (1 Thess. 1:10). God's wrath cannot be poured out as long as a single believer remains on the earth. Tribulation, on the other hand, has always refined the church. *"It is given unto you...not only to believe in Him, but to suffer for His sake"* (Phil. 1:29).

THE 3 WRATHS OF THE REVELATION		
ANTICHRIST	***THE BEAST***	***GOD***
The Tribulation	The Great Tribulation	The "Hour of Trial"
Destroys anyone in his way of becoming ruler of the world.	Destroys all opposing his right to God's throne.	God's anger poured out on the entire world.

11. "I am coming soon: hang onto the ground you've gained. Don't let anyone rob you of your crown. 12. I will make the one who overcomes a pillar in the temple of My God and he will hold that position forever. I shall write on him the name of My God and the name of the city of My God, the New Jerusalem, which comes down out of heaven from My God. In

addition, I shall also write on him My new name. 13. You who have ears, listen to what the Spirit is saying to the churches."

COMING SOON. Jesus' coming will be quick, all right, like lightning flashing across the sky (Matt. 24:27). The believer is exhorted to hold his ground and endure patiently to the end. That will either be when death occurs or when Jesus appears in the sky. Having come far enough to secure a crown (actually a job or position in Jesus' administration) through obedience, the believer must continue to press on. As with a runner in a race, there is no reward unless you cross the finish line. It is possible for a believer to think he's done enough at some point and let up (perhaps retire) and if he does, the job he's won could go to someone else. There'll be many fabulous jobs in Jesus' government, making it worth it to "endure to the end," no matter what it costs or takes in the way of personal sacrifice.

PILLAR. A pillar is not only a prominent part of a temple, it is also a permanent part. However, it is used here simply as a metaphor. The pillar speaks of a significant position in Christ's kingdom. Interestingly, there was a great temple in Philadelphia and the Romans did inscribe names on its pillars, so this would be a meaningful comment to the believers. The Lord says He'll write 3 things on the pillar: the name of His God, the name of God's city, and His own new name. From this the believer derives a tremendous sense of security. As a "pillar," he's a high ranking member of God's family. He also is a citizen of the New Jerusalem and enjoys an intimate relationship with Jesus. A CITY is one of the ways the church is pictured in scripture, thus the New Jerusalem that *"comes down from heaven,"* is a reference to the Lord's descent with His church. Again, the reader is asked to listen to the Spirit and understand that God holds out fabulous rewards for those willing to "endure to the end." All the letters say..."Hang in there and you won't be sorry."

LAODICEA: the worst of the lot.

Here is a church that demonstrates what wealth and power can do to Christians. Located at the junction of two major trade routes, Laodicea served as the banking and financial center of the province of Asia. It was the wealthiest city in Phrygia. It was also famous for its jet black wool from which were made expensive garments that were in great demand throughout the Roman Empire. Beyond that, it was widely known for an eye salve made from a powder mixed with olive oil. The Lord says this church lacks, in a spiritual sense, everything for which the city was famous.

14. "To the angel of the church at Laodicea write: These are the words of the Amen, the faithful and true witness, the originator and ruler of God's creation. 15. I know what's going on with you; how that you are neither cold nor hot. How I wish that you were one or

the other. 16. So because you are merely lukewarm, neither hot nor cold, I am ready to spit you out of my mouth."

ORIGINATOR. The Lord Jesus refers to Himself as the *"Amen,"* because He has the last word. Because He speaks for God, His word is absolutely true and final. He is reinforcing the "Amen," when He adds that He is *"the faithful and true witness."* This means that when He promises something, men can bet their lives He will do as He says. Most translations read that Jesus is the "beginning of God's creation." But the Greek word for *beginning* includes the idea that He is the starting point and ultimate source of all power and authority. He could just as well say... *"Everything is under My control!"* Consequently when He speaks to this blind church, they'd better put on their ears and respond.

LUKEWARM. The water in Laodicea was terrible. People spit it out in disgust. So the Laodicean church knew what he meant when he spoke of spitting them out of His mouth. *"You make Me sick,"* He says, *"you make Me feel like vomiting!"* Why would their lukewarmness make the Lord nauseous? Because they were like the Pharisees, whom He loathed. The Pharisees regarded themslves as religious, and they were *outwardly,* but inwardly they were full of impurity and sin. That kind of religion sickens the Lord. Here was a church that professed to be Christian, but excluded the Lord. It had no spiritual life. It was blind to its spiritual bankruptcy. A person who does NOT profess to be a Christian, but is aware of his lost condition, is far better off than these Laodiceans. The Lord is saying, *"I'd rather have you cold, admitting you don't know Me, than to see you playing games with religion."* The church fathers came to use the term *"lukewarm"* to describe unsaved people who professed to be Christians.

17. "You say, man am I rich! Look at the fortune I've made! I've got everything I need! And yet, if you only knew it, you are pitiful, poor, blind, wretched and naked. 18. My advice to you is, come and buy from Me gold that has been purified in the fire and then you'll be truly rich. Also buy white clothes to cover the shame of your nakedness and salve to put on your eyes so you can see your real condition."

MY ADVICE. Blind to their spiritual condition, these Laodicean professors were satisfied with their "spiritual" wealth. They said, *"We've got it made!"* Believing themselves spiritually rich, they felt secure in their phoney wealth. The very things the Lord counsels them to buy, shows they didn't know Him at all. The gold has reference to the divine nature, which we receive when we're saved. The white clothes needed to cover their shame, represent the righteousness of Jesus. And the eye salve speaks of the Holy Spirit Who alone enables people to see their true condition. This entire church is unsaved.

19. "All those whom I love, I correct and discipline. Therefore fire up your spirits, rouse yourselves from your complacency and repent. 20. Behold I stand at the door and knock; if anyone hears My voice and opens the door, I will come in and we will have supper together."

OPENS THE DOOR. What an amazing picture! The Lord has rebuked this church which has no personal relationship with Him. Yet, there He stands on the *outside* offering to come into the heart of any individual *inside* the church willing to invite Him. Jesus is *not* appealing to the church, but only to those *individuals* inside the church who really want Him. This is strong motivation for anyone struggling with salvation. In effect, Jesus is saying, *"Look, all anyone has to do to have Me for his friend and Savior is open his heart to Me. I won't force My way in. I simply knock and await an invitation."* In that part of the world, eating supper together symbolized the warmest kind of friendship. Obviously, this invitation is not limited to the Laodicean church, but extends to *"anyone"* today. It includes sitting down with Him at the "marriage supper of the Lamb" (Rev.19:7-9),

DISCIPLINE. *Change* is probably the most important word in the Christian life, but Christians resist change. In fact we have an expression that bears out our reluctance to change, *"Don't rock the boat."* By that we mean, we prefer things the way they are. This explains why our lives change so little year after year. But the Lord hates the *status quo.* He's a *boat rocker.* He uses painful things to rock the boat in our lives, because He knows we only do what we have to. We'd never give our children diabetes, cancer or arrange accidents. But God is not like us. His love for us is so great, He'll put us through *temporary suffering* if it will produce an *eternal* benefit. Throughout scripture, believers are told not to despise chastening (Prov. 3:11-12; Heb.12:5-6). Pain is the quickest way to bring about repentence (change) whether in God's little ones or our own.

21. "To the one who overcomes, I will grant to sit beside Me on My throne, even as I Myself overcame and sat down with My Father sharing His throne. 22. You who have ears, listen to what the Spirit is saying to the churches."

OVERCOMERS. Here's a promise that should motivate us to be serious about overcoming. It is no small thing to be a *"joint heir with Christ,"* and share in His reign. Don't visualize an actual throne with people sitting next to each other. Rather, picture a cabinet room with high ranking officers of the kingdom seated about a big table. The throne merely speaks of authority and power. Again, marvelous job opportunities await those who'll turn their backs on this world and go all out to serve the Lord Jesus. To have a place near Jesus, one must be an overcomer. But it's hard to overcome family, fun and worldly security. Very few will put Jesus ahead of those things, leaving the field wide open for those who really want to reign with Him. For the seventh and last time we are urged to listen for the Spirit's witness to Jesus' words to these churches.

SUMMARY. The seven churches were a cross section of all the churches in existence at that time. There were other churches in Asia besides the seven named by the Lord, but seven, being the sacred and complete number, was representative of the whole church throughout the world and down through all ages. The messages are a comprehensive warning to the entire church. We are to understand the *entire book* of Revelation is addressed to these seven churches. These letters were designed and meant to prepare the followers of the Lord Jesus for the trials due to come upon them before His return. His appeal is for every Christian to be an *overcomer.*

A strange mix of those early problems can be found in churches today and all Christians are being warned against them:

Ephesus—losing that first love
Smyrna—fear of Satan generated persecution
Pergamum—compromising with immorality
Thyatira—tolerating false teachers
Sardis—spiritual deadness
Philadelphia—letting opportunities slip away
Laodicea—leaving Jesus on the outside

It is said no church can rise higher than its pastor. But pastors range from faithful and truthful to those who are worldly and apostate. Believers would do well to consider the Lord's seven warnings as a check list to make sure their own church is on track. At the judgment, every Christian will have to give an account of HIMSELF as an overcomer, and won't be able to blame his pastor should he stumble through failure to heed this caution of the Lord (Rom.14:12).

WHY THE REVELATION CHURCHES?

Do you wonder why the church messages are included in John's book?

First, the apostle John was writing to his own people on the mainland. It would be absurd to think this book was so prophetic it had nothing to do with them. They were suffering serious persecution and John meant for his words to lift the burden of fear from their hearts. During the reign of Domitian, believers were dying for Jesus right and left. They needed to know their deaths were part of God's plan for them. Only then could they stand up for Christ no matter what it cost.

At the same time, it would be a mistake to limit the book to John's generation. Far worse persecutions have occurred throughout history, with each generation thrilling to the promised blessings and comfort of this book. Besides, the Roman persecutions and The Inquisition don't compare with the slaughter of believers in our time. Millions have died in Russia, Poland, China and a host of other countries. The Holy Spirit means for this book to be a blessing to anyone who reads it or hears it...*in any generation* (1:3).

John's own words tell us who it is *really for.* When he says...*"The time is close,"* we must conclude it is for the generation that will endure the specific persecutions described in his book. While every generation can apply the comfort to its own need, the people suffering under the beast will be the most bewildered by what is happening. With believers slaughtered on a WORLD-WIDE SCALE, the common cry will be...*"I thought God was supposed to be in control! Where is His hand in all this? Is this really what He wants for His people? Could we be making a mistake in standing against the whole world for the sake of Jesus?"*

With a counterfeit Christ performing eye-popping miracles in the power of Satan, only those who know *the Revelation* will understand what is happening and why. When hospitals are emptied; when counterfeit resurrections occur; when false teachers speak with many different tongues, masses of believers will be utterly confused and perplexed. Satan will plague their minds with thoughts such as:

..."Can't you recognize the power you see before your eyes? Why make your family suffer by clinging to the old fashioned idea that the crucified Carpenter is coming back? The real power is here. It's foolish to die for someone no one has seen for 2000 years!"

When you find yourself in the tribulation with no money, no food, and your children dying slowly and begging for relief, Satan's suggestions will have awesome power. What power can stand up to Satan's power? Only one power can match the power of The Liar—THE TRUTH. And the truth needed for the coming tribulation is found only in *the Revelation.* No where else can we get such precise information on the last days. This is the only book of prophecy in the New Testament.

So don't let it bother you that John is writing to seven churches in Asia Minor. The genius of God is seen in that this book blesses all who endure persecution for Jesus' sake...in any generation. But please understand it is a book of prophecy picturing things *that haven't happened to date (1992).* A persecution is coming with a severity never seen before. Therefore its message is designed *primarily* for those who will be persecuted most.

Not everything will be clear, but if you'll open your heart to the Holy Spirit, the central truths will surface in your spirit. You'll see that John is dealing with a specific time in the future. You will *also understand* that no matter how dark and evil those days become, our sovereign Lord will suddenly appear and smash the forces of evil and exalt His people! In producing this book, I seek to prepare God's people to face those days with total confidence in Jesus' promise...

"I AM COMING SOON!"

SO FAR SO GOOD

Two parts of Jesus' command to John have now been completed. He was instructed to write *what he had seen.* He did that when he described for us his vision of the glorified Christ in Chapter One. When he was told to write *what is now,* the Lord gave him seven messages to send to the churches that described their present condition, and he did that. Thirdly he was told to write *what is going to take place in the future* and get all that information to the churches. What is left is for the Lord to show him what is going to take place in the future.

REVELATION 4

WILL WHAT JOHN SEES NEXT PREPARE HIM FOR WHAT'S COMING?

John has been writing steadily, copying down all that Jesus told him to say to the churches. As if to rest his eyes, he looks heavenward. While reflecting on the messages he's just written to the churches, one can almost hear him say...*"Lord, is that all they're going to get, just challenges to be overcomers? You said You wanted me to write down the things that are going to come to pass. When will You show me those?"* The old apostle, greatly concerned for the churches in his charge, won't have long to wait. The Lord is ready to show him the grim judgments and suffering due to occur on earth just prior to His return, but they are *so terrible,* John needs to be prepared for what he is going to see. The next two chapters, 4 and 5, are intended to give him the necessary preparation.

4 **1. Almost immediately, as I was looking upward, there appeared before me a door standing open in heaven. Then the same voice I had heard earlier, the one that sounded as loud as a trumpet, said to me, "Come up here and I will show you what is going to happen in the future."**

COME UP HERE. John didn't have to wait long for an answer to his question. The voice he heard earlier bids him join the Lord in heaven. The first thing he sees is an open door. Whether he goes through the door or merely peers inside from the doorway, isn't clear. At the same time, he can also see the earth. If John is to behold future events, this is the best place to view them. Some might be tempted to think the words, *"Come up here,"* imply a rapture of the church at this point. But there's no basis for that. Why show the church what is going to take place, if the church isn't going to be here? What's more, the invitation is clearly to the throne room of *heaven,* not to a meeting in the sky, which Paul says will happen in the case of the *rapture* (1 Thess. 4:17).

2. I was in the Spirit that instant. And there in heaven I saw a throne set up and a person seated on it 3. Whose appearance blazed like light flashing from a diamond, or perhaps a ruby. There was also a rainbow around the throne that glowed with an emerald hue.

HOW WE ARE PROCEEDING

CHAPTER 1	CHAPTERS 2 & 3	CHAPTER 4	CHAPTER 5	CHAPTER 6

John has just received an astonishing invitation to the throne room of heaven. Before he is exposed to the staggering events of the future, he will be privileged to visit the command center of eternity. What he has seen so far, the revelation of Christ in Chapter One and the present condition of the churches, while overwhelming, is nothing compared to the earth convulsing events he will meet in Chapter 6 and beyond. What is coming is so incredible, the apostle needs to be convinced that God is really in control and that the approaching calamities fit His plan. That's why Chapters 4 and 5 are in this book. Even with this kind of preparation it will still be hard for John to believe what he sees.

THRONE. The first thing to catch John's eye is a throne. It may have been there simply to accommodate his human mind, for it is not likely the omnipresent God (Who is spirit) sits on any kind of a throne. But things need to be presented to John in terms a space/time creature can understand. At this point, the One on the throne does not appear in human form, but is portrayed in terms of an incredible radiance of precious stones. It is the radiance that is significant here, not the stones. Later, a scroll will be seen in His right hand (5:1). The "throne" is significant, for it represents the place of absolute authority, power and strength, giving John the certainty he needs *—God is in control—and has the power to carry out things according to His will.* That's the reason John was invited to the throne room. He will use the word "throne" more than forty times in this book.

4. Encircling this throne, were twenty-four other thrones, and on them were twenty-four elders clothed in white garments with crowns of gold on their heads. 5. Flashes of lightning and peals of thunder came from the throne in the midst of the circle. Before the throne were seven flaming lamps, which are the seven spirits of God. 6a. In front of the throne, there fanned out what looked like a gleaming sea of glass, clear as crystal.

ELDERS. A common identification of the elders suggests that 12 of them represent the 12 tribes of Israel and

12 the apostles. Under that view, the 24 would represent God's people of both the Old and New Testaments. They are wearing white robes, have crowns and are seated on thrones. However this will be true of all believers after they have been judged. It is difficult to see what believers would be doing in heaven at this point, since the judgments of the saints has not yet taken place. A better view, perhaps, is to assume John is the only earthling in the scene. In that case, these elders would be angelic beings of some kind. There is a hierarchy of beings in God's kingdom, just as there is in Satan's kingdom (Eph. 6:12).

SEVEN SPIRITS. Lightning and thunder play a significant role in heralding critical events in connection with the seals, trumpets, and bowls. The presence of the 7 spirits here is connected with God's anger. As noted earlier, they are the angels appointed to administer the judgments. Bear in mind, the context of this book—*judgment.* The sea of glass, gleaming like a sheet of ice, stretches from the throne to where John is standing. Its mirror-like surface reflects the dazzling colors about the throne generating an awesome atmosphere. They give John's mind a heightened sense of God's majesty. The dancing colors radiating off the glassy sea must have provided overwhelming splendor to the scene. The placid sea represents how smoothly and quietly things go when God is in charge.

6b. Then I noticed in the midst, right where the throne was located, four living creatures on each of the throne's four sides. They had eyes everywhere and could see in front of them and behind. 7. The first of these living figures was like a lion; the second like an ox, the third had a man's face, and the fourth like an eagle in flight. 8. Each of the four living creatures had six wings with eyes all over their bodies, even under their wings. Day and night they unceasingly glorify God, saying:

> ***"Holy, holy, holy, is the Lord God,***
> ***The Almighty, the One who was,***
> ***the One who is, and the One who***
> ***is yet to come."***

LIVING CREATURES. Again, we should not read human representations into these creatures. As with all of the other beings we're seeing in heaven, these are part of the angelic order that manages the affairs of heaven. These four seem to have charge of throne or heavenly activities in some way, which make them highly exalted. Further, they seem to be ministers of worship, leading the other agencies of heaven in praising God. With all those eyes, they know everything that's going on. Thus when they sing of the power and might of "THE ALMIGHTY," they are referring to the awesome judgments to be unleashed upon the earth during the tribulation period. John is silent on what the different features of these creatures mean.

9. As often as the living creatures give glory and honor and thanks to the One who sits on the throne and who lives forever and ever, 10. the twenty-four elders prostrate themselves before the One upon the throne and worship Him as the One who lives eternally. They cast their crowns before the throne, saying:

> ***11. "You are worthy, O Lord our God, to receive the glory and the honor and the power because You created all things that exist. And nothing exists except that which You called into being by Your will."***

GIVE GLORY. Observe the action: the four living creatures make statements *about God*, and then the twenty-four elders cry out praise *to God.* But notice the praise has to do with power and glory and God's sovereign control of His creation. The elders, by casting their crowns before the throne, are acknowledging they hold *delegated* authority which God can take away any time He wishes. Apparently every being in heaven is aware of God's anger; that His patience with sinful man is coming to an end. Later, they'll be saying... *"And your wrath has come."*

At the moment, it's as though all of heaven is tensely acknowledging God's right to judge His creation as He pleases, no matter how terrible those judgments may seem to anyone else. At the same time, it is refreshing to us, His saints, to realize that this same power guarantees our glorious future in the kingdom. That should take the sting out of the tribulation. John, who'll be writing down the awful things to come, will certainly need this assurance to keep his spirit under control.

MOVING ALONG

CHAPTER 1	CHAPTERS 2 & 3	CHAPTER 4	CHAPTER 5	CHAPTER 6

The window for chapter 4 is now open. And what do we see? A throne. And that's all you need to remember about this chapter. John was summoned to heaven simply to see this throne and hear heaven's testimony concerning the power of the Person seated on that throne. This scene is critical to John's preparation for the astonishing things he is about to see. Any doubt John may have had as to the reality of heaven and God's power to carry out His plan for man on the earth, is gone now. Now we're ready to see what the next window holds for the apostle.

REVELATION 5

In Chapter Four, John was in the throne room where He beheld, in symbolic sense, the awesome majesty of God. He described for us the twenty-four elders and the four living creatures, but he didn't give any clues as to who they were or whom they might represent. When we come to Chapter Five, John is still in the throne room, but the focus shifts to a scroll in God's right hand. This scroll, while primarily disclosing God's judgments, will also unveil His plan for the final days of this planet. Inasmuch as it lays out the future of the world, some call it the "Scroll of Destiny."

5 **1. Then I noticed that the One sitting on the throne had in His right hand a scroll with writing on the inside and the outside and was sealed with seven seals. 2. At the same time, a mighty angel was asking with a loud voice, "Who is worthy to break the seals of this scroll and discover its contents?"**

SCROLL. In this chapter, the scroll occupies center stage, at least until someone answers the angel's question. Daniel was told to *"Keep the words secret and seal the book until the time of the end"* (Dan. 12:4). Those seven seals guarantee that no one has ever gained access to what's inside. The fact that writing appears both inside and out indicates that nothing more is to be added. The revelation contained in the scroll is complete. But then a mighty angel asks: *"Is anyone anywhere, qualified to open the scroll?"* John, of course, breathlessly waits for someone to respond. He is eager to know what is in the scroll, for it contains the *"things that will take place in the future."* So far, all he has told the churches is that they must be overcomers. But they still need to know what they're to overcome. John won't be able to finish his job and give them that information if that scroll isn't opened. That would be heart-breaking for the old apostle.

3. But no one anywhere in all creation was able to open the scroll and look inside. 4. And because no one was found worthy to open the scroll and reveal its contents, I wept in bitter disappointment.

WEPT. John was purposely called to the throne room to get the details of end-time events so he could send them to the churches. Even without looking inside the scroll, John knows that Satan has been ruling over God's creation since Adam surrendered it to him in the garden of Eden. He had heard Jesus call Satan the *"prince of this world"* (John 14:30). John, himself, wrote *"The whole world is under the control of the evil one"* (1 John 5:19). God's plan had to include the wresting of the world from Satan and the establishment of Jesus' kingdom on earth. John was taught to pray, *"Thy kingdom come"* (Luke 11:2). How God intends to bring that to pass has to be in that "Scroll of

Destiny." If no one is qualified to open the scroll and get God's plan under way, would that mean SATAN WINS? Such a thought tears John apart.

5. But one of the twenty-four elders said to me, "Stop your crying and look! See, here is the Lion of the tribe of Judah, the Root of David. He has triumphed and won the right to break the seven seals and open the scroll."

SEE. What fabulous news! One of the elders comes to John saying, *"Stop crying, I've got great news for you! A man has been found who is worthy to open the scroll!"* Out of all humanity, this solitary individual, a Jew, comes with the credentials necessary to break the seals. The elder identifies this person with language from two Old Testament passages. The first is Gen. 49, where Judah, one of Jacob's twelve sons, is called a "Lion's whelp," and is promised that the scepter will not pass from him until all the nations obey him. The second passage, Isa. 11, says a descendant from the root of Jesse will rise like a standard and the nations will come to Him. So the Man is a Lion! This Lion, says the elder, is none other than the Messiah Who has triumphed over Satan and redeemed a family for God out of the human stream. The Lion, of course, is Jesus.

WAS JOHN EXPECTING TO SEE A LION?

6. Then, right in the midst of the living creatures and the elders surrounding the throne, I saw a Lamb standing upright. It was obvious

He had been slain in sacrifice, for He bore the marks of being slaughtered. He had seven horns and seven eyes, which are the seven spirits of God that go into every part of the world to do His bidding.

LAMB. The overwhelmed apostle, shifts his eyes from the scroll to look where the elder was pointing. He expected to see a lion, but instead he sees a Lamb! And it's a "little Lamb," at that. One so meek and helpless you wonder how it could triumph over anything. What's more amazing, the Lamb bore the marks of sacrifice. It had obviously been slain, yet here it was standing up in the midst of the angelic audience. It had risen from the dead. His seven horns, a symbolism from Daniel 7, indicate His irresistible power and authority and right to reign. His seven eyes are identified. They are the seven spirits or seven angels we saw in Chapter One. They will be seen again and again throughout the book, executing the judgments of God on the earth. Apart from watching over the churches during the tribulation, their primary mission is administering the judgments. Once more, this is a book of judgment.

7. He stepped forward and received the scroll from the right hand of the One Who sat on the throne. 8. As He did so, the four living creatures and the twenty-four elders fell down before the Lamb. Each of the elders had a harp and was carrying a golden bowl full of incense, symbolizing the prayers of God's people.

FELL DOWN. The Lamb, now identified as Jesus, moves forward to take the scroll from the hand of His Father. This guarantees the seals will be broken and the judgments will fall on mankind. As the Lamb moves to take His place on the throne, the atmosphere of heaven becomes electrified. The living creatures and the elders then prostrate themselves before Him. The *infinite worthiness* of the Lamb compels them to do so. They know what He has accomplished by the sacrifice of Himself. And since He did it as a helpless little Lamb, not as The Mighty God, they are overwhelmed with wonder, amazement and appreciation. Acting as intermediaries, the elders bring bowls of incense representing the prayers of God's people. For nearly 2000 years, the saints have prayed, *"Thy kingdom come."* And now the events leading up to that moment are about to begin. The harps indicate the elders are about to sing.

9. With these words they began singing a new song to Him:

"You are worthy to take the scroll and break its seals, for You were slain and by Your blood You purchased for God people from every tribe and language, nation and race. 10. And You have made them a family of priests and kings for our God, and they shall reign on the earth."

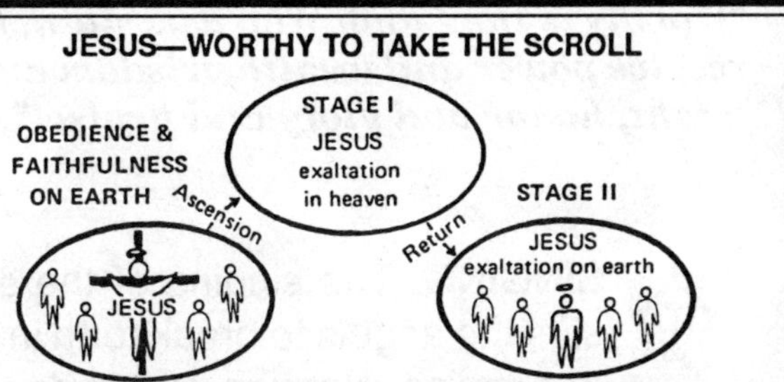

First see Jesus at His exaltation to the heavenly throne after His ascension. He is filled with joy, having earned this honor as a MAN! As God, it was always His, but to earn it as well—by obedience—is astonishing. But that is only part of His Joy. See the MAN Christ Jesus exalted again when He returns to earth to reign as King over all kings.

NEW SONG. Once the Lamb receives the scroll, and breaks its seals, the final days of this age will begin. It is the *worthiness of the Lamb* that inspires the elders to sing. By means of His death, the Lamb put in force a _new covenant_ that made it possible for people to become *as righteous as God* through faith in Jesus (2 Cor. 5:21). This will give God a real family, a genuine family, something He has always wanted. With the cross behind Him, Jesus is ready to inherit the throne of His father David (Luke 1:32). Since believers are *IN CHRIST,* they are "joint-heirs with Jesus," and will reign with Him. Here is one verse that specifically says *we will reign on the earth.* This obviously poses a problem for those who say we will not reign on the earth with Jesus.

11. Then to my ears came the voices of millions of angels. They surrounded the throne, the living creatures and the elders, 12. and were loudly singing:

"Worthy is the Lamb Who was slain, to receive power and wealth, wisdom and might, honor and glory and praise!"

SINGING. The singing of the elders stirs the angels to break forth in glorious praise. Heaven resounds to the words... *"Worthy is the Lamb!"* It may not be possible to express exactly what the angels are doing here. But John, who hears this, has never heard anything sweeter, stronger or louder before. The angels are attributing to the Lamb, the highest of all honor, glory and praise. These are not benefits heaped on the Lamb, *but qualities He already possesses.* Someone has written that the one thing that we, who possess nothing, can give to Him who possesses all...*is praise.* As the elders and angels add their voices in response, heaven swells in majestic song. However, the crescendo is yet to come.

13. And then I heard every creature, whether in heaven or on earth, whether in the ground or in the sea, join the chorus, singing:

"Praise and honor, glory and power belong to the One Who sits on the throne and to the Lamb forever and ever!"

14. The four living creatures said, "Amen," while the twenty-four elders fell down in worship.

EVERY CREATURE. The sound surges to full volume as a great roar from below rises to heaven to join the heavenly chorus. The whole universe now blends together for the final hymn of praise. No living thing is excluded, not even the bugs and worms. Since the Lamb's sacrifice redeems the whole of creation, it is fitting that the entire creation praise Him. The four living creatures who triggered all this praise, now bring it to a close with their "Amen." See how this worship is addressed to both the One Who sits on the throne and to the Lamb. Is that not a clue to the real identity of Jesus? When the earthly program is over, *"the mystery of Christ,"* will no longer be a mystery (Eph. 3:4; 1Cor.15: 24-28). When we meet Him in eternity (Spirit to spirit), we will behold His true identity.

HEADED FOR OVERCOMER TERRITORY

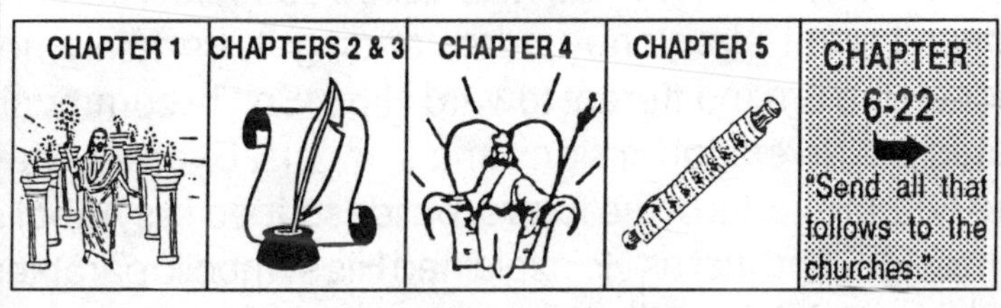

John's visit to the throne room was necessary preparation for what is coming. He has sampled the majesty of heaven. He has heard the testimonies of myriads of angels. He has seen the Lamb in the midst of the throne, with the heavenly host prostrate at His feet. He is now convinced the Lord is in complete control of the universe and easily able to execute whatever judgments on the earth He chooses. While John will be confronted with frightening scenes of the future, he won't hesitate to write down what he sees and send it to the seven churches as ordered (1:11). He has prepared the churches by warning them that they must be overcomers. When they read the rest of John's book (Chapters 6 - 22) they will realize they are headed for—*overcomer territory.*

GET READY FOR THE SEALS

When Jesus was on earth, He taught in parables. When His disciples asked about them, He would say, in effect..."I don't want OUTSIDERS to understand what I'm saying, but I do want you INSIDERS to understand." Then He would take His disciples aside and explain the meaning of His parables in plain language. By *"outsiders"* He meant those without the Spirit, whose hearts were hard toward God.

Similarly, the Revelation is veiled speech. The Lord doesn't want everyone understanding it, certainly not those who are indifferent toward Him. So He communicates His revelation in signs and symbols. Even so, they are actual events of the future, but described in symbolic language. And just as He explained His symbolic parables to His disciples in those early days, He has also explained the symbolic end-time events of the Revelation.

When did He do that? He did it when His disciples came asking, *"Tell us, when will this happen, and what will be the sign of your coming and of the end of the age?"* (Matt. 24:3). In very plain language, the Lord gave them a prophetic outline of John's scroll with its seven seals. His explanation is found in Matthew Chapter 24 where He lists the events that were to occur. Note the sequence:

1. False prophets or false Christs (vs.5)
2. Wars (vs.6) vs.7 may be the final world war
3. Famines (vs.7)
4. Pestilences (vs.7)
5. The Great Tribulation (vss.21-22)
6. Cosmic disturbances & earthquake (vs.29)
7. Sign of His coming & appearance (vs.30)

As we move through the seals, you'll find they harmonize with Jesus' words in Matthew 24. Consequently, that chapter may be useful in understanding what the seals mean. Fix in your mind that *the seven seals cover the balance of the book of Revelation.*

JOHN'S PRIMARY ASSIGNMENT

We now have a real handle on the book. First, Jesus revealed Himself to John. Then He gave him seven *overcoming* messages for the 7 churches. Next, John was summoned to the throne room where he beheld the scroll containing startling events due to take place on the earth. This was to prepare him for what he was about to see. Chapters 6 thru 22 present the future events John is to write down and send to the churches. One could ask why the Lord would send this information to those churches, if the church has been raptured from the earth as some suggest. The truth is, the church hasn't been raptured at this point, and won't be until the last trumpet sounds, as Paul insists (1 Cor. 15:52). Getting this truth to the churches is John's primary assignment.

The 4 Horsemen of Chapter 6

In this chapter we meet the famous four horsemen of the apocalypse, who will be presented to us one by one. As the Lord Jesus opens the first four seals, these horsemen gallop past us, laying out for us a future time which the Lord describes as *"the beginning of sorrows"* (Matt.24:8). The first seal introduces the antichrist as he erupts on the stage of the world. The other 3, his demonic henchmen, wreak havoc on the earth destroying a fourth of mankind. This destruction is the by-product of antichrist's reign. Even so, it is just the beginning. Later we'll see this same man indwelt by Satan and transformed into the beast.

REVELATION 6

In Chapter One, John beheld a vision of Christ in which he was instructed to write letters to seven churches in Asia. In Chapters Two and Three, he did that. In Chapters Four and Five, he was called up to the throne room of heaven where he saw the scroll sealed with seven seals. He heard Jesus declared worthy to break those seals and open the scroll. In this chapter, the Lamb will break six of the seals. As we explore the terrible times ahead for the church, bear in mind that God showers His grace on believers and His wrath on unbelievers. We will see the two groups side by side throughout the book of Revelation. The chapters ahead will picture the sufferings of the church, God's judgments on her enemies, and the final triumph of Jesus. While many Christians will die at the hand of antichrist, they will never suffer the wrath of God. Now let's watch as the action begins.

6 **1. I watched as the lamb broke the first of the seals, and I heard one of the four living creatures say, in a voice like thunder, "Come!" 2. I looked and there before my eyes was a white horse. Its rider carried a bow, and a crown was placed upon his head. He rode out conquering everything before him, for he was bent on total conquest.**

WHITE HORSE. As the Lamb breaks the first seal, the action begins. A white horse suddenly appears before John's eyes. The rider is clearly a conqueror, howbeit an unusual one. He has a bow, the symbol of human military power, *but no arrows.* He doesn't need them. He uses different weapons—promises, personal charm, and miracles. Because of this and his white horse, one might think this was Jesus. But when we compare this rider with Jesus in Chapter 19, we see all they have in common is their white horses. The Lamb is the OPENER OF THE SEALS, He is not the rider. Jesus wields the sword of judgment, this rider has only a bow. Jesus has many crowns, this rider but one. Besides, this rider is chiefly a deceiver.

ITS RIDER. This action precedes the Great Tribulation. That tells us the rider is the counterfeit Christ, the antichrist, as he begins his reign. At this point he will look very much like a savior. Operating in the power of Satan, his political and economic genius will cause the world to view him as a great deliverer. Actually, he will be the slickest deceiver ever to appear on this earth. Established as the ruler of the world, he will settle the Arab-Israeli dispute to the complete satisfaction of the Jews.

TOTAL CONQUEST. The apostle Paul says this man cannot appear until God removes the restraining force holding him back (2 Thess. 2:7). He will not conquer until he is *allowed* to conquer. After that, he will easily and quickly become the ruler of the world. Bringing this man to power is God's doing and should be viewed as a herald of impending judgments. This rider, the antichrist, will bring a lot of suffering to the world. Some may find it difficult to accept a 2000 year gap between the 69th and 70th weeks of Daniel, but it is important to remember that the thunderous events of the 70th week have not yet come to pass. They are still future. Regardless of any theological arguments, we have yet to see a ruler gain control over the entire world.

3. And when the Lamb broke the second seal, I heard the second living creature say, "Come!" 4. Out came another horse, this time a fiery red one. Its rider was given a huge sword and empowered to remove all peace from the earth by inducing men to slay one another.

RED HORSE. As the second seal is broken, John sees a red horse whose rider is the *prince of war!* This man (assuming he is a man), is able to generate a period of intense warfare on the earth. He is commissioned to remove peace from the earth, probably by unleashing the destructive instincts of one man upon another. God is not the only one who uses men to accomplish His will. The devil also uses men. What's more, Satan has a descending order of beings that form a chain of command (Eph. 6:12). This suggests the riders of these horses may represent demonic princes of some sort.

DIRTY WORK. We can expect antichrist, since he is coming in the power of Satan, to use demonic agents for his dirty work (2 Thess. 2:9). That way he can pose as a *"prince of peace,"* while his subordinate on the red horse charges forth as the *"prince of war!"* Now we know why the rider on the WHITE horse needs no arrows. All of his ambitions are accomplished by means of demon-inspired wars. The "huge sword" symbolizes the broad scope of these wars. What follows war? Famine and death as we'll see. Keep in mind all this is symbolical. There are no actual horses, neither are there any riders. We would never fathom these things if they were given to us in the abstract, so symbols such as these are needed to accommodate our finite minds.

5. As He broke the third seal, I heard the third living creature command..."Come!" 6. This time I saw a black horse and its rider was holding a pair of scales in his hand. A voice that seemingly came from the four living creatures said, "For a day's work a man may buy a quart of wheat and he may also buy three quarts of barley for a day's work, but leave the oil and the wine alone."

BLACK HORSE. The rider of the black horse comes out holding balance scales in his hand. The symbolism is clear—food is so scarce it must be parceled out. The price is inflated, roughly ten to fourteen times the normal price. Scarcity, following in the wake of war, generates nearly famine prices. A quart of wheat was the bare minimum for a man per day. A day's wages, would also buy him three quarts of the less nutritious barley for his family. At the same time, the Lord (it's His voice), places limits on this horseman, ordering him not to damage the vineyards or the olive orchards. Grains grow on the surface, but grapes and olive trees have deep roots. It appears this devastation is not to go below the surface of the earth, a definite limitation.

7. When the fourth seal was broken, I heard the voice of the fourth living creature say, "Come!" 8. I looked once more and saw a pale horse whose rider's name was Death, and following close behind was Hades. A fourth of mankind was placed under the power of these riders, that they might kill with the sword and famine, and with pestilence and wild beasts.

DEATH. This horse has the color of a corpse—pale. The rider is authorized to produce massive death, but his authority is limited to one fourth of mankind. His inseparable companion is Hades, the pitiless receptacle of death's victims. Hades is a Jewish term for the abode of the wicked dead. Whom do we blame for all this death and destruction? Antichrist, of course. War, famine and death are simply the by-products of his reign. The red, black and pale horsemen merely symbolize the ruin that follows in the wake of this evil ruler. Since they are so destructive, we must see them as servants of Satan, and the more so, when we realize the restraints have been removed from antichrist and his subordinates. Their chief work is to obey antichrist and bring about unrestrained evil.

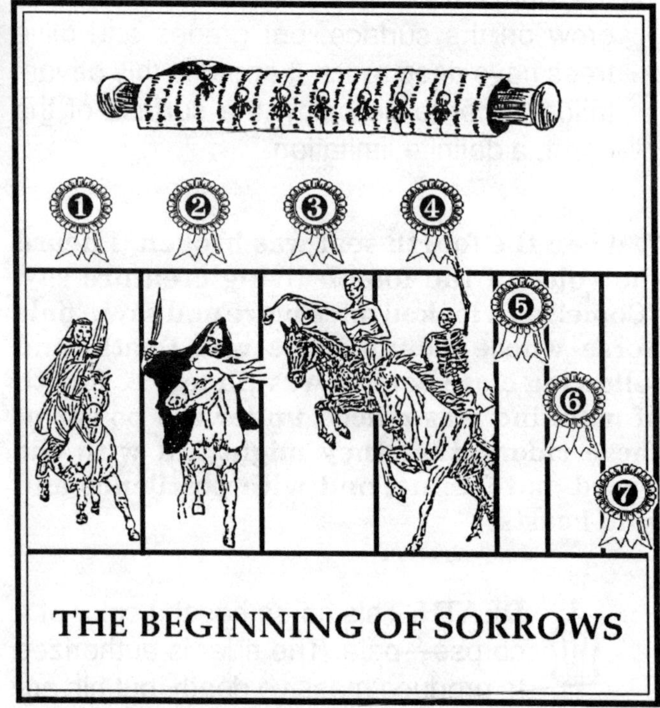

THE BEGINNING OF SORROWS

COMMENT: Antichrist is the center of all this destructive activity, with the other three horsemen merely the by-products of his evil reign. Wars, famine and death are the natural consequences that flow in the wake of this evil ruler. Do not regard them as principal characters. They simply represent the devastation brought about by antichrist. Long before Jesus appeared on earth there were conquerors, wars, famine and death. Not only did these appear during the early centuries of the church, but often during the centuries down to our time. It is possible to read about these four horsemen and feel their destructiveness fits many situations in human history. But one has not truly laid hold of the Revelation unless he can see that most of it can only be APPLIED TO THE FUTURE. John's four riders will yet appear to do on a world-wide scale, what earlier riders did within limited scope of history and geography.

WON'T THIS KIND OF DESTRUCTION TRIGGER FEAR IN CHRISTIANS?

9. And when He broke the fifth seal, I saw an altar and beneath it were the souls of those who had been martyred for declaring the word of God and for their faithful witness.

BENEATH THE ALTAR. The four horsemen will generate fear in every heart not prepared for "perilous times" (2 Tim. 3:1). The terrorizing horsemen will plunge the world into a frightening time and many Christians, worried about their futures, will need encouragement. While John's purpose is to encourage believers, he is obliged to reveal their peril as well. Something dreadful is at hand, the Great Tribulation! Beneath the altar John sees the souls of many martyrs. In ancient Jewish rituals, the blood of the sacrifices was poured out at the base of the altar. And since "the life is in the blood," John is symbolically saying, the deaths of these martyrs is the same as sacrifices offered to God (Lev. 17:11). This scene is symbolical of all those who have died for Jesus from earliest times and will include those about to die for Him at the hand of the beast.

10. They gave out a loud cry: "How long, O Sovereign Lord, holy and true, will you wait before judging the inhabitants of the earth and avenging our deaths?" 11. They were each given a white robe and told to enjoy their rest a little longer until their total number had

been completed, that is, until the remainder of their brothers were put to death as they had been.

HOW LONG? Some of these martyrs have been there a long time. For centuries they've seen the wicked prosper and the righteous suffer and want to know how much longer God will wait before vindicating His name? It's as though they were saying, *"Look at what men are getting away with!"* They're concerned for God's reputation. That's what they mean by—"avenging our deaths." It is not personal vengeance they seek, they want God's honor upheld. From where they sit, it's obvious "the inhabitants of the earth" are hostile toward God. So they want Him to bring judgment on the whole world—which He will. <u>This seal marks the beginning of the Great Tribulation, during which millions of Christians will be slaughtered</u>. The central feature here is the death of God's people. Later John will flashback to this period and explain how this slaughter comes about.

TOTAL NUMBER. To these impatient souls, God is saying in effect, *"You'll just have to wait until everyone destined to be a martyr is killed! I can't pour out my wrath until the family is complete!"* From this it's clear the Lamb's book of life contains a specific number of people who make up the family of God (Rev.17:8;21:27;Phil.4:3). Until that number is complete, God will put up with this unbelieving world. During the Great Tribulation it will cost believers their lives to identify with Christ, since they will be forced to choose between antichrist and Jesus. This is why we must distinguish between tribulation and wrath. The wrath of God follows the Great Tribulation (Matt. 24:29). In the coming tribulation, those who confess Christ will have the privilege of dying for Him. Today's Christians should prepare for this. If they are expecting a rapture/escape from this tribulation, they are clinging to a very recent and faulty view of Scripture. Nothing in the Word even hints such a thing.

ROBES AND REST. Each of the martyrs receives a white robe, representing the righteousness of God. It is *given* because no one can earn it or is worthy of it. All believers receive this robe as a part of the "salvation package." The martyrs are not uncomfortable, they are enjoying a blessed rest. They are to continue resting until joined by the tribulation martyrs. When the family is almost complete, the Lord will move. When He appears in the sky with these resting saints, then those who have not yet been martyred will be raptured from the ground in a flash, to join the host in the air (1 Thess. 4:17). The world-wide slaughter of believers will no doubt make the number of raptured saints relatively small. However, it will include those Christians who are seized and pressed into slavery (13:10). The rapture is actually a clean-up operation, an act of God to get every last saint off the earth before He pours out His wrath! The believers are not "children of wrath" (Eph. 2:3; 1 Thess.1:10).

GOD HAS HAD ENOUGH

**12. I watched while the Lamb broke the sixth
seal. With that, there was a tremendous earthquake. The sun turned black as sackcloth
made of goat hair, and the full moon was as
red as blood. 13. The stars of the sky seemed to
fall to the earth like unripe figs blown off a
tree when whipped by a gale. 14. The starry
sky vanished like a scroll being rolled up, and
every mountain and island was shifted from
its place.**

SIXTH SEAL. This seal marks THE END OF THE GREAT TRIBULATION and heralds God's intervention into the natural world. The vindication of God's name is about to occur. Unrepentant man has defied Him long enough. When this seal is broken, the entire universe is shaken up. Catastrophic movement occurs world-wide as a *great* earthquake dislocates mountain ranges. The earth is racked with convulsions, the seas don't know where they belong. The islands, which are mountain tops, disappear. This awesome earthquake merely foreshadows a far greater one ahead (16:18). Changes occur in the skies as well: the sun is darkened, the moon turns blood-red and the sky recedes. All these events are described in Old Testament prophecies (more than 60 of them) as signs that herald the coming Day of the Lord.

①	②	③	④	⑤ ⑥
WHITE HORSE	RED HORSE	BLACK HORSE	PALE HORSE	ALTAR • QUAKE War on the Saints The Great Tribulation

This chart focuses on the 5th & 6th seals which mark the beginning and ending points of the Great Tribulation. The dotted line is merely to distinguish between the two seals. The souls under the altar signal the beast's war on the saints, whereas the earthquake announces that God is ready to intervene. Later John will describe in detail the awful things confronting the church.

15. At this, the kings of the earth with their nobles and captains, the rich and the powerful, and all men whether slave or free, hid themselves in caves and among the rocky projections of the mountains. 16. "Fall on us," they begged the mountains and the rocks. "Hide us from the face of Him Who sits on the throne and from the wrath of the Lamb! 17. For the great day of their wrath has come and who can stand against it?"

FALL ON US. This seal is God's attention getter. Men will now get their eyes off of the beast and his miracles and get a taste of what God can do when He is upset. They're going to see His thunderbolts of anger. The things described in these verses (12-17), were foretold by the Lord as signs of His second coming. In Luke 21:25-28 we find the Lord detailing those signs just as they are itemized here. These signs are but a sample of the coming wrath *and they all know it.* That's what's remarkable. The enemies of God realize the day of His wrath is approaching! The day of terror is all but upon them and still they won't repent. It's not death they fear, for they want the mountains to crush them. What they fear is *the presence of the Lamb.* As Adam and Eve hid themselves from the presence of God, so does man's guilty conscience make him dread *facing God.* Men would rather die than be confronted by Him. They prefer death by a crushing avalanche to facing Jesus. God has their attention now. But it won't change anything.

COMMENT: Don't be upset with the apostle for saying so little about the Great Tribulation at this point. Remember he's an old man relating this as he sees fit. Besides, he is ever mindful that the guards will be examining his writing before allowing it to leave the island.That's another reason why the book seems so jumbled. You'd think he would immediately go to the 7th seal in the next chapter, but he doesn't. Instead, he interrupts the flow of the narrative to tell us about 2 groups of people and how they fare during the Great Tribulation. The 7th and last seal won't be opened until chapter 8. When we get to Chapters 12, 13 and 14, John will flash back to the Great Tribulation and bring us up to date on what really happened during those awful days.

THE TRIBULATION IS BEHIND US

We have just passed through a terrible time of history—*the Great Tribulation.* The question arises: *how will believers make out when the beast vents his wrath against those opposing him?* At this point, John pauses in his explanation of the seals to deal with that question. We have now come to the first of a series of 5 interruptions John makes in this book. Chapter 7 is the first break in the story. During this "time out," before the opening of the seventh seal, John explains what happens to two groups of people: 144,000 Jews and an innumerable multitude from all races and nations specifically identified as "coming out of the Great Tribulation."

SEAL #1	SEAL #2	SEAL #3	SEAL #4	SEAL #5	SEAL #6	TIME OUT—CHAPTER 7	SEAL #7
THE REIGN OF ANTICHRIST "The Beginning of Sorrows" (Matt. 24:8)				The Great Tribulation			
				BEGINNING OF TRIBULATION	End of The Great Tribulation		

Here's an overview of the seals. While the 7th seal has not yet been broken, we nonetheless can sense what God is doing. The first 4 seals, the *"Beginning of sorrows,"* that Jesus spoke of in Matthew 24, picture antichrist unleashing his wrath on all as he exercises power over the entire world. The first seal opens with him in power, while the next three seals picture the terrible fruits of his reign. His covenant with Israel spans the first 4 seals. In seals 5 and 6, the beast vents his rage against the saints for 42 months, bringing on the Great Tribulation. With the 7th seal, God gets into the act with His trumpet judgments and bowls of wrath. Bear in mind, the scroll contains all the future events John was told to record and send to the churches.

REVELATION 7

(John's first interruption)

7 1. After this I saw four angels stationed at the four corners of the earth, holding its four winds in check and not allowing them to blow on land or sea or any tree. 2. Then rising from the East, I saw another angel bearing the seal of the living God. He shouted to the four angels who had been given power to lay waste to land and sea. 3. "Hold up on those winds! Don't do anything to harm the land or the sea or the trees until we have placed the seal of our God on the foreheads of His servants!"

FOUR WINDS. Before discussing the seventh seal, which takes us into the Day of the Lord, John knows his readers are wondering about the *spiritual safety* of believers suffering under the beast. So he takes "time out" to show how safe believers are during the Great Tribulation. It is needed, because practically all of them will be killed. They need to know that death in no way threatens their salvation. The Jews, bewildered when the false messiah declares himself to be God, are asking themselves, *"If the beast was not the Messiah, who is?"* So God holds back the four winds, giving the Jews time to rethink the claims of Christ. The salvation door is still open and a lot of shaken Jews could be saved.

THE SEAL. God seals certain believing Jews against physical harm that they might get the truth of Jesus to their fellow Jews, who are confused about Jesus. These Jewish evangelists will operate right under the nose of the beast, and for that they'll need divine protection. Thus they are sealed by God. Without supernatural protection, they wouldn't last five minutes. These Jewish servants are believers. Since the seal is that of the *living* God, we know they are believers. When their task is done, the protection will be removed. Then, like the two witnesses coming later, they'll be killed (11:7). John doesn't say HOW these servants are sealed, however there is no need to suppose any physical mark is placed on them. If the protection is supernatural, it will be apparent to everyone quickly enough.

HOW MANY JEWISH EVANGELISTS WOULD BE NEEDED FOR THIS JOB?

4. Then I learned how many had been sealed this way—one hundred and forty-four thousand from all the tribes of Israel. The tribes were listed like this:

5.From the tribe of Judah 12,000
from the tribe of Reuben 12,000
from the tribe of Gad 12,000

6.from the tribe of Asher 12,000
from the tribe of Naphtali 12,000
from the tribe of Manasseh 12,000

7.from the tribe of Simeon 12,000
from the tribe of Levi 12,000
from the tribe of Issachar 12,000

8.from the tribe of Zebulun12,000
from the tribe of Joseph 12,000
from the tribe of Benjamin 12,000

TRIBES. You hear talk of the missing tribes of Israel, but if they are really missing nobody told John. Nor did they tell James, who writes "*To the twelve tribes scattered among the nations*" (James 1:1). They are not lost to God, who has been regathering Jews from all over the world for centuries. By the time these are sealed, the real mix of Jews will be known only to God. The number 144,000 may be symbolic, but there's no reason to insist that it is. 144,000 should be plenty. Using Jewish evangelists to reach a mass of disillusioned, shaken Jews makes sense. Besides, the choice is so clear cut. It shouldn't take long to harvest those willing to turn to Jesus. The tribes are listed in no less than 18 different ways in the Old Testament, so the order named here is not significant. What is significant, is that a good number of Jews are going to be saved to swell the ranks of believers.

IT SOUNDS LIKE GOD IS USING THE TRIBULATION TO HARVEST SOULS, RIGHT?

9. After this I saw a multitude so vast no one could count it. These were people from all races and tribes, nations and languages, standing before the throne and the Lamb. They

were clothed in white and had palm branches in their hands 10. and they shouted:

> ***"The power that saved us belongs to our God who sits on the throne and to the Lamb!"***

MULTITUDE. John's eyes move to a different scene, this one in heaven. He beholds an enormous mass of people clothed in white robes, which tells us they are Christians. Biblically, white robes represent the righteousness of God. These people are in heaven and thrilled to be there. They know by experience the saving power of the Lamb and happily shout His praises. Before they reached heaven, salvation was a truth they had to embrace by faith. But now they are enjoying the reality of heaven and looking directly into the face of Jesus. Their praise is more than just acknowledging their safe journey through death. They are thinking of the evil world they've left behind. Their salvation is from EVERYTHING EVIL. No wonder they shout. When we join this crowd, we'll do some shouting too! Now let's see how the angels react to their shouts of praise.

11. All the angels gathered around the throne and around the elders and the four living creatures suddenly prostrated themselves before the throne and worshipped God.

> ***12. "Amen!" they said. "Praise and glory and wisdom and thanksgiving and honor and power and might be to our God forever! Amen!"***

13. One of the elders turned to me, asking "Who are all these people dressed in white robes and where do they come from?" 14. I replied, "If you know who they are my Lord, please tell me."

"These," he said, "have come out of the Great Tribulation. They have washed their robes and made them white in the blood of the Lamb. 15. And now they stand before God's throne serving Him day and night and worship Him in His temple. He Who sits on the throne will shelter them with His presence. 16. Never again will they suffer hunger and thirst. Never again will the noonday sun beat upon them, nor any scorching heat, 17. for the Lamb, who is in the center of the throne will shepherd them, leading them to springs of the water of life. And God will wipe away every tear from their eyes."

THESE HAVE COME OUT. Who's in this crowd? Every believer martyred in the Great Tribulation, including the 144,000 Jewish evangelists and any other Jews they introduced to Jesus. The overwhelming majority will be Gentiles, of course. And all arrive in heaven by way of martyrdom. These are the tribulation saints. John was thinking of the tribulation when he was urging those in the seven churches to be overcomers. For them, overcoming didn't mean escaping death, but facing it and being willing to die for Jesus rather than accept the mark of the beast. Overcoming is the big word in those church letters. With this multitude beyond counting, it's clear God will take a huge harvest out of the Great Tribulation. The Great Tribulation is His harvesting machine. In the earliest days of the church, persecution caused Christianity to spread like wildfire. Now it will happen again. Above all else, it is the joy of this glorious assembly that John wants us to see.

SHEPHERD THEM. Why does John use "shepherd" and "shelter" language? Later he will expand on the dreadful nature of the Great Tribulation and the slaughter of the saints, so these words are preparatory. Here the happy saints are shouting..."Jesus saves!"...*after they've been martyred!* This is meant to comfort any of us called upon to defy the beast and suffer martyrdom. We need this kind of encouragement. Later we'll learn the beast is given authority to make war against us and kill us (13:7,10). Even so, Jesus will shepherd us through the experience. In Chapters 12, 13, and 14, which *flashback* to the Great Tribulation, John will give us the terrible details. This will be the most severe test for God's people, for it is the wrath of Satan vented against the saints. While permitted by God, it will not be His doing. God doesn't move against man until the next seal, seal #7.

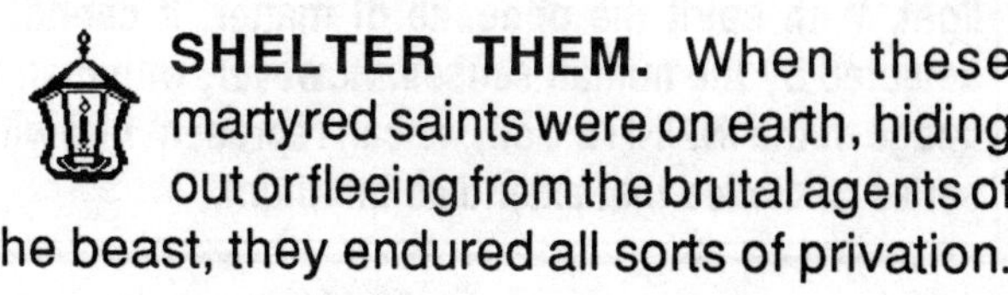

SHELTER THEM. When these martyred saints were on earth, hiding out or fleeing from the brutal agents of the beast, they endured all sorts of privation.

Bitter cold and icy rain in some places, scorching hot sun in others. Hunger and thirst always dogged their steps. However this reference to their physical needs is symbolic of...*eternal refreshment!* Man is not a body, he merely uses one as an "earth suit." With it, he gets about in space and time. Physical needs belong only to the physical body. The *soul* of man has an eternal hunger that can only be satisfied by the Eternal One Himself. This passage is saying that every longing of our hearts will be satisfied when we're with Jesus. Consequently, anything we might suffer at the hands of the beast is not worthy to be compared with the satisfaction and joy that will be ours in that day.

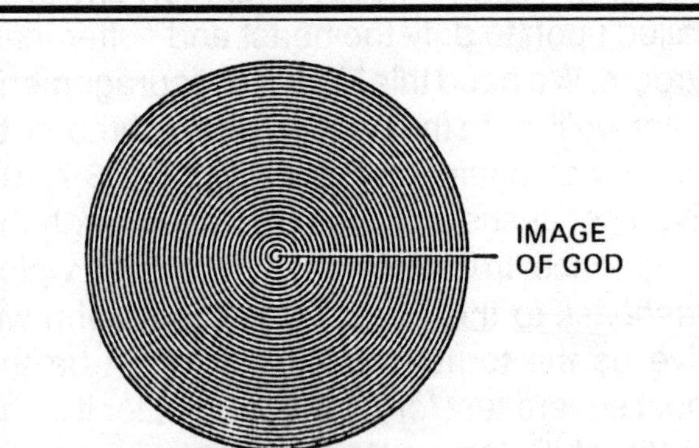

Since God is Spirit, His image must also be spirit (John 4:24). Therefore we don't know what man, as the image of God, is really like. We see his body, but no one has ever seen a spirit. Our eyes can only see things that reflect light. With spirit the opposite of matter, it cannot be detected by the human senses. However, with man the image of the INFINITE God, we can represent him with a series of circles that extend ad infinitum.

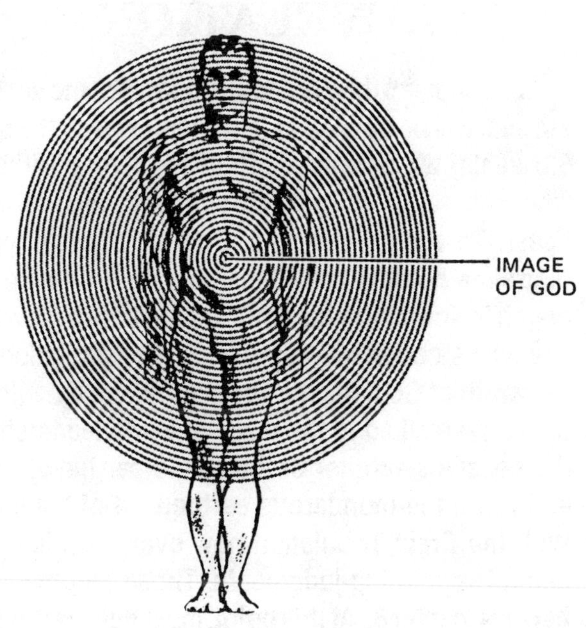

Observe how the circles, which represent the image of God, extend beyond the human body. That's because man, like God, is a spirit, and there is no way to compress an infinite and eternal spirit inside a physical, corporeal body. Man is more than a body, MUCH MORE. Because we are limited to the physical realm with its 5 senses, we have no way to be aware of what we are in the spirit. It is for this reason that the apostle Paul could say that we *"Sit together in heavenly places in Christ Jesus"* (Eph. 2:6). We take God's word for it that our spirit has its own life and our body (a creature of the field) has its own life. The death of the body, then, has no affect on the life of the soul. Jesus said, *"Fear not those who can kill the body, but cannot kill the soul"* (Matt. 10:28). This can be a comforting truth when our physical lives are threatened.

REVELATION 8

In Chapter 6 the Lord broke open 6 of the seals. The 7th seal will be opened in this chapter. With the 5th and 6th seals, we passed through the Great Tribulation, where the saints endured the wrath of antichrist and the beast. To accomplish this, God simply removed the restraints holding back Satan's man. He immediately began to spew forth his wrath against the believers and any who stood in his way. The Great Tribulation is not the wrath of God, it's the wrath of Satan. It begins with antichrist exalted to the place of world leadership and the beast's slaughter of the saints per the 5th seal. It ends with the thunderous earthquake of the 6th seal. With the Great Tribulation now over, God is ready to begin His warning-judgments. Those judgments start here in Chapter 8. At this point, most believers will have joined the Lord—*by slaughter.* Those surviving the slaughter will be removed later—*by rapture*—at the last trumpet (1 Cor. 15:52). So get set to watch God unleash His judgments, but remember these are warning-judgments only, they are not His wrath. His wrath doesn't come until the last trumpet sounds in chapter 11.

8 **1. When the Lamb broke open the seventh seal, all heaven was silent for about half an hour.**

SILENT. This is a surprise. Silence is not what we might expect at this point. Why? The noise in heaven has been building from Chapter 4 when the four living creatures began their "Holy, Holy, Holy." The

24 elders joined them and before long the angels were adding their voices. The intensity has been building for 4 chapters and now all of a sudden everything is quiet. What's up? We're about to see the place that prayer has in the plan of God. You know what it is like when we pray—everything becomes quiet. When we pray, we stop everything and talk to God. For His part, God also stops everything and listens to us. And that's what's happening here. Of course here the truth of the power of prayer is magnified many times by the sudden silence. We needn't suppose the Lord actually spent 30 minutes listening to the sum total of His people's cries. Rather, it is a symbolic scene that shows how the prayers of God's people really do move His hands. That will become clear as we watch the action.

2. Then I saw the seven angels that stand in the presence of God and seven trumpets were handed to them.

COMMENT: Having reached the 7th and last seal, we come now to the seven trumpets. The seven trumpets *are the 7th seal*, and the seven bowls of God's wrath *are part of the 7th trumpet*. This view does no violence to scholarship or to John's words. The easiest way to handle the *seals, trumpets and bowls* of the Revelation, is to view the 7 seals as covering the whole of John's revelation. The 7th seal consists of the 7 trumpets, the last of which contains the wrath of God. This is the big seal. With this seal we will be exposed to everything God wants us to know about the last days of planet earth. The flow chart at the end of Chapter 11 shows the events packed into this last seal, seal #7.

TRUMPETS. The seven angels are not just now arriving on the scene. They've been here all the time. It's their task to deliver God's warnings and pour out the bowls of His wrath. However, the focus here is not on the angels, but on the trumpets handed to them. This is the first action to take place after the half hour of silence. Trumpets have always been significant throughout the Bible. Since the day they announced God's presence at Mount Sinai, they have symbolized His intervention into human affairs. While it is true that God runs practically everything by natural laws and natural order, He can thrust Himself into the human program any time He chooses. He is now ready to do just that with His trumpet warnings. While they may seem like judgments, they are nonetheless warnings.

3. Then another angel who was holding a golden censer, came and stood by the altar. He was given a large amount of incense to add to the prayers of God's people and present them as an offering on the golden altar before the throne. 4. The aroma of the incense, mingled with the prayers of the saints, rose up before God from the angel's hand. 5. Then the angel took the censer, filled it with live coals from the altar and hurled it to the earth. This was followed by a crashing roar as thunder rumbled across the sky. Lightning flashed all around and there was a terrible earthquake.

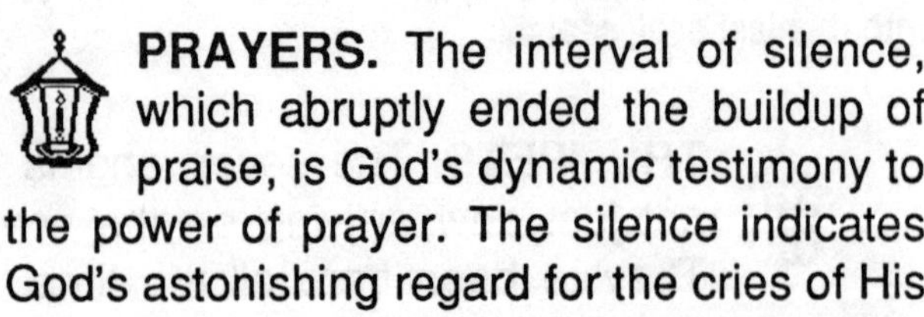

PRAYERS. The interval of silence, which abruptly ended the buildup of praise, is God's dynamic testimony to the power of prayer. The silence indicates God's astonishing regard for the cries of His people. It is not by chance that this silence occurs just before the sounding of the trumpets. Those trumpets will bring terrible calamities to earth as God's *direct response* to the cries of His people. Observe that the angel sends the prayers of the saints up to God before anything else happens. The 30 minutes of silence is representative of God's careful attention to what His people are saying. Note further, that the prayers are mingled with incense and come from beside the altar. Having symbolically weighed their prayers, God is now ready to act. He will now intervene in human affairs by firing warning shots (trumpets) across rebellious man's bow.

LIVE COALS. The angel holding the golden censer (actually a fire pan), scoops up hot coals from the altar. He is ready to throw it down on the earth, but first he tosses handfuls of incense on the glowing coals of the altar and a cloud of fragrant odors rises up before God. This is representative of the prayers of God's people, including the cries of those under the altar wanting God to avenge Himself. These are mingled with prayers of those who have long cried... *"Thy kingdom come."* See how the silence is strategically placed precisely as the Lord is about to answer their requests. As a *symbolic gesture* to the saints that the "Day of the Lord" has arrived, the angel hurls his fire-filled censer to the earth. The thunder and lightning and earthquake signal those on earth that God Himself is now ready to deal with rebellious man.

6. **And now the seven angels who had the seven trumpets prepared to sound their warning blasts.**

PREPARED TO SOUND. In verse 2, the seven angels received their trumpets. Now they are ready to blow them. As the angels step forward to lift their trumpets to their mouths, one can visualize an orchestra leader raising his baton. Before that baton comes down, we have a moment to consider again that we are in the seventh seal and that this seal contains the 7 trumpets. When the last angel sounds his trumpet, John's scroll will be fully opened and loud voices in heaven will proclaim... *"The kingdom of this world has become the kingdom of our Lord and His Christ!"* (11:15). Later we will see that everything God plans to do with this world is summed up in that last trumpet. So I say again, those 7 seals cover the entire Revelation.

GOD GETS INTO THE ACT

7. **When the first angel blew his trumpet, hail and fire mixed with blood were hurled upon on the earth, setting a third of the earth on fire. A third of all the trees were consumed as well as every blade of green grass.**

HAIL/FIRE/BLOOD. With the first trumpet, we have God's first angry intervention into our world system since the flood. Though He is fed up with unrepentant man, it's still not time for His wrath to be poured out. So God's first attacks are not directed against man, but against nature. The first trumpet destroys one-third of the vegetation. Some will no doubt die in this plague, but the purpose behind it is to give man an unmistakable warning. John is reporting what he sees. God gave him these visions and yet the data had to be processed through John's mind. So it is not surprising that John would use language out of his background, i.e., hail and fire mixed with blood. Apparently that imagery is drawn from the plagues of The Exodus. We'll see more of this as we proceed.

8. When the second angel blew his trumpet, something that looked like a great mountain engulfed in flames, was thrown into the sea.
9. A third of the sea turned into blood, killing a third of all the living creatures in the sea, and a third of all the ships was destroyed.

SEA. Again the target is not human life. As serious as this is, God still means for it to be a warning. As His judgments increase in intensity, we'll see the hardness of men's hearts increase as well. The fact that only one-third is destroyed, indicates God is still after repentance. These plagues are meant to warn men that God's full wrath is yet to come. As plagues came before the exodus of the Israelites from Egypt, so do these plagues come before the exodus of the church from this world. Will Christians then be affected by these plagues? Yes.Those who have not already perished by the sword will have to depend on their knowledge of this revelation to protect themselves the best they can. Those serving as slaves will have to rely on God's grace to bear whatever comes (13:10). While believers will be protected from the *demonic assaults* still to come, they are not immunized against natural calamities.

10. Then the third angel blew his trumpet and a huge star, blazing like a torch, fell from the sky. It fell upon a third of the rivers and springs. 11. This star was given the name "wormwood," because it fouled a third of the earth's drinking water. Many people died from drinking this tainted water.

WORMWOOD. In verse 8 a flaming mountain was hurled into the sea. In this case a glowing meteorite plummets through the earth's atmosphere to strike the world of nature at another point. The third plague is directed against the world's fresh water supply. The star is called "wormwood," because it embitters the water. Normally "wormwood" is not poisonous. For people to die from drinking this water, this star must do more than make the water bitter. It is likely poisoned in some way, as well. This plague, coming directly from heaven, is directed against the natural world. Still we find people dying. The number of those dying from this plague will be slight compared to those who will die when God's wrath is poured out. In that day, deaths will be in the hundreds of millions.

12. When the fourth angel blew his trumpet, a third part of the sun was struck, along with a third part of the moon and a third part of the stars so that the light of each was blacked out by one third. Thus the light of day and light by night were reduced by one third.

LIGHT. With the fourth trumpet plague, God is still dealing with the natural realm. This time He strikes the heavenly bodies, the light sources of the universe. This results in an increase in the duration of darkness for those on earth, creating shorter days. This is an obvious change in the laws of nature. It also signals a change in God's next dealing with people on the earth. We should not think of this as a "dimmer switch," with men moving about in dimmer light. But rather as absolute darkness, a darkness corresponding to Satan's kingdom of darkness. Jude speaks of "an eternity of blackest darkness" reserved for the servants of Satan. We now have a bridge (darkness) from the warning strikes against *nature*, to demonic strikes against *men*. The next trumpet will herald God's strike against men, using demonic forces for the job.

13. As I watched, I heard an eagle give out with a loud cry as it flew across the mid-heaven:

"Woe, woe, woe to the inhabitants of the earth because of the trumpet blasts which the next three angels are about to sound."

EAGLE. An eagle is a bird of prey, the kind that flies in the mid-heaven. This eagle seemingly circles where those below can see it and hear its loud calls. What he is announcing is the next three trumpets and because they will *come against man directly*, he calls them woes. They are going to be awful. This announcement by the eagle (not an angel), while a tiny interruption in the sounding of the 7 trumpets, is sufficient to tells us a change is coming. Thus, the verse indicates a transition from *physical attacks* to *spiritual attacks*. That an eagle makes the announcement, rather than an angel, also signals a change is at hand. God's first four plagues were directed against nature and intended as *warnings*. But the next three trumpets are directed *against men*. That's what makes them woes.

THE TRUMPETS

God Gets Into The Act

AGAINST NATURE				AGAINST MAN (WOES)		
EARTH	SEA	RIVERS	SKYLITE	DEMONS	PLAGUES	WRATH

Chapter 8 brings us to the 7 trumpets, which herald God's intervention into the affairs of men. He now gets into the act Himself. His first 4 trumpets were warning shots fired against nature and they occur in such a way that no doubt is left but what God is doing this. With the screaming eagle, men are warned that the next 3 trumpets will bring terrible plagues against all refusing to repent.

ALL THE SEALS AT A GLANCE

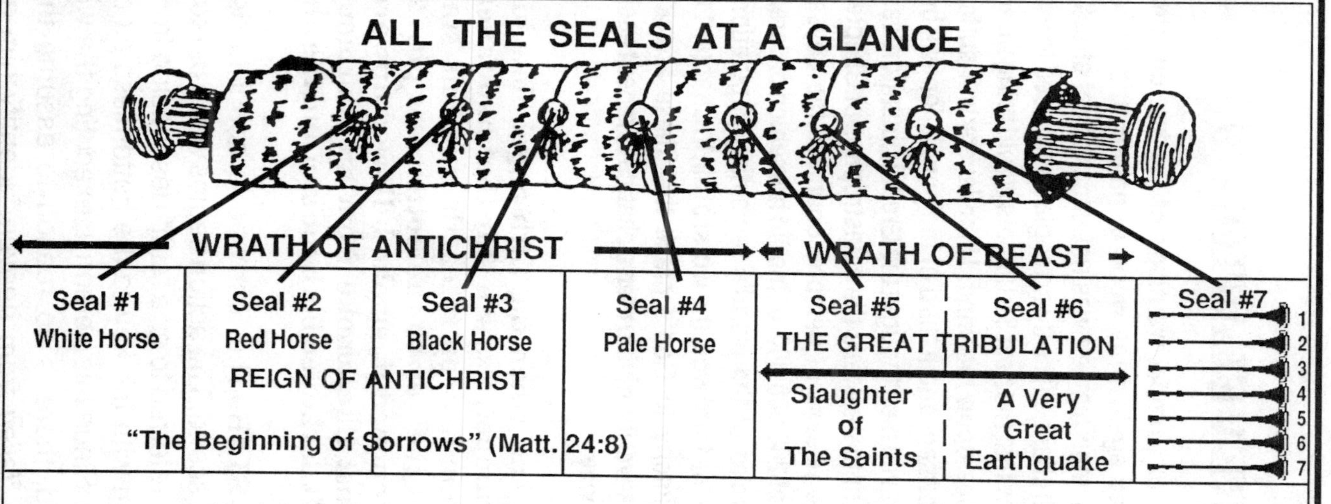

WRATH OF ANTICHRIST				WRATH OF BEAST		
Seal #1 White Horse	Seal #2 Red Horse	Seal #3 Black Horse	Seal #4 Pale Horse	Seal #5	Seal #6	Seal #7
	REIGN OF ANTICHRIST			THE GREAT TRIBULATION		1 2 3 4 5 6 7
"The Beginning of Sorrows" (Matt. 24:8)				Slaughter of The Saints	A Very Great Earthquake	

We may now survey the whole scroll with its seven seals. The first 4 seals usher in the four horsemen and picture the devastation that occurs with antichrist in power. This corresponds to the period Jesus describes as... *"the beginning of sorrows" (Matt. 24:8).* During this time, the earth suffers what may be described as *the wrath of antichrist.* The next two seals, 5 & 6, cover the Great Tribulation. During this time, believers experience the *wrath of the beast.* Then God intervenes with His trumpets, 6 of which are warning shots, while the 7th unleashes His wrath.

REVELATION 9

God's four trumpet warnings of the last chapter were directed against the world of nature, and while people died, man himself was not under direct attack. Now that will change. The flying eagle announced to the people below that the next 3 trumpets would bring three dreadful woes upon mankind. Unbelievers will suffer agonizing torment and a third of the population will be killed. If unsaved men thought the Great Tribulation was rough, wait until they face the catastrophes of Chapter Nine: 1.) the release of demons bound in the abyss, 2.) an army of 200,000,000 demonic horsemen ordered to kill one third of the world's remaining population. We'll look at the third woe, the worst of all, in Chapter 11. It is a testimony to God's grace that these attacks increase in severity, giving men a chance to repent each step of the way.

9 **1. And when the fifth angel blew his trumpet, I saw a star that had fallen from heaven to earth, and this star was given the key to the bottomless pit. 2. When he opened it, smoke billowed upward from it just like smoke from an enormous furnace. It darkened both the sun and the air.**

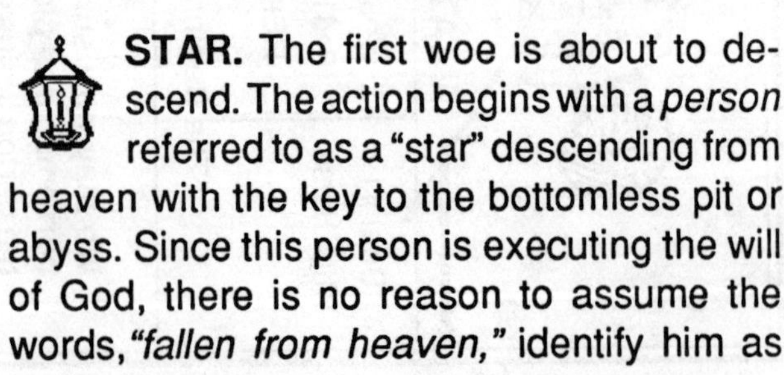

STAR. The first woe is about to descend. The action begins with a *person* referred to as a "star" descending from heaven with the key to the bottomless pit or abyss. Since this person is executing the will of God, there is no reason to assume the words, *"fallen from heaven,"* identify him as

Satan or one of the devil's servants. It is safer to consider him as one of the many angels who carry out God's will in the book of Revelation. What's more, his job is not all that different from the angel blowing the trumpet. He is likely the same angel we find in the first verse of Chapter 20, the one who comes down from heaven with a great chain and the key to the abyss. The word "fallen" here, means nothing more than to descend.

3. Then out of the smoke, locusts came forth swarming over all the earth and they were given the power of scorpions. 4. They were ordered not to harm any grass, plant or tree, but to attack all those who did not have God's mark on their foreheads. 5. They had no power to kill anyone; but they did have power to inflict men with painful torments for five months. The agony of that pain will be like that which a man feels when stung by a scorpion. 6. In those days men will seek death, but won't be able to kill themselves. They will long to die, but death simply won't be available.

SMOKE. When the angel unlocks the abyss, the first thing we see is dense clouds of smoke gushing upwards and darkening the sky. Out of the smoke, locusts swarm across the earth, but they are not after plant life. They've been ordered to leave the vegetation alone. That locusts normally feed on plant life makes these locusts most unusual. And since they are commanded to go after men, they can only be demonic locusts. These demon-locusts are well equipped to inflict severe pain, having the power of scorpions. A literal scorpion has a stinger at the end of its tail and when it strikes, it injects a painful poison into its victims. But the pain of demons is different; it is *not physical* it is *spiritual and emotional.* These strike the spirit and the imagination, using *fear* as the principal venom.

AGONY. It is *torment* the people suffer, not torture. These locusts are *demons,* afflicting men on the inside. The demons are instructed *only to torment,* not kill. That tells us they are under the sovereign control of the Lord. Internal suffering, especially apprehension, despair, hopelessness and fear, can be worse than physical pain. Especially when there is no limit to the intensity of the torments. These can drive people to suicide. However, in this case, death is impossible. That's what makes the woe so awful.The fact that they are limited to five months is further evidence that God is managing this plague.

COMMENT: *"Where do these demons come from? How did they get into the abyss in the first place?"* The answer is: they're put there. By whom? By believers who know how to use the authority given them by the Lord Jesus. The New Testament is rich with statements concerning the believer's authority over Satan and his demons. While Christians can order *the devil away,* they CANNOT send him into the abyss. God is using him. But demons are another matter. They *can be* ordered into the abyss and told to stay there. And there they stay until someone let's them out. That's what we're seeing here. The first woe is God's first judgment directed against men. He sends it by opening the abyss and allowing these demons to attack all who do not have God's seal. They

are so numerous, because for 1900 years many of God's people have been delivering themselves by ordering these demonic agents into the abyss. The rest of the demons, who were not sent into the abyss, will probably make up the demonic cavalry turned loose as the second woe.

FOREHEADS. Should Christians be concerned about this judgment? No. The assault is against those WITHOUT *the seal of God on their foreheads.* God's seal is not physical, but spiritual. *Forehead*, refers to one's thoughts, just as the *right hand* refers to his actions. However, Christians have a spiritual seal...*"The Lord knoweth them that are His!"* (2 Tim. 2:19). With these demons operating *inside people*, they instantly recognize God's seal. What's more, the Lord indwells the believer. God's promise that Christians will never be tempted beyond their ability to cope, blunts these internal attacks (1 Cor. 10:13). No wonder unbelievers, with no such protection, would want to die.

WHAT KIND OF LOCUSTS ARE THESE, ACTUALLY?

7. The features of these locusts resembled horses dressed for war. As I viewed them, they seemed to be wearing gold crowns on their heads, and their faces were a lot like human faces. 8. They had long hair like that of a woman and their teeth were like those of lions. 9. Their breastplates seemed to be made of iron and the sound of their wings was like the roar of many chariots charging full speed

into battle. 10. It was their tails, however, that did the damage, for they had stingers and those stingers were like the stingers of scorpions. And with these tails they had the power to hurt people for five months. 11. They served under a king who was the angel (a demon) of the abyss and whose name in Hebrew is Abaddon and in Greek, Apollyon (meaning the Destroyer).

RESEMBLED. It's difficult to describe unseen spirits, so drawing on his knowledge of the prophets and Israel's past experiences with plagues, John calls these demons, "locusts" (Joel 1:4- 2:11). So far all he has told us is that they came out of the smoke. Only now does he describe them for us. They are not small. He sees them the size of horses. But notice his use of the world "like," which tells us something other than literal horses is intended. John is picturing demons empowered to deliver diabolical, supernatural pain. What a scorpion's sting does to a man's foot or hand, the sting of these demons does to a person's soul.

THE DESTROYER. The protective armor of the horses suggests there is no way for pagan man to strike back at the demons. The unsaved have no weapons for repelling these torments. With this kind of power, there is little doubt of the success of the demon mission. If they were allowed to kill, much of unrepentant mankind would have been dead before the five months had passed. But they are not allowed to kill, even though their commander is—"The Destroyer." Called the *king of the abyss*, this demon is undoubtedly a high ranking angel in Satan's chain of command. It seems he is responsible for managing the demons confined to the bottomless pit. Bear in mind that all demons are fallen angels.

12. The first woe has now passed, but there are still two more to come!

TWO MORE. Now we know why the last three trumpets are called "woes." They are divinely-directed strikes against man. If the first woe seemed terrible, what must the remaining two be like! One might be tempted to think that with all the demons out of the pit, the worst is over. But John says there are more woes to come. With man's unrepentant defiance building, we can expect the intensity of God's judgments to increase as well. This means the next woe will be even more terrible.

WHAT ELSE IS TO BE LOOSED ON MANKIND?

13. And when the sixth angel blew his trumpet, I heard a voice speaking from the four horns of the golden altar that stands in the presence of God. 14. The voice was saying to the sixth angel, as he stood there holding his trumpet,

"Release the four powerful angels imprisoned at the great river Euphrates!"

RELEASE. As the 5th and 6th trumpets bring demonic attacks upon the world's population, one thing is clear—God is controlling these activities. When the 6th angel sounds his trumpet, a voice from the altar orders him to release four mighty demons of destruction. The altar is the same from which the martyrs urged God to avenge Himself on the unrepentant inhabitants of the earth. What is happening confirms that the prayers of God's people play a big part in end time events. That the four angels are imprisoned at the great river, indicates they are fallen angels. There's no hint that God's angels are ever bound. This 6th angel, obviously more powerful than the demonic angels, is commanded to turn them loose on mankind.

15. So these four angels, who had been held in readiness for this very year, month, day and hour, were turned loose to kill a third of all mankind. 16. And the total number of their cavalry-men was two hundred million. According to what I heard, that really was the number.

TO KILL. The demonic angels now released, have one job to do—kill. The demons of the 5th trumpet could only *torment,* these are loosed only to *kill.* Their objective is to reduce the earth's population by one third. In John's day, the earth's population was around 180 million and a third of that would be roughly 60 million. John, of course, had no idea the world's population would be around 6 billion in our day. Had he known, it would have seemed impossible to kill 2 billion with the weapons of that day. However with 200 million horsemen, a number greater than the population of his day, killing 10 apiece would do it—if we allow the number of the cavalry-men to stand. God's hand is again seen in that the four angels were prepared for a precise moment in history, the exact year, month, day and hour. When that moment arrives, this horde will be loosed.

17. Here's what I saw in my vision: the breastplates of the riders were fiery red, blue and sulphur yellow. The horses' heads seemed to me to be like the heads of lions, with fire, smoke and sulphur coming from their mouths. 18. A third of all mankind was killed by the three plagues of smoke, fire and sulphur pouring from their mouths. 19. While the power to kill was limited to their mouths, they also had power in their tails. Their tails were like serpents and had heads that could inflict real damage.

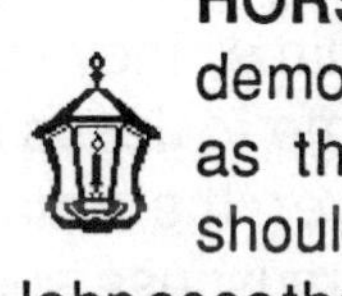

HORSES. John sees a vast horde of demon cavalry-men stretching as far as the eye can see. We probably shouldn't see the horses and riders as John sees them. He's trying to describe something taking place 2000 years in the future. He would know nothing about cars, tanks, planes or bombs. Electricity, submarines and guns would overwhelm him, so he does the best he can with what he knows. What is clear, is that we've got three powerful plagues (weapons, perhaps) capable of mass killing. It would seem that 200,000,000 demon riders would be sufficient to goad the world into a devastating war. Killing a billion and a half people might require nuclear weapons. However, the 6th trumpet will leave the remaining two-thirds of the population alive to change its mind about God—*if they are so inclined.* Let's see if they are.

20. But the rest of mankind, those surviving these plagues, refused to renounce the gods they had made with their own hands. They continued to worship demons and idols made of gold and silver, brass, stone and wood—idols that can neither see, nor hear nor walk.
21. What's more, they refused to turn from their murders, their sorceries, their sexual sins and the robberies they had committed.

REFUSED. At least three billion people survive the plagues of the 6th trumpet. One would think such a slaughter of souls would shake men to the place where they would consider changing their way of thinking and living. By this time, they've all heard God's invitation to come to Jesus and be part of His family. However, the situation on earth is so bad that God must use supernatural means to get the gospel to every creature. An angel will do it from mid-heaven, appealing to the survivors to honor God and come to Him before it's too late (14:6). It seems that once the heart of a person has hardened into hostility toward God, not even the plague of death will lead him to repentance (1 John 5:16). If men won't worship the true God, what then will they worship? Gods of their own making, of course. The worship instinct in all men compels them to worship something.

WORSHIP DEMONS. It has always been the desire of Satan to be worshipped. So great is this ambition, he once offered to give Jesus ALL the kingdoms of the world, all those He came to redeem—if He would fall down and worship him (Matt. 4:8,9). Satan devotes much of his demon force to deceiving men into devil worship. Of course, it has to be disguised. That's why men worship idols and images. Travel anywhere in the world and you'll find people worshipping something, even if they have to make it with their own hands. The span ranges from snakes to the sun and everything between. India alone has millions of gods. Yet behind them all, is Satan. He is forced to settle for this secondary worship until the day arrives when he can offer himself to the world as God (2 Thess. 2:4).

REVELATION 10

(More preparation for John)

To appreciate what is said in this chapter, we need to consider God's patience through all that has happened. It is astonishing to weigh His efforts to get man's attention. The Great Tribulation (5th and 6th seals) is behind us with nearly all believers slaughtered or taken captive. The 7th seal brought us to the 7 trumpets where God intervened with His warning judgments. His first 4 trumpets devastated a third of the natural realm. The 5th trumpet (1st woe) brought INTERNAL torment to men, while the 6th trumpet (2nd woe) saw the destruction of a THIRD of the world's population. Did that lead men to repent? No. It had little effect on them. God's patience is now at an end. The stage is set for Chapter Ten.

10 **1. Then I saw another mighty angel
coming down from heaven. He was
enveloped in a cloud with a rainbow
over his head. His face shone like the sun and
his legs were like pillars of fire. 2. He had a
little scroll lying open in his hand. With his
right foot planted on the sea and his left foot
on the land, 3. he shouted with a loud voice
like that of a roaring lion. This caused the
seven thunders to roar back a reply. 4. I was
all set to write down what the seven thunders
said, when a voice from heaven instructed
me,**

"Do not write down what the seven thunders said. Instead, seal up the message."

ANOTHER ANGEL. We've encountered mighty angels before, but this time John watches one descend. Apparently the apostle is observing this from the earth. This is a colossal angel, one who seemingly has authority over the sea and the earth. His descent from heaven adds to his authority, but that's all we know about him. Even though we find striking similarities in the Old Testament, we won't try to guess this angel's identity. If we really needed to know, John would have told us. The significant item here is the little scroll. It's small, indicating the message is short. It is also open, suggesting the message is not a secret.

SEVEN THUNDERS. Whatever this mighty angel shouted, it brought a response from the 7 thunders. Having been told early on to write down what he saw, John was prepared to copy the words of the thunders. However the angel orders him to refrain. From this we conclude the message was not for believers. Having reached the 7th trumpet where everything will be disclosed, we can assume nothing in their words applied to the saints or to John. The thunders are probably roaring their reaction to the little scroll. One can almost hear them saying... *"Yes, it's time for God to pour out His wrath on unrepentant man!"* From their heavenly position, they know God's patience has come to an end and unbelievers are the only ones who need to hear it.

**5. Then the mighty angel I saw straddling the
land and the sea, raised his right hand toward
heaven 6. and swore by Him who lives forever, who created heaven and earth and the
sea and everything in them,**

> ***"There shall be no more delay! 7. It's
> time for the seventh angel to blow his
> trumpet, and when he does, the hidden
> purpose of God will be fulfilled just as
> He made it known to His servants the
> prophets!"***

SWORE. Look what we have here! *An angel using the oath!* That's remarkable. Rarely does God employ oaths, but when He does, it's significant. We now have the angel's sworn testimony that God is all through with delays. No time left for man to repent and be saved. He's had his chance. The salvation door is ready to be slammed shut (Matt. 25:10). With the sounding of the *"last trumpet,"* all surviving believers will be changed and caught off the earth to meet the Lord in the sky (1 Cor. 15:52; 1 Thess. 4:17). This has to occur before God can pour out His wrath on the unbelievers. Believers are not "children of wrath" (Eph. 2:3). Since Jesus bore the wrath of God for all who put their trust in Him, it is unthinkable that a single child of God would be left on the earth when God's wrath is vented against this God hating world! That's the real purpose of the rapture.

PURPOSE FULFILLED. We're all set for the 7th trumpet, and when it sounds it will herald the *completion* of God's purpose in the entire earthly program. TIME itself, is an earthly concept, for it has a beginning and an ending. Anything that begins and ends is finite, not eternal. God is using "PROGRAM EARTH" as a device for screening out of the earth's billions, those who really want Him. And He uses the the faith-method (not the sight method) to do it. The last trumpet, number 7, will take us all the way to the end of John's Revelation, unveiling the whole purpose of God. It will not only include the Lord's return, His wrath and His earthly kingdom, but even the END of the earthly program. Human history is shut down as the earthly program is closed out. We'll see this in the next chapter.

DOES THE ANGEL HAVE FURTHER INSTRUCTIONS FOR JOHN AT THIS POINT?

8. Then the voice which I heard speaking to me from heaven, spoke once more from heaven, saying,

> ***"Go and take the little scroll lying open in the hand of the angel straddling the land and the sea."***

9. So I approached the angel and asked him to give me the little scroll. He answered,

> ***"Take it, and eat it. It will give you a bitter stomachache, but in your mouth it will be sweet as honey."***

10. So I took the scroll from the angel's hand, just as he told me—and ate it! Sure enough, it was sweet as honey in my mouth, but once I swallowed it, it gave me a bitter stomachache.

EAT THE SCROLL. That's one way of getting a message inside a person. John obediently does as the angel asks. *In his vision*, he actually takes the scroll and eats it. Not only does John acquire the message, but he can *taste* the sweetness and *feel* the bitterness of it. It becomes a part of his very being. God would have all of His preachers smolder with both sides of the gospel—the blessings of obeying God's voice and the consequences of refusing His voice. John is not through prophesying. However, when he preaches he will *feel* the impact of the words himself. The message he will preach will be that contained in the scroll.

SWEET/BITTER. The apostle Paul comments on the sweet/bitter aspects of this kind of preaching. *"We are the aroma of Christ to God among those who are being saved and those who are perishing. To the one, we are the smell of death; to the other the fragrance of life"* (2 Cor. 2:15,16). That is precisely the effect John's words will have. To believers, his words of Jesus' return to take vengeance on His enemies will be music to their ears. To those refusing to repent, his words will carry *"the smell of death."* The scroll, being little, will likely focus on a small portion of the events covered by the big scroll, namely Chapters 5 and 6. It will be like turning a microscope to a higher power. Certain details of the big scroll, which John didn't give us before, will be magnified for a closer look. Some of it won't be pretty.

11. Then I was told,

"You must go on preaching, giving forth prophecies concerning many peoples, nations, tribes and kings."

GO ON PREACHING. If John thought he could quickly bring the message of the last trumpet and his work would be finished, this is a surprise. He learns from the angel that he must bring the message of the *small scroll* to all men regardless of their rank or place in the world. That little scroll is a portion of the big scroll and spells out the terrors of the Great Tribulation. When we come to Chapter 12, John will FLASHBACK to the 5th and 6th seals. At the same time, he understands he should reveal those horrors with the compassion of a man who knows how God feels about His creation. Possibly he is reminded of the words of the prophet Ezekiel: *"As I live, says the Lord God, I have no pleasure in the death of the wicked. I would rather that the wicked mend their ways and live"* (Ezek. 33:11). Knowing the wicked will NOT repent at his preaching, and that God must destroy them, will make this a painful task for John.

PROPHECIES. John's *little scroll* messages will bring relief to believers. Christians suffering under the beast will be comforted to hear of Jesus' glorious return and the defeat of Satan. Even though they are being hunted down and killed, they'll know the kingdom is just ahead. The unsaved, on the other hand, will hate John's message. It will spell out the fate of those who reject God's offer. The lake of fire awaits them with the smoke of their torment ascending to heaven forever (14:11). Now we understand why the scroll tasted as sweet as honey in his mouth, but was so bitter in his belly. He *FEELS* both the blessings for the believers and the horrors awaiting the unsaved.

COMMENT: We shouldn't think the message of the little scroll contains the whole of John's preaching. There is much more for John to preach after the sounding of the 7th trumpet. The scroll is simply a flashback that expands on the Great Tribulation. Authors seek to maintain the flow of their narratives and use the flashback as a way of filling readers in on something that was glossed over earlier. Keep in mind that we are still within the scope of the 6th trumpet, the second woe. The final woe, the last trumpet, has yet to sound. Also note the angel's instructions to John do not end with this chapter. The eating of the little scroll and the command to continue preaching are only *part* of the angel's instructions. The rest continues on in Chapter 11.

REVELATION 11

(Still more instructions for John)

As this chapter opens we are still waiting for the 7th trumpet to sound. We are on hold as the mighty angel continues to instruct the apostle John. In Chapter 10, John got into the act himself as he ate the little scroll. He is still part of the action as Chapter 11 opens. Having been told that he must prophesy even further, John receives some strange orders. He also receives some prophetic insight as to what will happen to the city of Jerusalem during the tribulation. What's more, he will learn of two powerful witnesses who will operate in Jerusalem during the 42 months of the beast's reign. These instructions are intended to aid John in giving out his *little scroll* message. In Chapters 12, 13 and 14, we'll get the details of that message. Now let's see what further instruction the angel has for John.

11 **1. Then I was given a long reed to use as a measuring rod, and was told: "Go measure the temple of God and the altar and count those worshipping there. 2. But omit the courtyard outside the temple and do not measure it, because it has been given over to the Gentiles. They will trample the city underfoot for forty two months."**

MEASURE. John is given a long bamboo reed and ordered to go measure the temple. The temple disappeared in A.D.70. To this day none has been built, so the reference is to the tribulation temple—or as some call it, antichrist's temple. Daniel 9:27 implies the temple will be rebuilt during the tribulation and 2 Thess. 2:4, seems to confirm it. In early times, when a prophet was told to measure something, it pictured either the preservation or the destruction of that object. With the tribulation period one of destruction, this temple is marked for destruction. While some see a protected church here, it is hard to see born again believers getting involved with Jewish rituals. It is better to view this temple as part of the restoration of Judaism under antichrist's covenant with Israel.

TRAMPLE. Why measure the temple for destruction? It's doomed. When the world ruler appears on the scene and makes his agreement with Israel, a false peace will exist for the Jews. Eager to pass himself off as their Messiah, the beast will encourage the rebuilding of the temple and the restoration of the sacrificial system. For 3 1/2 years Jews will prosper under this arrangement. Then, following the 3 1/2 years, the world ruler (the beast) will break the agreement and declare himself to be God. As he assumes God's place in the temple, the Jews will realize their mistake. The next 42 months will be an awful time for them. The world ruler will seize the city (Jerusalem), and it will become a Gentile trade center. The ancient prophets describe this 42 month period as a time of great trouble and distress for Israel.

Jeremiah refers to it as *"The time of Jacob's trouble"* (Jer. 30:7). The outer court is not measured since it was already in use by Gentiles.

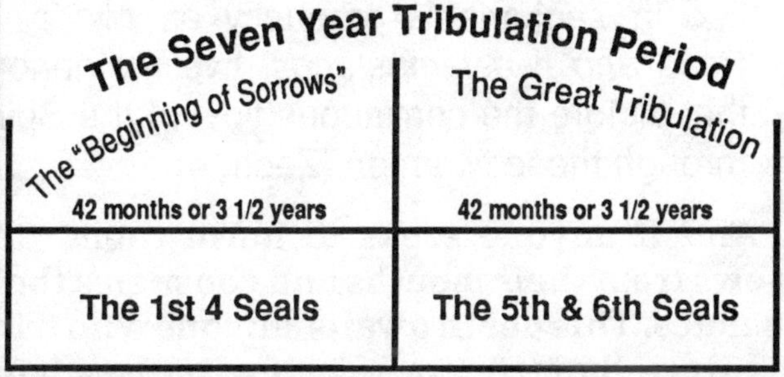

The Seven Year Tribulation Period

The "Beginning of Sorrows" 42 months or 3 1/2 years	The Great Tribulation 42 months or 3 1/2 years
The 1st 4 Seals	The 5th & 6th Seals

The term "the tribulation" refers to two 42 month periods. The first of those periods the Lord labeled "The Beginning of Sorrows" (Matt. 24:8). And indeed, it is only the beginning. The next 42 months cover the reign of the beast, the time referred to as the Great Tribulation.

3. "In the meantime, I will give my two witnesses power to prophesy for those twelve hundred and sixty days, clothed in sackcloth."
4. These are the two olive trees and the two lampstands that stand in the presence of the Lord of the earth.

TWO WITNESSES. Do we know who these two witnesses are? No. But they are described as having the same kind of power as Moses and Elijah, who appeared with Jesus on the Mount of Transfiguration (Matt. 17:3). Whoever the witnesses are, they will need supernatural power and protection to witness at a time when believers are being hunted down and killed. It will surely infuriate the *beast* to have them preaching against him and urging people to repent (sackcloth symbol) and turn to Christ. They could reap a nice harvest of souls during their 1260 days (42 months) of ministry, for the salvation invitation is still open. These two witnesses are identified in Zechariah's prophecy as *two olive trees and two lampstands*, two metaphors that picture the continuous flow of the Spirit through these two men (Zech. 4).

5. And if anyone seeks to harm them, fire spews from their mouths and consumes their enemies. This death awaits anyone who tries to injure them. 6. These two witnesses have the power to close off the heavens, so that no rain falls during the days of their ministry. What's more, they have the power to turn the waters into blood and to smite the earth with any kind of plague as often as they wish.

HARM THEM. As time goes by, the beast's hatred for the two witnesses will mount higher and higher. Servants of the beast will launch repeated attacks against these two men. But the fire-breathing witnesses will be too much for them. Their enemies will be consumed, much as the enemies of Elijah were consumed with fire from heaven (2 Kings 1:12). Further, they have the power to stop all rainfall, bringing drought to the land as occurred in Elijah's day. That would confirm their ministry (1 Kings 17:1). They can also turn water into blood and smite the earth with any plague they wish, feats reminiscent of Moses' time in Egypt (Ex.7:20,21). These are judgment *actions* backing up their judgment *message*.

**7. Then when they have finished their testi-
mony, the beast who comes up out of the abyss
will attack them, conquer them and kill them.
8. Their bodies will lie in the open street of the
great city, which in prophetic language is
called Sodom or Egypt, the city in which their
Lord was crucified. 9. For three and a half
days, people from every nation, and tribe, and
language and race, will gaze at their corpses
and will not allow them to be buried. 10. Then
all those who dwell on the earth will gloat
over them and celebrate their deaths by ex-
changing presents, because these two prophets tormented them so.**

BEAST OF THE ABYSS. In Chapter 13, we will meet the beast of the abyss. For now, we'll understand he is Satan's man, the antichrist, the chief enemy of believers in the last days. That he is from the abyss will explain his demonic nature. The angel explains that these two witnesses will be raised up to minister during the last half of the tribulation when it would mean certain death for anyone to witness for Jesus. The beast, who will certainly make every attempt to silence these two, is finally allowed to kill them. With their supernatural power, it would be impossible even for armies to conquer them. But when their ministry ends, their physical protection is withdrawn and they are easily attacked and slain. It is God Who removes their protection, so again we see Him in control. Later we'll learn why it was a blessing for them to die such a death.

NOTE: During the 1260 days of ministry by the two witnesses, there will be no Jews in the city. As long as it served the purpose of the beast to pass himself off as the Jewish Messiah he was content to favor the Jews. But when he presumes to take God's place in the temple, he no longer needs the Jews (2 Thess. 2:4). They will denounce him immediately, bringing the beast's full wrath down on them. They'll flee the city, looking to God for protection, which He will give. The covenant between antichrist and the Jews is now broken. Only the two witnesses are able to offer the gospel invitation.

CORPSES IN THE STREET. About the only way one can disgrace a dead man is to deny his body burial and expose it to the scorn and abuse of his enemies. The bodies of the martyred witnesses are not buried, but put on display in the broad street of the "great city." The sight will be televised to the entire God-hating world. Thus they are viewed by every race and nationality. The three and one half days correspond to the three and one half years of their ministry. The beast has had 7 years to establish Jerusalem as the center of world power. He had to locate here if the Jews were to acknowledge him as Messiah. To be recognized as Messiah was critical to his plan to assume God's place in the temple. It was his ambition to make Jerusalem (the "great city") his capitol, as well as the political and financial center of the world. After all, it is the "city of the great king," the "seat of God" in the world. What other city could fit this man's ambitions?

CELEBRATE. The pagan world will be thrilled to see the two witnesses out of business. They can then breathe easier and get on with their sin. With Satan indwelling the beast, evil will rush to its climax. Can you imagine this world being ruled by a totally evil master? The apostle describes the childish glee of the rejectors over the demise of the witnesses. One can only guess the extent of world depravity when the two witnesses need supernatural protection to do their job. Should the witnesses take a harvest for Jesus, it is certain all who say "Yes" to His invitation will be killed by the beast's agents in short order.

11. But after the three and a half days had passed, the breath of life from God entered their bodies and they rose to their feet, to the great terror of all who saw them. 12. At that point, they heard a loud voice from heaven say to them:

"COME UP HERE!"

And they ascended to heaven in a cloud in the full view of their enemies. 13. At that very moment there was a violent earthquake, and a tenth of the city collapsed in ruins. The number of people killed by the earthquake was seven thousand. Those who were not killed were filled with fear and acknowledged the God of heaven was doing this.

TERROR. The merriment of the pagan world doesn't last long. When 3 1/2 days pass, God breathes life into those dead bodies and they rise to their feet.

The beast and the rest of the world must have been stunned as this event appeared on satellite TV. Great fear settles over the earth. Since killing a person is the last thing you can do to him, what can you do with someone who rises from the dead? Nothing. Here is final proof that God is the supreme authority over life and death! What encouragement this holds out to us as we approach the dreadful hour ourselves! Remember, we have paused at the 6th trumpet while the mighty angel explains these things to John. When he finishes his explanation, the 7th trumpet will sound.

ASCEND. Look at this! Something is up. We've got bodies rising and ascending as the last trumpet is set to sound. That should ring a bell. With television cameras capturing the action, the two witnesses obey a loud voice from heaven ordering them to... *"COME UP HERE!"* With the world watching, the two ascend exactly as did their Lord—IN SLOW MOTION. This is not a "twinkling of the eye" catching away, such as will happen to us when the archangel's voice summons us. This is done slowly so that the viewers will connect it with the earthquake that follows immediately. What an awesome sight! Is this a rapture? Indeed. Will our rapture also occur at the last trumpet? It will indeed, says the apostle Paul (1 Cor. 15:51-52).

EARTHQUAKE. The slow ascent of the two witnesses is accompanied by the earthquake. Imagine the impact on those watching on world-wide TV. Even though the earthquake is localized, it's not all that small. The "great city" of the beast doesn't fare too well. A tenth of his city is reduced to ruins and 7000 of his people killed. What a news story! The result: terror strikes the hearts of those left alive. They won't like it, but there's no denying God's power now. They are forced to acknowledge His overpowering majesty. Those inclined to repent because of this, had better act quickly. Why? This event heralds the last trumpet. When that trumpet sounds, it will be too late. For the *SALVATION DOOR* is slammed shut at that very moment (Matt. 25:10). The faith-method ends with the Lord's appearance at the last trumpet. *"Every eye shall see Him,"* as the TV cameras focus on His appearance in the sky! Salvation *by faith* is no longer possible now. From this point on, everything will be *by sight*.

THIS COMPLETES THE ANGEL'S INSTRUCTIONS TO JOHN

14. The second woe has now passed. The third woe is at hand.

THIRD WOE. We've covered some ground since the 6th trumpet sounded. To us it may seems like a lot of time has passed, but it hasn't. Don't let the occasional interruptions move you from the steadfast flow of the narrative. We're now ready for the *third woe.* As we listen to the last trumpet, John will give us a brief outline of the rest of the book—*and that's all.* Immediately following the message of the 7th trumpet, there will be another interruption, another interlude. John will use that interlude to unveil the contents of the "little scroll," using Chapters 12, 13 and part of 14 to do it. That is the FLASHBACK referred to earlier and it will return us to the Great Tribulation. In those 3 chapters, we'll learn the frightening details of what life will be like in the days of the beast. You should understand that all we're going to get from the 7th trumpet *at this point,* will be a scant outline of the rest of Revelation. Now let's hear what the last trumpet has to say.

WILL THE LAST TRUMPET CREATE MUCH EXCITEMENT IN HEAVEN?

15. Then the seventh angel blew his trumpet. With that, loud voices raised a great cry in heaven:

> ***"The kingdom of this world has now become the kingdom of our Lord and His Christ, and He shall reign forever and ever."***

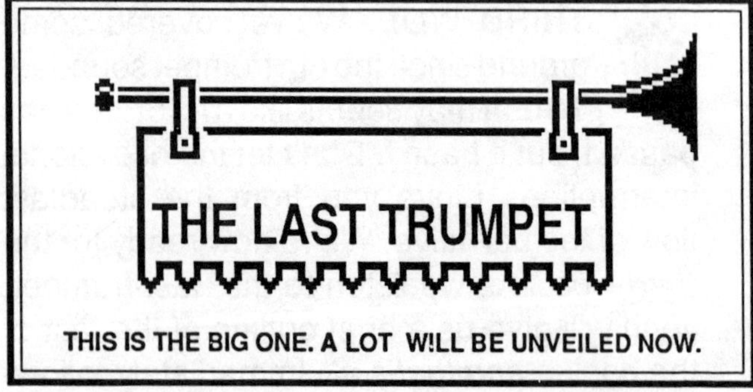

THE LAST TRUMPET
THIS IS THE BIG ONE. A LOT W!LL BE UNVEILED NOW.

LOUD VOICES. The mighty angel of Chapter 10 told us the sounding of the 7th trumpet would unveil God's hidden purpose. And that's exactly what we're going to get. However, there won't be much detail. Instead, we're going to get a *brief outline* of all that is yet to come. Excitement in heaven has been mounting as we come to this moment. It is enough to provoke noisy cries from the hosts of heaven. Their outburst triggers a response from the 24 elders who then disclose the rest of God's plan. Tremendous things are about to take place and the elders will sketch them for us. We understood the 7th trumpet would bring on the 3rd woe, but now we find it is going to bring us much more than that.

PROPERTY. The angelic host shouts the fact that the kingdom of this world has been removed from Satan's hands and transferred to Jesus. At first glance it sounds like the elders have jumped the gun, for the actual transfer hasn't happened yet. The Lord has yet to subdue Satan and seize his assets. However, the angels, knowing that Jesus' death secured all right and title to Satan's domain, consider it as good as done. That's why the 7th trumpet evokes such excitement. The great moment has finally arrived for the Lord to take possession. It also signals it's time for Him to make His appearance in the sky. We'll be with Him and we'll watch as He pours out His wrath on the unbelieving world below. No wonder the angels find it hard to contain themselves. Now let's see what the ELDERS' PACKAGE is all about.

16. Then the twenty-four elders sitting enthroned before God, prostrated themselves before Him in worship, saying:

***17. "We thank You, Lord God almighty,
You who are and Who were, for assuming Your great power and commencing
Your reign. 18. The nations were angry
with You, but now it's time for Your wrath to explode against them. It is also time for the dead to be judged, and beyond that, the rewarding of Your servants the prophets, Your saints and all who honor Your name, both small and great. Now is the time to destroy those who destroy the earth."***

POWER. Normally the twenty-four elders remain seated, but now they are on their faces before God. They understand the moment of God's wrath has arrived. With the sounding of the last trumpet, the Lord will appear in the sky and every eye will see Him. We will be with Him and the world will see us too. From our vantage point in the sky, we will witness the outpouring of His wrath. When that is completed, Jesus will begin His descent to earth with all of His saints. His mighty power will be demonstrated when He defeats Satan in what is called the battle of Armageddon. With Satan captured, the Lord will begin His reign over the earth, using a NEW

JERUSALEM as His capitol. The old Jerusalem, the capitol of the beast, will be wiped out in the great earthquake of the last bowl of God's wrath. That will be the worst quake the world has ever seen (16:18). The phrase... *"And who is to come,"* usually found in this series, is omitted, because the elders no longer see the Lord's coming as future.

COMMENT: Satan has always wanted to be God and worshipped as God. This ambition led to his downfall. Before Planet Earth was here, he attempted to seize God's heavenly throne and establish himself as Lord of all, but that failed. Even so, he was not destroyed. His tempting and deceiving skills were too useful to throw away. They provided God with something He never had before—a way to bring forth a race of TESTED SOULS. Thus the devil was permitted to operate in the spirit realm, but with his attacks limited to the *spirits of men.* Though restricted, his passion to be worshipped did not diminish and he remained jealous of God. Before long, in the coming "flashbacks," we'll see him cast out of the spirit realm and limited to the physical realm, where his rage will create havoc for a short time. We call that time—*the Great Tribulation.* This tribulation period can honestly be described as the wrath of Satan. He will even go so far as to raise an army of men, with which he hopes to intercept the Lord's return to earth. That too will fail. In the end, Satan will be destroyed.

IT'S TIME. The elders, having announced that it was time for certain things to happen, sketch out for us the rest of John's revelation. When we list the events in the order *in which they occur,* the elders' package unfolds like this:

1. The Lord Jesus appears and God's *wrath* is poured out on the world's God-hating population (Rev. 16:1).

2. The Lord descends from the sky with ALL of His saints (both resurrected and raptured) to engage Satan's armies consisting of the *multitudes angry with God* (1 Thess. 3:13).

3. Billions die as Satan's forces are vanquished (14:20).

4. The Lord *rewards* His saints, assigning them jobs in His kingdom.

5. The Lord establishes His headquarters in Jerusalem and begins His *reign* over the world.

6. His saints will serve Him on earth for 1000 years (Rev. 20:6), at the end of which Satan is released (Rev.20:7). The nations *again rise in wrath* and Satan leads them in a final rebellion against God. This time he is seized and cast into the lake of fire (Rev . 20:10).

7. All the wicked dead are then raised *to be judged* at the Great White Throne and are assigned their places in the lake of fire, according to their works (Rev. 20:12). At this point, the earthly program ends and the eternal program begins.

Go back over verses 17 and 18, comparing what you see there with this list, and you'll find the *elders' package* is actually a nice outline of what is yet to come.

WILL GOD BACK UP THE ELDERS' STATEMENT?

19. Then the temple of God in heaven was thrown open and the ark of His covenant inside His temple was in plain view. This sight was accompanied by flashes of lightning, peals of thunder, an earthquake and a violent storm.

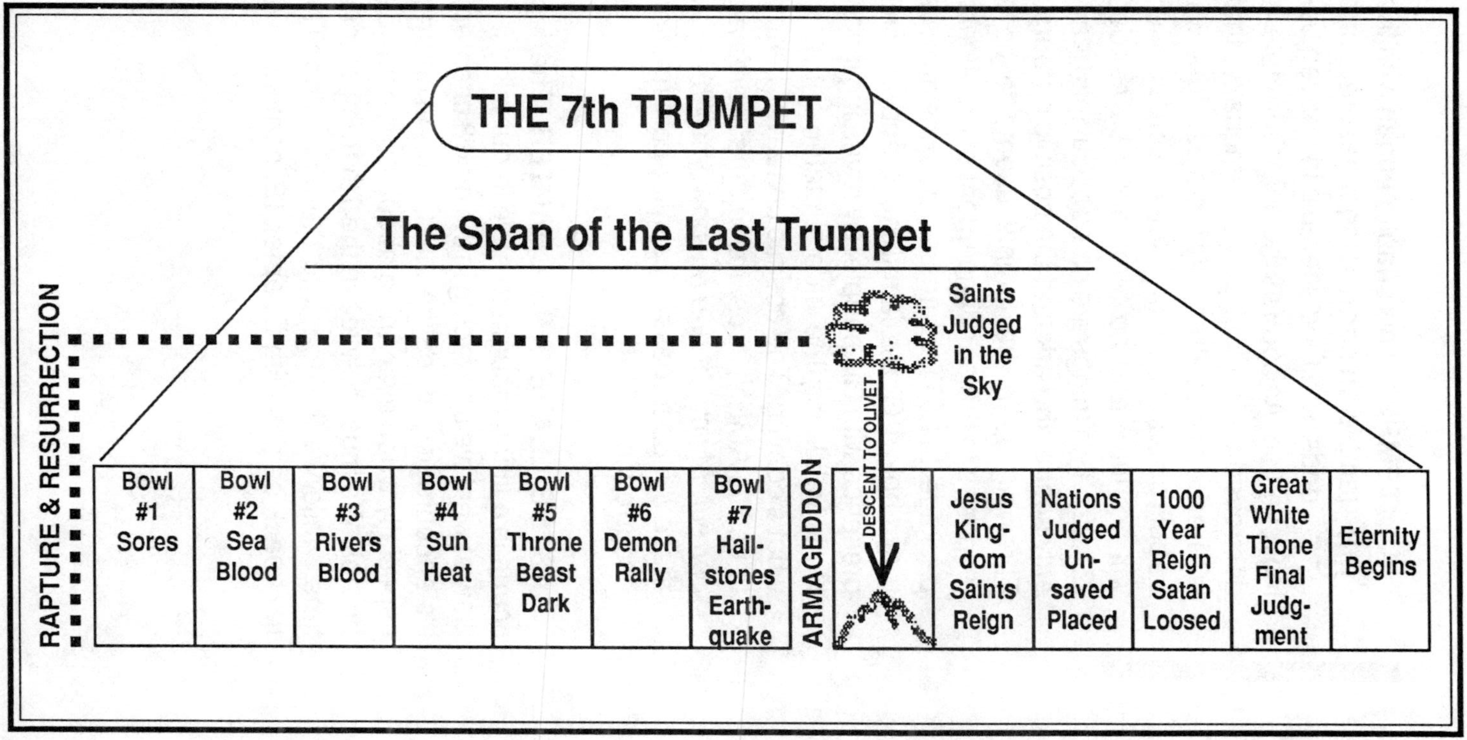

THE 7th TRUMPET

The Span of the Last Trumpet

RAPTURE & RESURRECTION

Saints Judged in the Sky

DESCENT TO OLIVET

Bowl #1 Sores	Bowl #2 Sea Blood	Bowl #3 Rivers Blood	Bowl #4 Sun Heat	Bowl #5 Throne Beast Dark	Bowl #6 Demon Rally	Bowl #7 Hail-stones Earth-quake	ARMAGEDDON		Jesus King-dom Saints Reign	Nations Judged Un-saved Placed	1000 Year Reign Satan Loosed	Great White Thone Final Judg-ment	Eternity Begins

TEMPLE. This chapter began with the temple on earth being measured, and ends with God's temple in heaven being revealed. As soon as the beast's temple is destroyed by the last great earthquake, that will be the end of all earthly temples. None will be built on earth after that, for the Lord Himself will be here, and no temple will be needed (21:22). Two things are noted about this heavenly scene: the ark and the cosmic outburst. Throwing open the temple seems to be a response to the announcement of the *elders' package.* In Old Testament times, the ark was a symbol of God's faithfulness and abiding presence with His people. By revealing it now He is validating the elders' statement as to what's coming. The cosmic upheaval seems to be His AMEN, *"Yes, the elders' words are correct. My might and My power will bring all these things to pass!"* A similar confirmation occurred in Acts 4:31.

AS WE LEAVE THIS CHAPTER. The last scene is a fitting thought to have in our minds. In view of what we'll be facing in the next 3 chapters, it's encouraging to realize that God is in charge, especially when everything about us is in terrible turmoil. We must now leave the 7th trumpet for a time, while we flashback to the tribulation. The flashback begins with Chapter 12, coming next.

THE FLOW OF THE BOOK

SEVEN SEALS
(Everything from Chapter 6 to the end of the Revelation)

SEAL #1 ANTICHRIST
SEAL #2 WAR
SEAL #3 FAMINE
SEAL #4 DEATH
SEAL #5 GREAT TRIBULATION BEGINS (Slaughter)
SEAL #6 END OF THE GREAT TRIBULATION (Cosmic Uproar)
SEAL #7 THE 7 TRUMPETS

#1 EARTH SCORCHED
#2 SEA BLOODIED
#3 RIVERS POISONED
#4 CELESTIAL DARKENED
#5 DEMONS LOOSED (1ST WOE)
#6 DEMONIC CAVALRY (2ND WOE)
#7 THE LAST TRUMPET

(THE RAPTURE)
7 BOWLS (3RD WOE)
ARMAGEDDON
JESUS DESCENDS
THE KINGDOM SET UP
1000 YEAR REIGN
FINAL JUDGMENT

ETERNITY BEGINS

UNDERSTANDING THE FLOW OF THE BOOK

This book is deliberately mysterious. It had to be to get it off the Island of Patmos. All of its mysteries are under the seven seals. As each seal is opened, the story moves steadily to its climax. However, we will encounter occassional interruptions and flashbacks. It is the 7th seal that reveals God's direct intervention into this physical world to punish it and to rule over it.

The first four seals are the "beginning of sorrows," referred to by Jesus in Matt 24:8. With the first seal, antichrist bursts forth on the scene to reign over the earth. The next three seals feature the destruction that flows in his wake. Then comes the GREAT TRIBULATION which is spread across the 5th and 6th seals. Seal #5 marks the beginning of the Great Tribulation with a massive killing of the saints, while seal #6, with its cosmic upheaval, warns that God has had enough of man's rebellion. With the seventh seal, God gets into the act with His trumpets. His first four trumpets are warning shots fired at the *natural realm.* The last three trumpets are called *WOES*, because with those God directs His plagues against *man himself.* The seven bowls of God's wrath ARE the third woe.

As you read, it will *seem like* the seals flow into the trumpets. BUT THAT IS NOT THE CASE. The 7 trumpets *are IN* the 7th seal and the last of those trumpets, trumpet #7, *contains* the 7 bowls of God's wrath—plus a lot more prophecy. It would be easy to say, "*The 7th trumpet is the seven bowls of wrath,"* but that would fly in the face of those "great voices" that speak when the 7th trumpet sounds:

"The kingdom of this world has become the kingdom of our Lord and His Christ, and He shall reign forever!" (11:15).

What's more, the twenty-four elders go on to announce the judgment of the nations and the rewarding of the saints. A whole package of prophecy flows out of that 7th trumpet. Please note that it is the kingdom of *this world* that has become Christ's kingdom. His kingdom consists of the kingdoms of *THIS WORLD,* not the kingdoms of some eternal realm.

As you look at the chart, observe that the 7 trumpets ARE IN the 7th seal. Then look at the last trumpet and note how the 7 bowls of God's wrath are simply *one item* on the list. A lot of prophecy unfolds with the last trumpet. Observe also how the 7 bowls are all emptied *BEFORE* the battle of Armageddon begins. Only then does Jesus descend to set up His kingdom to begin the millennium. When the millennial kingdom ends, a thousand years later, the great white throne judgment takes place. Once that task is out of the way, the Lord Jesus surrenders the kingdom to His Father and eternity begins when God will be "all in all" (1Cor. 15: 24, 28).

On the basis of Paul's statement, I put the rapture as the first item under the last trumpet:

"Listen! I will unfold a mystery: we shall not all die, but we shall all be changed in a flash, in the twinkling of an eye, at the LAST TRUMPET. For the trumpet will sound

and the dead will rise imperishable and we shall be changed" (1 Cor. 15:52).

My decision to place the rapture at this point *assumes* the last trumpet referred to by the apostle Paul is the same last trumpet of the Revelation. This assumption could be wrong, but it seems to be the proper point in the Revelation where the *dead rise* and we are *"changed."* In any event, it all takes place under the 7th seal.

If you will fix the chart in your mind and watch for the occasional interruptions and flashbacks, the book of Revelation will be stripped of considerable mystery. Actually the book is quite orderly. You will particularly enjoy the later chapters where you'll find yourself descending with the Lord from the sky and making yourself at home in the New Jerusalem. No matter what you might have to suffer before the Lord appears, it will be worth it all when you find yourself reigning with the Lord on the restored earth. The 1000 years won't exactly be heaven on earth, but they'll seem like it.

> **NOTE: With the sounding of the last trumpet, you and I are out of here, but John has not yet given us any details on the catching away of the church (the rapture). That's the first thing he'll take up when he finishes his flashback. When we get to 14:14, he'll be back on track.**

NOW GET READY FOR JOHN'S FIRST FLASHBACK

REVELATION 12

(Here is the first flashback.)

It is not uncommon for writers to pause in their narratives and return to earlier scenes so as to give readers important background information. That's what John is about to do and his information is critical. He brought us to the 7th trumpet with its summary of what is to come, but now he feels the need to go back and bring us up to date. The church, having suffered persecution all along, descends into deep tribulation before the Lord returns. To encourage Christians to be steadfast and ready to die for Jesus, is the whole purpose of this prophecy. Having assured us that God is in control and the power of evil will be broken and banished, John is ready to reveal what the church must go through before the Lord appears. Here now is his flashback to the tribulation.

FLASHBACK to the Great Tribulation

12 **1. A great and wondrous sign appeared in heaven: a woman wearing the sun for a robe, with the moon under her feet and a crown of twelve stars on her head.
2. She had a child in her womb and in the anguish of her labor, cried out to be delivered.**

WOMAN. When John refers to the "woman" as a SIGN, he is telling us we are dealing with highly symbolic figures. So who is this woman? The mention of the sun, moon and twelve stars (12 sons of Jacob) tell us. SHE IS ISRAEL, including spiritual Israel. There has always been a spiritual germ inside Israel that blossomed into the New Testament church. Here though, we are looking at NATIONAL ISRAEL who's task it was to bring the Messiah into the world. Clothed with the sun, this woman stands in stark contrast to her ancient enemy, the prince of darkness—Satan. The moon under her feet pictures dominion. The crown indicates her status among the nations, she is the royal nation, as God views all the nations. As the sun clothed woman cries out to be delivered, a second sign appears in heaven.

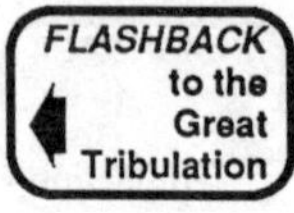

3. Then a second sign appeared in heaven: a huge, fiery red dragon with seven heads and ten horns. On each of his seven heads was a royal diadem 4. and with his tail he scooped a third of the stars out of the sky and hurled them upon the earth. The dragon stood in front of the woman who was in childbirth so that he might devour the child the moment it was born. 5. But when she gave birth to a male child who is to rule all nations with a rod of iron, that Son was snatched up to God and His throne. 6. The mother fled to a place in the wilderness that God had prepared for her.

DRAGON. When it comes to the dragon, we can forget symbolism. John tells us who he is—Satan. In verse 9, he gives us 2 more names: the devil and the old serpent. Apparently he wants no mistake concerning the identity of the dragon. As for his seven heads and ten crowns, we'll be looking at those in the next chapter. For now we'll understand they have to do with the world-wide nature of his reign and his claim to be ruler of the world. His crowns are phoney in that he has *appointed himself* "king of kings." It is a testimony to his skills of deceit that he could induce a third of the angels, millions of them, to join his initial rebellion against God. Here we see him casting that same one-third to the earth, thereby providing himself with a formidable army of evil spirits to use against the believers.

DEVOUR. The dragon stands in front of the woman eager to seize her child once it's born. There's no doubt as to whom Satan is really fighting—GOD. He felt if he could kill the child (Jesus), there'd be no way God could redeem the world. This explains the assaults on Jesus from the flight into Egypt, right up to the cross. Of course, he didn't know that Jesus' death would be the very means by which God would redeem the world (1 Cor. 2:8). When Jesus died at Calvary, Satan thought he had won. But when Jesus rose from the dead and ascended to heaven, the devil realized his mistake and knew he was doomed. From that point on he set out to destroy all who followed Jesus. While God's people have been slaughtered in droves in the past, those slaughters will be nothing compared to what the devil will do through the beast during the Great Tribulation.

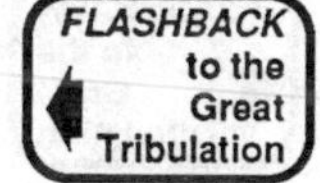

ROD OF IRON. The mother of the manchild is forced to flee. But where? The text says a place in the wilderness. Apparently God means to protect NATIONAL Israel. With unsaved Jews *unsealed*, physical protection is needed to guarantee a remnant will be alive to enter the kingdom. God made *physical* promises to Israel that He must keep. He also made *spiritual* promises in Christ, which the Jews rejected. The statement that the child will rule the nations with a rod of iron, identifies Jesus as the Messiah-ruler of Psalm 2:9. Once God's wrath (the bowls) has been satisfied, Jesus the true Messiah, will descend to His headquarters in the New Jerusalem. The people in those nations surviving God's wrath will enter the kingdom unsaved. They will *still have their old natures* and remain sinners. The new nature will no longer be available at that time. To establish a righteous kingdom, per the prophecies, the Lord will mandate righteousness, backing it up with force (the rod of iron). The unregenerate population of the kingdom won't like it, but they'll have no choice.

7. Later a fierce war broke out in heaven. Michael and his angels fought against the dragon. The dragon and his angels fought back, 8. but they were no match, and they lost their place in heaven. 9. The huge dragon, that ancient serpent, whom we call the devil or Satan, who leads the whole world astray, was hurled down upon the earth, and his angels with him.

ANGELS AT WAR. War breaks out in the spirit realm as Michael and his angels battle the dragon and his angels (the demons). What has this got to do with the tribulation? This heavenly war occurs at the beginning of the Great Tribulation, the midpoint of Daniel's 70th week. Apparently Satan attempts to regain his former position in the heavenlies, but is unsuccessful. As a result he loses his freedoms as the "ruler of the kingdom of the air" (Eph. 2:2) and is forced to operate "on the earth." No one can function on the earth without a body, so the devil must acquire one, or at the very least, indwell one. But whose? Ah—there's only one body he wants—that of the antichrist. Later we'll learn of antichrist's fatal wound and resurrection, and his transformation into a beast. It's Satan's indwelling that makes him a beast. The dragon's angels (evil spirits) must also indwell bodies. With no chance of regaining a place in the heavenlies, Satan launches a furious assault on the church. The next chapter reveals his awful slaughter of Christians.

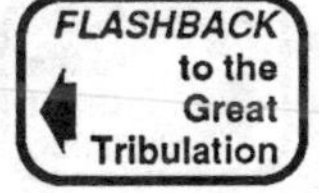

Comment: Consider Satan's blunders. At one point, in ages past, Satan enjoyed a high position in heaven, perhaps next to God Himself. But he became greedy and coveted God's throne. As a result, he was kicked out of heaven and forced to operate in the realm of the human spirit, holding the title of "Prince of the power of the air" (Eph. 2:2). In that role he was limited to the surface of the globe. But he blundered again. When he went up against Michael and his angels, it cost him his freedom to operate in the spirit, forcing him out of the spirit realm. This occurs at the beginning of the Great Tribulation. Forced to operate in a body, he no longer would have access to men's spirits. After that, he must rely on fleshly means to persuade people to go along with him. It

also means his persecutions would have to be *physical*. From this point on, a man's choice would be between the voice of God on the inside and the voice of the beast coming from the outside.

LEADS THE WORLD. What a testimony this is to Satan's power to deceive. While he cannot touch anyone's salvation, he can lead sincere believers to waste their lives in living for self and family, careers and the pursuit of pleasure. He has reduced the church to an impotent mass of meetings in buildings once a week, but with little commitment the other six days. With believers under constant attack in Satan's world, the need to stand up to him is obvious (Eph. 6:11-17). Being a Christian provides no automatic protection against this experienced enemy. He must be RESISTED (Ja. 4:7). He has false prophets everywhere teaching the *comfortable life.* This is why the church has minimal effect on crime, corrupt politics, the immoral entertainment world, the drug scene, and homosexuality. It's all due to Satan's power to deceive. The Christian life is a fight. It's a struggle to deny self, forego pleasure and live for Jesus, but few are taught to fight. Satan has seen to that. God has few hardened troops (2 Tim. 2:3).

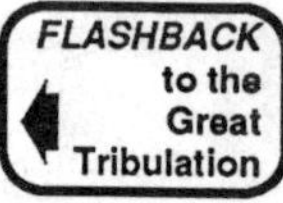

IS HEAVEN HAPPY OVER SATAN'S OUSTER?

10. Then a voice boomed across heaven, proclaiming:

"The moment has arrived! God's salvation, the setting up of the kingdom and

the power and the authority of His Christ may now be displayed, because the accuser of our brethren has been cast out of his place. Day and night he stood accusing them in God's presence. 11. However, they overcame him by the sacrifice of the Lamb and by their own witness to the truth. In the face of death they chose not to cling to their lives. 12. Therefore, rejoice O heaven! Rejoice also you citizens of heaven! But woe to you people of the earth and sea, for the devil has come down to you in great fury knowing he has but little time left!"

MOMENT HAS ARRIVED. By now we should be used to these outbursts of praise. Heaven is understandably excited over the fact that God's plan for the last days is soon to go into effect. An unidentified voice, triggered by Satan's ouster, proclaims the results of the devil's removal from the spirit realm. The voice declares three things will now happen in order: 1.) God's deliverance (salvation) of Israel, 2.) the establishment of God's kingdom on earth, 3.) Jesus' authority and power, which has never been seen before. It will be seen by all as He rules over God's earthly kingdom. Forced to occupy a body, Satan will now use PHYSICAL MEANS to afflict the objects of his wrath. While heaven is delighted with Satan's banishment, those on the earth are in for a bad time. The Great Tribulation (Satan's wrath) is about to break upon the church. Bear in mind, we are flashing back to the beginning of the Great Tribulation.

ACCUSER OF OUR BRETHREN. On first reading, one might think Satan is making accusations about us to God. There's no way God would listen to that day and night. Besides, it would be worthless, for God doesn't remember sins He's forgiven. Actually, Satan's accusations are directed to our *consciences*, for our consciences *are* in the presence of God (Heb. 4:13). They are spirit and God sees everything that goes on there. Once Satan's activity is limited to the flesh, he will be powerless to address accusations to the believer's *conscience*. From that point on, believers will never again be made to *feel* guilty. However, until the day the devil is removed from the spirit realm, he will continue to plague our consciences with guilts—unless we know how to deal with him.

OVERCAME HIM. Those who truly understand that Jesus' sacrifice removes forever the GUILT OF ALL SIN, can stand up to Satan. They can laugh at his accusations and point to God's Word where it says our consciences are cleansed "*once for all*" (Heb. 10:2,10,14). When a person reaches the place where he is willing to stand on God's Word, even staking his life on it, the devil's accusations have no power. Even so, it's tough to resist an accusation that comes from *your own mind*—unless you're wise to the way Satan works. If a person can do that, he has no problem with Satan's accusations. If he doesn't he'll be plagued with guilts. Today, millions of Christians suffer from guilts, because they are ignorant of the devil's methods and don't know how to deal with him.

THE VOICE HAVING SPOKEN, WILL JOHN RESUME THE STORY?

13. So when the dragon found himself cast down upon the earth, he went in pursuit of the woman who had given birth to the male child. 14. But the woman was given wings, similar to those of a great eagle that she might fly to her place in the wilderness to be looked after and kept out of reach of the serpent for three and a half years.

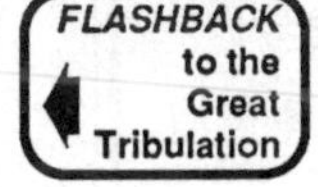

PURSUIT. Why would the devil go after the mother (Israel) so furiously? Why so hostile toward the Jews? He resents her place in the plan of God. To this point Israel has accepted the antichrist as Messiah. But once he claims to be God, the Jews will turn against him and denounce him as a pretender. Satan's man, antichrist, previously made a covenant with the Jews, but now with Satan indwelling him, he will break it. From this point on, he will do his best to wipe out Israel. This means God will have to provide some protection for her if He wants any Jews left to enter the millennial kingdom. Now that Satan has been removed from the spirit realm, his great advantage is gone. He knows his days are numbered and he'll do his best to frustrate God's plan any way he can—even though he's in a body.

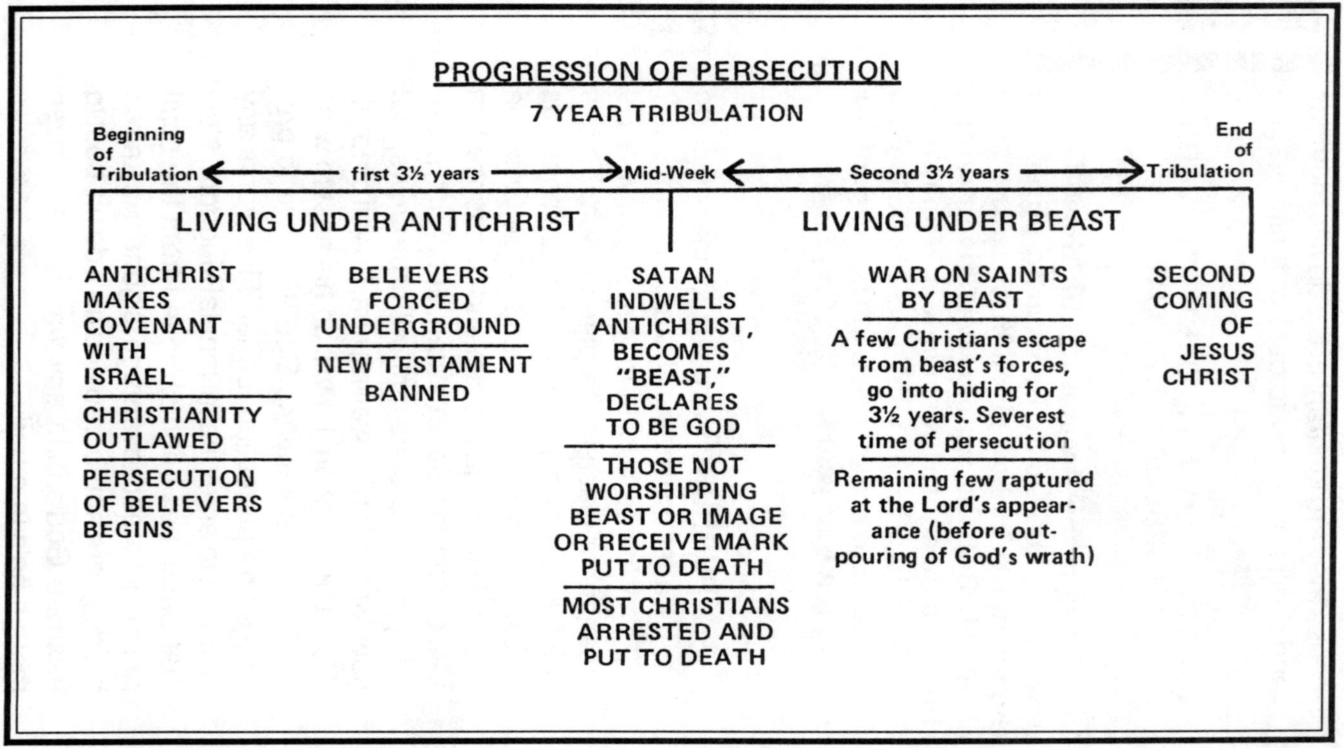

PROGRESSION OF PERSECUTION

7 YEAR TRIBULATION

Beginning of Tribulation ← first 3½ years → Mid-Week ← Second 3½ years → End of Tribulation

LIVING UNDER ANTICHRIST			LIVING UNDER BEAST	
ANTICHRIST MAKES COVENANT WITH ISRAEL	BELIEVERS FORCED UNDERGROUND	SATAN INDWELLS ANTICHRIST, BECOMES "BEAST," DECLARES TO BE GOD	WAR ON SAINTS BY BEAST	SECOND COMING OF JESUS CHRIST
CHRISTIANITY OUTLAWED	NEW TESTAMENT BANNED	THOSE NOT WORSHIPPING BEAST OR IMAGE OR RECEIVE MARK PUT TO DEATH	A few Christians escape from beast's forces, go into hiding for 3½ years. Severest time of persecution	
PERSECUTION OF BELIEVERS BEGINS		MOST CHRISTIANS ARRESTED AND PUT TO DEATH	Remaining few raptured at the Lord's appearance (before outpouring of God's wrath)	

WINGS. When God gathered Israel before Him at Mt. Sinai, He told the people, *"I bore you on eagles' wings and brought you to Myself"* (Ex.19:4). The *wings* in John's passage are symbolic of God's protection and deliverance. The term *wilderness* reminds us of the way the nation Israel was provided for during her forty years of wandering in the desert. Israel's supernatural past is in John's mind as he reflects on the fury of the beast directed against her. Many Old Testament scriptures that speak of Israel's place in the kingdom, flash before John as he contemplates her three and one half years as the target of rage. God must protect her from the wrath of the serpent (Satan) in some way, if He means for her to be the empress of the world during His earthly reign.

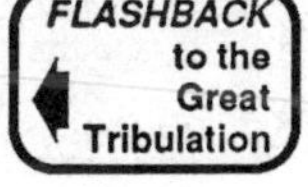

15. Then from his mouth, the serpent spewed a flood of water after the woman, thinking to sweep her away on its tide, 16. but the earth came to the woman's rescue. Opening its mouth wide, the earth swallowed the dragon's flood. 17. Though still furious with the woman, the dragon went elsewhere to make war against the rest of her children—those who keep God's commandments (His Word) and cling to the testimony of Jesus. 18. And the dragon was seen standing on the seashore, waiting.

FLOOD. Though we don't know how, Israel will be protected by God in some way. Perhaps as she was protected in Egypt during the plagues. In any event, the serpent (the beast) will not be able to harm her. So he'll try something else and it will come from his *mouth*. What comes from a man's mouth? WORDS. And the beast will use words in an attempt to reach Israel. But what kind of words? LIES! And they'll come like a flood—lies flowing like water! This is what Satan does best—lie. With 6000 years of experience in lying to men, it's natural that he would seek to deceive Israel with lies. But what does he want? What a triumph if he could woo her back and get her to acknowledge him as God. But that's hopeless. Israel learned this lesson from her Babylonian captivity. She will turn a deaf ear to his promises and pleas—and they will fall as harmlessly as water into the thirsty sands of a desert.

FLASHBACK to the Great Tribulation

REST OF HER CHILDREN. With Israel out of the serpent's reach, the beast will turn his attention to Christians wherever he can find them. He has a neat strategy for catching them. He identifies his own people with a special *mark*, so that his enemies stand out through having none. Then comes the church's most terrible hour. She won't have divine protection such as Israel will enjoy for those three and one half years. Thus the slaughter of the saints will begin in earnest. Most will be slain, as we'll see in the next chapter. Others will go into prisons or slavery. However the saints will have something the Jews won't have—*the seal of God.* No matter what happens to them *physically*, they are eternally safe, sealed for eternity. That these are Christians is obvious, for they are identified as keeping God's Word (commandments) and clinging to Jesus' testimony. For two thousand years, believers have clung tenaciously to the Lord's testimony, *"I will return!"* This is the great hope of the church. The next scene finds the dragon standing on the seashore, waiting for someone to appear.

FOR WHOM IS THE DRAGON WAITING?

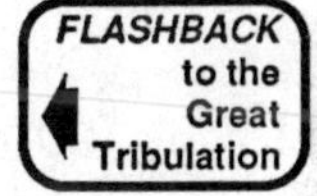

BACKGROUND ON THE BEAST

Before we tackle Chapter 13, let's talk about the animals John will mention. They are not animals, of course, they're people. They're world leaders with great power and authority. But where would John get such an idea? From the prophet Daniel. The ancient prophet used animals to represent world empires. In Daniel 7, he depicts 4 world empires in the form of 4 beasts. Daniel's 4th beast, far more terrible than the other three, had ten horns, matching John's beast.

In the Revelation, John combines in one animal ("the beast") the various features of Daniel's four animals. In John's beast we find the swift, bloodthirsty stealth of a *leopard*, the crushing, unstoppable force of a *bear* and the born to rule demeanor of a *lion*. The heads represent seven world empires, while the ten horns symbolize the final kingdoms out of which the world ruler (antichrist) will come. One of those ten horns is the antichrist/beast who is scheduled to wage war against the saints until the Son of Man arrives. Any Christians left alive at the Lord's coming will be raptured off the earth so that the Lord can pour out His wrath—but they are likely to be few in number.

It's important to remember that this letter was written to the 7 churches of Asia, not merely to the generation that will live under the beast. It would be ridiculous to assume the only message intended for them was the first three chapters, and then add 19 additional chapters that had nothing to do with them.

For John, the beast had to be the Roman Empire, for she was the persecutor of the church in that day. The emperors increasingly began to accept titles of deity and John's readers could identify them. They rejoiced to hear that these godless forces would be destroyed when the Lord arrived. A later generation faced martyrdom from the Roman Catholic church during the Inquisition period. In fact, those of every suffering generation have been able to feel John's words applied to them.

At the same time, it would be unfair to the final purpose of John's book if we didn't realize its true fulfillment was still in the future. In describing the evil empire as a PERSON...a person such as this world has never seen, John shoves the ultimate purpose of his book into the future. The powers, and particularly the universal scope of this man's reign, are still to occur in history. We have yet to see a world ruler with such supernatural power and charm that the entire world follows him; a man so amazing that it takes three different animals to describe him!

John's beast, with its seven heads and ten horns, describes a man with the whole world in his hand. He is Satan's man, as we'll see—the personification of evil. The sad thing is, the pagan world will love him, for he promises to satisfy every evil longing of the human heart. For a Christian to live under such a man would be unthinkable, were it not for the Lord's promised return. That He is returning in great power and glory to vanquish every enemy, is the comforting blessing of this book.

Most scholars hold Chapter 13 to be the most important chapter of the book. Here we meet the most amazing man that has ever been on this planet, except for Jesus, of course. At the same time we observe that he has no real power of his own, other than his commanding presence and charm. His power is derived from the dragon who gives him *"his seat and great authority"* (13:2). Though John speaks of his awesome authority and power, believers are not to entertain fearful thoughts of the beast. He is, after all, a defeated enemy.

Jesus said, *"Now shall the prince of this world be cast out"* (John 12:31). The apostle Paul affirmed, *"The God of peace shall bruise Satan under your feet..."* (Rom. 16: 20). The writer to the Hebrews asserts that Jesus was manifested to *"destroy him that had the power of death, that is, the devil"* (Heb. 2:14). And in his epistle, John declares that Jesus was manifested *"that He might destroy the works of the devil"* (1 John 3:8). The final defeat of the devil and all those associated with him, was surely a vital part of John's teaching to his congregations. It was to encourage his people to be overcomers, even if that meant dying for Jesus. That Satan is a defeated enemy, guarantees Christians that they will ultimately win.

REVELATION 13

(We are now entering Slaughter Alley)

In the last chapter we met the seven-headed dragon (Satan) and learned of his hatred for Jesus, Israel and the church. Israel escaped to a place out of his reach where she was protected by God. But the church, without any such protection, remained fair game for the dragon. This chapter, which might be called “Slaughter Alley,” is the central scene of the Revelation. Here we witness the head on collision between the dragon and the church with the resulting slaughter. We will also meet the dragon’s two agents, through whom he will carry out his vendetta. These agents are pictured as terrifying beasts, one out of the sea and one out of the earth. However, they are not animals. They are two of the most charming, amazing men this world has ever seen. One will be the world’s greatest political figure, the other will be the world’s greatest religious figure. Their ability to deceive the world and devastate the church will be absolutely overpowering—and God will allow it. The beast out of the sea will be the antichrist, the one out of the earth will be his false prophet. Their joint power to crush the church will be irresistible.

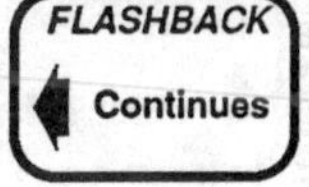

13 **1. Then I saw a beast rising out of the**
sea. It had seven heads and ten horns
with a royal diadem on each of its
horns. On each head was written a blasphe-
mous name. 2. The beast I saw resembled a
leopard, but it had bear’s feet and a lion’s
mouth. To this beast, the dragon gave his own
power and throne and authority.

THE BEAST. As Chapter 12 ended, Satan was standing on the seashore, waiting for someone. Bear in mind he has been ejected from the spirit realm and must now operate in the flesh—with serious limitations. To help him achieve his ambition, he needs an agent dedicated to his cause, someone totally yielded to his will. Limited to the flesh, he must wait for the right man to appear. We now meet that man. Apart from Jesus, this will be the most remarkable person ever to appear in the world. Yet John describes him as a beast and beholds his rise out of the sea. The churning restlessness of the sea pictures the unstable political conditions usually needed to bring tyrants to power. This beast's seven heads clearly relate him to the dragon of Chapter 12.

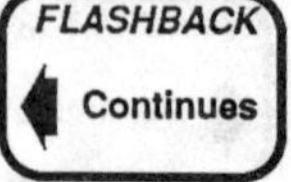

COMMENT: Even though antichrist has been rising to the place of world leadership (with the dragon's help), the moment the devil is ejected from the spirit world Satan can no longer control the timing of human events. Operating in the flesh imposes severe limitations on the devil. This is why he had to <u>wait</u> for the beast to "rise" from the sea (rise to power). This is the one man Satan needs to achieve his objective. No other man will do. So it was a matter of waiting on the natural course of events to produce this man. Used to running things as the "god of this world," it must have been tough on the devil to suddenly find himself no longer able to manipulate circumstances (2 Cor. 4:4).

BLASPHEMOUS. The beast's seven heads, the number of completeness, mark him as the world ruler. Ten other rulers are associated with him as indicated by his horns. Their diadems (crowns) fixed on their horns rather than on their heads, denote the completeness of their power. Horns equal power in Scripture. But why all this kingly power? What's it for? We know what Satan wants. His one ceaseless ambition is to be worshipped as God. He can't stand to have GOD worshipped as God. He is determined to be the one worshipped, no matter what it takes. To those who love the Lord, the height of blasphemy is for a man (or any creature) to claim God's place for himself. Yet we're seeing claims of deity on each of the beast's heads. This tells us the beast is totally dedicated to Satan's ambition. He is committed to seeing that the devil is worshipped throughout the world—*as God.*

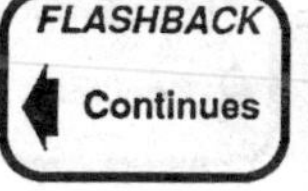

POWER, THRONE AND AUTHORITY. As powerful as this beast is with his world-wide rule, he still needs more power for the job. So the devil confers all of his power on him. We should understand this to be supernatural power. Totally familiar with *metaphysical magic,* the dragon would have much to teach him. With 6000 years of experience in the spirit world and *deceiving men*, Satan would have a lot to pass on. The devil also gave his man authority over the angels cast out of heaven with him. More than that, he gave the beast *his throne.* Pharaoh made Joseph his #2 man, but never gave him the throne. From this we deduce that Satan doesn't want just *any*body. He wants to indwell the beast. It makes sense. The beast is the recognized leader of the world. Once in that body, the next step up for Satan would be God's throne.

COMMENT: In an ordinary body, Satan would be a newcomer to this world. He would have no standing, no credentials of any kind. An angel in his own right, with great prestige in heaven, Satan would be nothing more than an ALIEN on earth. If anyone asked, he'd have a difficult time explaining who he was and how he got here. However, by indwelling the beast and working through his body, no one would suspect a thing. That way, he'd be in a position to demand the worship of the world and no one would suspect it was Satan himself claiming the deity.

3. One of the beast's heads appeared to have received a death blow, yet its fatal wound had been healed. Amazed at this miracle, the whole world followed the beast in wonder and awe. 4. They worshipped the dragon (though unaware they were doing so), because he gave his authority to the beast and they worshipped the beast as well. Together they exclaimed:

FLASHBACK Continues

"Who is like the beast? Who could possibly make war against him?"

FATAL WOUND. Here is a remarkable thing. Apparently an assassin gets to the beast and he receives a fatal head blow. Because of security precautions, the killer would have to be someone in the Satanic circle. Undoubtedly the assault is arranged by Satan for he wants to be inside that body. The news stuns the world. But the shock is quickly replaced by wonder. The beast rises from the dead and guess who's inside his body? Satan. To this point, the political leader was the antichrist, but now he is the BEAST (12:9). With a resurrection to his credit, his claim to be Messiah would be acceptable to the minds of most. Men are so awed by this demonstration of power that the whole world finds it easy to follow the beast. When the beast rises from the dead, the natural thing would be to accept his claim to deity and worship him.

COMMENT: Satan waited for this body for some time. His descent from the spirit-world into this body had to be executed with precision. The timing had to be just right. When the body seemingly recovers from the fatal wound, Satan will be inside it. Then there will be two people inside—SATAN AND THE BEAST. The personality of the beast will be dominated by Satan. Outwardly, however, the beast will appear to be the same person, except that his passion to be worshipped will be greater. As the beast is worshipped, Satan will appropriate the worship to himself. Later, when the beast sees the Lord in the sky, the devil will prompt him to rally his forces world wide to challenge the Lord in combat. The armies of the beast will be defeated and the bodies of the beast and the false prophet will be killed. At that point, the beast and the false prophet will be thrown into the lake of fire (Rev. 19:20). Satan will be locked in the abyss for 1000 years (Rev. 20:3). Since the Lord plans to use him for a final test at the end of the millennium, he is put on hold. When He is released at the end of the 1000 years, he may or may not be confined to a body. If he is, then it would again have to be the body of a recognized leader. On the other hand, the Lord may allow THE DECEIVER to operate in the spirit so as to move in and out of the spirits of men (Rev. 20:7). Satan's indwelling of the beast could well be a temporary arrangement needed solely to secure the worship of men.

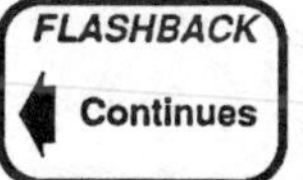

MAKE WAR. The antichrist was a brilliant, charismatic leader before he was indwelt by Satan. When you add the power of Satan to his talent and charm, he has to be the most incredible person this world has ever seen. When that same person rises from the dead, plus being able to perform signs and wonders, what folly it would be to war against him. At this point, the beast is in a position to impose his will on the entire world. Who'd dare oppose him? Imagine Christians forced to live under a ruler who was evil personified! How awful for those Christians who refuse to acknowledge anyone other than Jesus as the true God. Now you know what this chapter is all about.

ONE OF HIS HEADS. While only one of the beast's heads received the death blow, it is the beast who is resurrected. John will confirm that it was the beast who was struck down and yet lived (13:14). The words translated "death blow," as used here, are the same as used in Chapter 5 where it speaks of the Lamb "as though it had been slain" (5:6). The situation with the beast is parallel to that of Jesus whose "death stroke" was healed. A real problem arises when one tries to identify the head that receives the death stroke with Nero or some other emperor. John doesn't say the HEAD is restored, but that the BEAST is restored. Later in Chapter 17 an angel will give us an interesting interpretation of the beast's seven heads (17:8-17). When we see the relationship between the beast and his seven heads the mystery will clear up.

5. Then the dragon, using the beast's mouth, uttered monstrous blasphemies against God's character and was given authority to exercise control over the earth for forty-two months. 6. During this time he continued to blaspheme God's name, His dwelling place and those who live in heaven. 7. The dragon also gave the beast power to make war on the

saints and conquer them, and to rule over every tribe, nation, language and race throughout the entire world. 8. All the inhabitants of the earth will worship the beast—all, that is, except those whose names were written in the Lamb's book of life, the Lamb that was prophetically slain from the foundation of the world.

COMMENT: The model for the beast is the "little horn" of Daniel 7, who had a mouth uttering great things (boasts), and words against the Most High (blasphemies). Four times in this chapter the beast is given the authority to do things, which tells us he is subject to God's timetable. Proud people tend to exalt themselves by putting other people down and that's what the beast is doing here. He puts down God's name by ascribing evil to His character. He makes fun of God's dwelling place and regards angels and saints as clowns. He laughs at the idea that people become children of God through faith in Jesus. But his worst blasphemy is his own claim to deity. The beast doesn't know it, but his reign by God's permission, lasts only 42 months. Strange as it may seem, all this fits God's plan. Believers can endure such things patiently when they know it is only for a short time and from God's hand. That's the real comfort of this book.

FLASHBACK Continues

MAKE WAR. In Chapter 6, the souls under the altar asked how long God was going to wait before avenging their blood. They were told to wait a bit longer until the rest of their brethren had been KILLED as they had been. Now that is happening. Operating with the dragon's authority, the beast is authorized to begin the slaughter of Christians—and receives the power to do it. Thus we see where the blood-washed multitude of the Great Tribulation came from (Chapter 7). Because of his world-wide rule, the beast will be able to find and kill or imprison all those who refuse to worship his image (vss. 10,15).

The exceptions are the sealed 144,000 Jewish evangelists, the 2 witnesses and the Jews protected by God in their "wilderness place." All other believers will be ordered killed or imprisoned. Any managing to escape will make up the tiny group raptured before God's wrath is poured out.

ALL WORSHIP. The command to worship the beast is universal. No one is exempt. This is the strategy for identifying the Christians. They are the only ones who won't worship the beast. At the same time, it is also God's strategy for separating out those who truly love Him and mean business. No one can remain undecided when things reach this point: it's either love Jesus and die or forget Jesus and worship the beast. There'll be no middle ground in that day, no fence to straddle. On the plus side, there is a special reward for those who die under these circumstances (14:13) and later we'll see them enjoying that special reward (20:4). The names of those faithful to Jesus during this trial have already been written in the Lamb's book of life. When the earthly plan was laid out, God foreknew His own and they bear this seal, "The Lord knows all those who are His" (2 Tim. 2:19). All those named in this book will refuse to worship the beast.

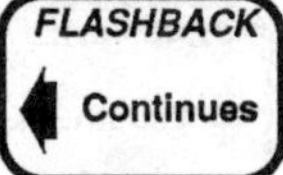

9. You've got ears, so listen carefully! 10. Anyone destined to be a prisoner will be arrested and taken to prison; and anyone destined to die by the sword will be killed by the sword. This will require the utmost patience and endurance on the part of the saints.

DESTINED. John pulls no punches. A faithful shepherd, he tells it like it is. Wise readers will prepare themselves to die for Jesus or be pressed into slavery. As Hitler didn't kill all the Jews, but pressed a good number of those skilled in the sciences and arts into service, so will the beast enslave talented Christians. John's counsel applies more to our present generation than to any other. Mounting signs indicate a one world government is taking shape, and that will set the stage for antichrist. When that hour arrives it will be too late for believers to prepare themselves. Wise ones will begin storing God's Word in their hearts against the time when all Bibles are banned. Sudden arrest and mass executions will catch many off guard. Even so, John doesn't want his readers overwhelmed by his warnings of slaughter, so he says, in effect,

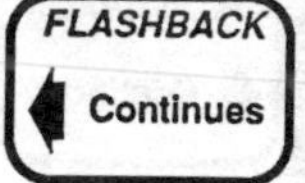

> "Look fellows, the Lord knows we're like sheep led to slaughter. He has made that plain enough. No matter what happens, whether death or prison, accept it as God's will and don't try to avenge yourselves. Actually, it is a great opportunity to honor the Lord with patient endurance and show the world that we are glad to die for Jesus. All we're doing is trading temporary life for eternal life and God guarantees we won't be sorry."

WE'VE MET THE POLITICAL LEADER, NOW WHERE IS THAT RELIGIOUS LEADER?

11. Then, rising up out of the earth, I saw another beast. This one had two horns like a lamb, but it spoke with the fearsome voice of a dragon. 12. It wielded all the authority of beast #1 on his behalf and used this power to compel the inhabitants of the earth to worship the first beast—the one whose death blow was healed.

ANOTHER. While it is universally agreed the apostle John borrows his figures from the book of Daniel, he comes up with another beast, one not found in Daniel's visions. His use of the word "another," indicates...another of the same kind. Both are of the same ilk, committed to Satan. However, beast #2 is equipped with a special skill: deceiving people with religion. Satan is not at all opposed to religion. He likes it. He uses it. It is one of his more effective tools. Later we'll see this beast out of the earth identified as the false prophet (20:10). Like the first beast, he too will have a single objective: getting the world to worship Satan as God. It's the only reason he's on the scene.

FLASHBACK Continues

LAMB. John calls the false prophet a beast, but he too is a man. And though a false prophet, he is an amazing prophet and fabulously successful. He has two horns *like a lamb,* but don't let those horns fool you. Lambs don't have horns. It's a disguise. Far from being a harmless lamb, he is a beast with enormous power. Those horns represent power. He wants to appear attractive and non-threatening so that people will be drawn to him. But who is he? He's the PUBLICITY AGENT for the first beast. He will carry the *religion ball*, while the first beast carries the political ball. Armed with the *power of religion,* his one task is to bring the world to its knees before beast #1—totally unaware they are really worshipping Satan as God. The first beast will give him all the authority and power he needs to get the job done.

13. He accomplishes this by performing great and miraculous signs, such as bringing fire down from heaven to the earth with everyone watching him do it. 14. Able to perform such wonders on behalf of beast #1, he deludes the inhabitants of the earth and persuades them to erect a huge statue in honor of this beast who received the fatal sword thrust and yet lived.

WONDERS. The term miracles probably shouldn't be used in connection with this false prophet, though what he does certainly appears to be miraculous. They are more properly wonders. He will likely heal the fatal wound of the first beast which will catapult him to the top of the religious world. Then, as he duplicates the prophet Elijah in bringing down fire from heaven, empties hospitals of their sick and restores certain dead people to life, his credentials will be established. Who'd challenge the knowledge and power of such a man? Just as they don't dare make war on the beast, neither do they dare to question the false prophet. This man will be to the beast what the Holy Spirit is to Jesus.

PERSUADED. It doesn't take much to see that today's culture is being prepared for this man and his signs. There is a hunger for the miraculous in many of our churches and public gatherings. Much of what we see today is beyond the biblical pattern. Deceptive religion is already being used by Satan. Miracle hungry people will see plenty of wonders at the hand of the false prophet. Paul spoke of the religious deception that would accompany the days of antichrist... *"The coming of the wicked one is the work of Satan; it will be attended by all the powerful signs and miracles that falsehood can devise..."* (2 Thess. 2:9). This man will counterfeit the miraculous acts of the apostles with all kinds of healings, the casting out of demons, and speaking in actual tongues. Satan knows all the world's languages. Yet it will all be to one purpose, to deceive the world into worshipping Satan via the image of the beast. The image will look like the beast.

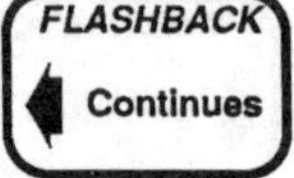

15. Beyond that, he was allowed to give the breath of life to the statue of beast #1, so that it could speak. And he ordered all who refused to worship the statue to be put to death. 16. He further decreed that everyone, small and great, rich and poor, free man and slave, should receive a mark on his right hand or his forehead, 17. and no one would be allowed to buy or sell unless he displayed the mark of

beast #1, which is the name of the beast or the number of his name. 18. Now this calls for discernment: let anyone who has insight figure out the number of the beast, for the number represents a man's name. And here's the number—666.

STATUE. The statue speaks—an idea often found in ancient literature. This startling magic transcends that of those magicians who mocked Moses by turning their dead rods into live snakes (Ex. 7:10-12). This dead statue not only comes to life, but speaks. And it's all done by magic. This statue is probably what Jesus and Daniel refer to as the "abomination of desolation" (Matt. 24:15; Dan. 9:27). It is also "the lie" of 2 Thess. 2:11. Imagine superstitious man's response to a talking statue! At once the world is divided into two camps: those who bow down to the image and those who remain true to Jesus. That decree draws the line in the sand. There is no middle ground, no fence to straddle. Believers must now be prepared to back up their faith with their lives. This is the "patience and endurance of the saints" (vs.10).

FLASHBACK Continues

MARK OF THE BEAST. The false prophet's success doesn't rest solely on his statue that speaks. He backs up his decrees with a surefire device for exposing all who refuse to worship the beast via the image. A visible mark is placed on the right hand or the forehead of all the beast-worshippers. Then it is decreed that no one can buy or sell unless he displays this mark. If a man's head is covered, his hand would be exposed as he offered money to pay for goods. The actual form of the mark, whether a tattoo or an implanted computer chip, is immaterial. The device is thorough enough to prohibit the simplest commercial transactions. The message is clear: worship the beast or die. Receiving the mark was a clear indication the choice had been made.

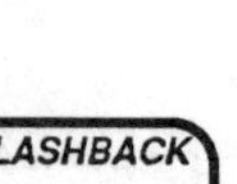

666. Probably no number in history has received more attention than this one. It is the number of a certain man, some future individual, and he has a name. But who is he? 2000 years of speculation have brought us no answer, though some very good men have been tempted to play with the numbers. There is no way to know whom John had in mind. Perhaps a name came to his early readers, but the Holy Spirit didn't allow John to write down any name. That was wise. At best, we can only ascribe a symbolic meaning to the number. SIX is the number of man and in 666 we have a trinity. At the very least the number symbolizes the claim of the satanic trinity (dragon, beast, false prophet) to be God. A little more time will reveal the identity of this man.

FLASHBACK
Continues

COMMENT: Believers will surely go underground, but ultimately most will be caught and killed. The few who survive as hideouts or prisoners until the Lord appears in the sky, will be raptured from the earth. Not a single Christian is to be left when the bowls of God's wrath are poured out on this unbelieving world. Obviously the consequences for refusing the mark of the beast are severe. But God always gives us the

grace to bear whatever He asks of us. However, His grace is not given IN ADVANCE. His usual pattern is to wait until the last minute, so as to extract the most from our faith. Why? So He can reward us for it. On the other hand, the consequences for ACCEPTING THE MARK are far worse. The consequences of that decision last forever, whereas any suffering the beast might inflict is temporary. If he kills us, we're out of here and safe, because we have the mark of God. In the next chapter we'll consider the mark of our God.

THE SCRIPTURE TRAIL THROUGH SLAUGHTER ALLEY

As hard as it is for Christians to accept, the key thought of the book of Revelation is dying for Jesus. The message to Christians throughout the book is—faith is going to be very expensive during the reign of the beast—it can cost you your life. But that idea is more tolerable when we're certain it is God's will for us. The Revelation provides its own map for going through slaughter alley:

FLASHBACK Continues

13:10... *"If anyone is to be killed with the sword, with the sword he must be killed. This calls for patient endurance on the part of the saints."*

12:11... *" They overcame Him by the blood of the Lamb and by the word of their testimony: they did not love their lives so much as to shrink from death."*

7:14... *"These are they who have come out of the Great Tribulation: they have washed their robes and made them white in the blood of the Lamb."*

6:11... *"...they were told to wait a little longer, until the number of their fellow servants who were to be killed as they had been, was completed."*

2:10... *"Do not be afraid of what you are about to suffer. I tell you, the devil will put some of you in prison to test you and you will suffer persecution for 10 days. Be faithful even to the point of death and I will give you the crown of life."*

Every Christian must ask himself..."*Which mark will I choose? That of the beast or the seal of the living God?"*

COMMENT: When the beast is *"given power to make war on the saints and to conquer them"* (13:7), it is easy to understand why this chapter is called "Slaughter Alley." It is also clear that preparing Christians to die for Jesus is the central thrust of this book. We have just come through the most difficult, most significant chapter of the Revelation. When we get to verse 14 of the next chapter, we'll breathe easier. There we'll see the removal of the church just before the 7 bowls of God's wrath are poured out. We'll be with Jesus when He descends to dispose of the beast and false prophet.

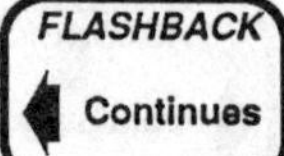

REVELATION 14

(The flashback continues)

John realizes his readers are absorbing considerable threat and need a tension release. The tribulation message is frightening, to say the least. To prevent discouragement and to make the word of the coming holocaust more bearable, he sprinkles scenes of their final triumph throughout the document. That way, readers not only get a breather, but the reward of faithfulness is kept before them. Verses 1-5 provide such a breather with its word of cheer. After describing the dragon and the slaughter of the saints by the two beasts, John feels they need a word about the future. By-passing, for a moment, the awful tempest due to break forth on the world, he leaps ahead in time to present a cheery view of the ultimate victory of the Lamb and all who follow Him. The scene opens with the Lamb and His followers standing on the heavenly Zion, surrounded by the music of redemption. People can pretty much handle anything if they know they're going to win eventually.

FLASHBACK
Continues

14 1. Then I looked, and there before me
on Mount Zion stood the Lamb and
with Him 144,000 who had His name
and His Father's name written upon their
foreheads. 2. And I heard a sound from heaven,
louder than the roar of a huge waterfall or the
crash of rolling thunder. Yet what I was hearing also sounded like harpists stroking their
strings. 3. This massive choir of 144,000 was
singing a brand new song before the throne,

the four living creatures and the twenty-four elders. However no one but the 144,000 ransomed from the earth could learn this song. 4. These are men who have kept themselves spiritually pure, refusing to defile themselves with women. They follow the Lamb wherever He goes, having been purchased from among men as first fruits to God and the Lamb. 5. No lie was found in their mouths; they stand before God's throne completely free of any fault whatsoever.

144,000. The 144,000 seen here could easily be confused with the 144,000 Jewish evangelists of Chapter 7 who were sealed for PHYSICAL SAFETY. The group before us was NOT sealed for that reason. Can we be sure? Of course—they were all martyred during the Great Tribulation. They were sealed for SPIRITUAL SAFETY as sons of God. Without physical protection, such as the Jewish evangelists enjoyed, they defied the beast, forfeiting their lives in the process. They are seen standing with Jesus on the *heavenly* Mount Zion, ready to receive their reward for faithfulness unto death. They sing a song peculiar to all who stand up for Jesus regardless of the cost. John uses a precise Hebrew expression—144,000—to show that not one of His sheep has been lost (John 6:39).

COMMENT: In handling the number 144,000, there are two ways to go: it can be taken literally as we did in the case of the Jewish evangelists, or it can be taken figuratively/spiritually as in the light above. In the case of the Jewish evangelists, where the actual tribes are named, the literal use of the

word seems proper. But concerning those with the Lord on the *heavenly* Mount Zion, the entire scene is spiritual. That the entire crowd is undefiled "with women," overrules the literal and makes the figurative sense the proper one. Since the message is meant to bring spiritual comfort in the wake of the terrible nightmare of Chapter 13, the spiritual application is the appropriate one.

FATHER'S NAME. John stresses the fact that these men bear the mark of God in obvious contrast to the mark of the beast in Chapter 13. It doesn't really matter that one is on the outside and the other is on the inside. A mark is a mark no matter where it is. The fact that God sees it, is enough for those who are truly His. Men are either marked by God or marked by Satan. Those marked by God have refused to worship the beast or participate in any of his pagan idolatry, at the cost of their lives. Having God's name written on their foreheads means they belong to God.

FLASHBACK Continues

REFUSE TO DEFILE. All these suffered the scorn and rejection of the world and were slain for Jesus' sake, even as He was slain for theirs. Here they are seen with Him as He promised..."*That where I am, you may be also*" (John 14:3). John honors these saints by describing them under three figures: 1.) *virgins,* 2.) *followers of the Lamb,* 3.) *first fruits.* They are *(spiritual)* virgins in that they have not defiled themselves by getting involved with the worship of the beast and the harlot associated with him. Like sheep following their shepherd, they have walked where He walked. They are also "first fruits" in that Jesus purchased them by His blood and presents them as a offering or gift to God. That "no lie" is found in their mouths, stands against "the lie" Satan uses to deceive the world.

COMMENT: Bear in mind that Chapters 12, 13, and 14 flash-back to the Great Tribulation. Verses one through five of Chapter 14, which picture the Lamb and His people together on the heavenly Mount Zion, was simply a breather. With verse 6, John resumes his comments on the Great Tribulation. As we pick up the action, God is sending His final word to the pagan world. Three angels will pass before us in quick succession, each with a different message. The first, flying in mid-heaven where all can see him and hear him, calls on men to worship God, rather than the beast (vss.6-7). The second declares the destruction of Babylon (vs.8). The third describes the terrible suffering awaiting all who accept the mark of the beast (vss.9-11).

FLASHBACK Continues

6. Then I saw another angel flying in mid-heaven proclaiming the final offer of the everlasting gospel to all those on earth, to every race, tribe, language and nation.

7. "Fear God," he cried in a loud voice, "and acknowledge His greatness, for the hour of His judgment has come. Worship Him who made heaven and earth, the sea and the springs of water!"

WORSHIP HIM. At this point, very little gospel business can be done on earth. Apart from the two witnesses and the 144,000 Jewish evangelists, no one can say anything about Jesus without being killed. To give men a final chance, God must now use angels. At this late date, it is not likely anyone would pay much attention to the words of men. Thus the challenges and warnings must come directly from heaven. Obviously the salvation door is still open. The first angel's proclamation appeals to common sense. The pagan population is worshipping an image that can speak, but is unable to create anything. So the angel appeals to their untaught consciences at a level they can understand, saying in effect:

> "If you're going to worship someone, why not worship the One Who made heaven and earth, as well as the seas you navigate and the water you drink? The beast has not produced anything like that. He merely offers those things that cater to your sinful flesh. Can't you see that what you're doing doesn't make any sense?"

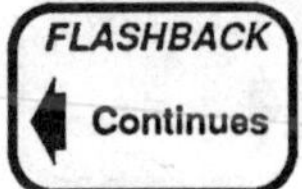

8. Then another angel, the second, followed behind him, crying out...

> ***"Fallen, fallen, is the great Babylon! She who has made all nations drink of the maddening wine of her passionate evils"***

THE SECOND ANGEL. The second angel, coming immediately behind the first, proclaims the fall of Babylon to those on earth. To John and his readers, Rome would be the "great city" that corrupts the earth with her religion and persecution of those who believe in Jesus. The wine of Babylon refers to the intoxicating appeal of Rome's wealth and idolatries. In speaking of

Babylon's fall, the angel is referring to the destruction of the city by the 10 kings serving the beast (17:16). Once the beast becomes the world-ruler, he will have no further use for Rome. Only one city interests him—Jerusalem. Therefore he orders Rome levelled, which took only "one day" (18:10,17,19). Ruling from Jerusalem is critical to the beast's plan to be recognized as God. From the "city of David," he will control all religion and commerce. Inasmuch as Rome would be a serious competitor, she had to go. We'll review her fall in Chapter 17.

9. Still another angel, a third, followed the first two, shouting...

"Whoever worships the beast and his statue, or receives the beast's mark on his forehead or hand, 10. he too shall drink, but the wine he drinks will be the wine of God's anger, poured undiluted into the cup of His wrath. They shall be tormented with burning sulphur in the presence of the holy angels and the Lamb! 11. The smoke of their torment will rise forever and ever. There shall be no relief, day or night, for those who worship the beast and his image or bear the mark of his name."

12. This will horribly test the patient endurance of God's people—those who keep His commandments and remain loyal to Jesus!

WHOEVER WORSHIPS. The warning of the 3rd angel counters the orders of the false prophet. He commanded that all who refused to worship the beast should be killed, and used the mark of the beast to discover the Christians. But angel #3 announces a *FAR WORSE FATE* for any who *DO* accept the mark. Such a person would not only drink the 7 bowls of God's wrath, but will suffer *eternal torment* in the lake of fire. All the beast can do is kill a man and after that, do no more to him. But God can punish a man *after* he dies.The same genius that designed heaven with its future glories, also designed the lake of fire with its eternal agonies. This warning is directed primarily against the pagan population, but any *"Christian"* playing games with the beast's orders, thinking to accept the mark on his hands, while at the same time rejecting it in his heart—*had better heed this warning.* Believers are challenged to reject that notion and realize it is better to die for Jesus at the hand of the beast, than risk the wrath of God.

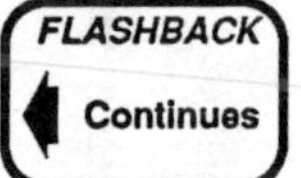

TORMENT. We don't like the thought of God making people suffer eternally for refusing His love, but neither dare we tamper with His teaching on hell. Jesus' most awesome statement on hell was... *"If you do not believe that I am He, you shall die in your sins"* (John 8:24). That's what hell is—unsaved people dying in the greeds, hatreds and jealousies of their corrupt human natures. Jeremiah described that nature as *"deceitful above all things and desperately wicked"* (Jer. 17:9). Those in hell will feed on their own viciousness without one drop of satisfaction for their souls. Made in the image of God, man has *infinite appetites* that can only be satisfied by the *infinite* God. Therefore, anything one might suffer *temporarily* at the hands of the beast couldn't begin to compare with the *eternal emptiness* of being cut off from God forever! The figures of *lake of fire, sulphur and brimstone* are apocalyptic terms for the terrifying reality of hell. Imagine being consumed with jealousy and hatred forever! If heaven lasts forever, then the corresponding reality, hell, also lasts forever.

THE THREE ANGELS

GOSPEL PREACHED FROM THE SKY

FALL OF BABYLON ANNOUNCED

WARNING AGAINST ACCEPTING THE MARK OF THE BEAST

These 3 announcements confirm this is a flashback. We can pretty well pinpoint that John has taken us back to a point just after the beast has begun his reign. Once the beast establishes his absolute rule, no one will be preaching the gospel openly. He will certainly not allow any competetive religion—that's why Babylon had to be destroyed. The image of the beast has been set up and his followers are receiving his mark. The warning of the 3rd angel against receiving that mark would be pointless unless the marking program was in full swing. This is what provokes John's comment, *"This calls for patient endurance on the part of the saints...who remain faithful to Jesus"* (14:12).

HORRIBLE TEST. The apostle John wants desperately to comfort his readers in the face of the coming nightmare, but he knows it is going to be a frightful test of their patience and faith. When it's clear that standing up for Jesus means certain death, one looks at his family and wonders how he can do it to them, or how they would bear up under it. But he determines to die anyway, because the consequences of turning his back on Jesus are far worse than anything the beast can dish out. The anguish of the moment seems unbearable. But doesn't God give us grace to bear it? Indeed, but He doesn't give it *in advance.* Usually He waits until *the very last minute...*so that He can extract the most from our faith. That way He can reward us *the most* on the other side of the experience. He aches to give us the maximum our faith can earn.

FLASHBACK
Continues

COMMENT: John took his readers back to the Great Tribulation, because he wants them to fully understand the horror of life under the beast. At the same time he cautions any Christian against thinking he might save himself or his family by compromising with the situation. The only course open for believers is *death or captivity (13:10).* There is no middle ground. This is what he wants his readers to understand. The central thrust of his book is preparing his readers to die for Jesus! It also explains why the theory of a pre-tribulation rapture is so appealing to modern Christians. Who wants to think of a situation so bad that angels must shout the gospel from the sky. And where no one but an angel can warn people of the consequences of accepting the mark of the beast. Praise God John obeyed the call to write down for us those things that will "soon come to pass." Now we see why John began this chapter with a heavenly scene of the Lord surrounded by His redeemed family. Every Christian needs to know it will be worth it all when we see Jesus.

NOW THAT THE ANGELS HAVE SPOKEN, WILL THERE BE ANY FURTHER WORD FROM HEAVEN?

13. Then I heard a voice from heaven saying:

"Write this down! Blessed are the dead who die in the faith of the Lord from now on. Yes, says the Spirit, they are indeed blessed. They may now relax and rest from their struggles and battles, for the record of their good deeds in this life does follow them."

FROM NOW ON. Those who die for Jesus in any age can expect generous treatment at the hand of the Lord, but those dying as martyrs *during the Great Tribulation,* seem to be in a unique situation. It appears the Lord places a special value on their death. Their death is like His own in that these Christians *know they are going to die.* They live on *death row* as He did, which apparently makes this death a remarkable service in His eyes. It takes a lot of people to run a government and this death might well qualify a person for an important place near Jesus in His kingdom. However, not all Christians will honor the Lord in this death the same way. Their attitudes will range from dying with great joy and thankfulness for the privilege, all the way to reluctant acquiescence. Even so, each person will receive a special honor *based on his attitude* at the time of his death. These words from heaven are meant to challenge readers to go out of this life as conquerors of death through faith in Jesus.

RECORD. God keeps strict records. We'll see that when we get to Chapter 20. The record of each man's work on earth is vital to his future with the Lord. For the place we give Him here determines the place He'll give us there. Our rank and future job in the kingdom will be based on our faithfulness in giving the Lord Jesus His rightful place in our lives. If we put Him ahead of fame, fortune, family and fun, we can expect to hear His *"WELL DONE"* and be thrilled with His reward. But it all has to be done in this life. There are no second chances in Christianity, no make-up classes. Once we're out of here, the next stop is the judgment seat of Christ. No changes can be made after that, for His judgment stands forever. We enter heaven just as we are at the point of death and never change. That's why Paul calls death, *"the last enemy"* (1 Cor. 15:26). Whatever we're going to do for Jesus, we have to do now.

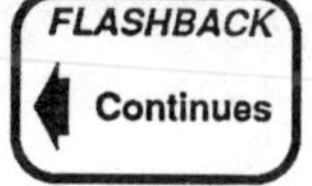

The flashback to the beginning of the Great Tribulation has ended and John resumes his narration.

NOTE: From the severity of the angel's warnings and the timing of the heavenly voice announcing a special reward for those who die for Jesus rather than accept the mark of the beast, it's clear we are approaching the hour of God's wrath. This chapter ends with John showing what will happen JUST BEFORE God's wrath is poured out and what happens AFTER it is poured out. He will do it using the figure of two harvests. John the Baptist did a similar thing to show the end time separation of saints from unbelievers. Referring to Jesus, John said, *"His winnowing fork is in His hand, and He will clear His threshing floor, gathering His wheat into the barn and burning up the chaff with unquenchable fire"*

(Matt. 3:12). We are about to witness those two harvestings: 1.) first the removal (rapture) of the church and 2.) the destruction of God's enemies.

THE SEPARATION OF THE WHEAT FROM THE TARES

14. While I watched, the scene changed and a white cloud appeared before me and seated on this cloud was a figure like "a son of man." He had a crown of gold on His head and a sharp sickle in His hand. 15. Then from the temple another angel came out calling in a loud voice to Him that sat on the cloud, saying:

> ***"Swing Your sickle and reap, because reaping time has come and the harvest of the earth is fully ripe."***

16. So the One Who was seated on the cloud, swept His sickle over the earth and the crop was harvested.

SON OF MAN. The person sitting on the cloud is clearly the Lord Jesus. The "sign of the son of man," is a cloud (Matt. 24:30). The title,"Son of Man," was the Lord's favorite title for Himself. This person is *human*, not an angel. The golden crown marks Him as a conquering king, and here He is seen gathering His own unto Himself. This is not a judgment. No fire is involved in this first gathering. This is the Lord appearing in the sky, ready to remove every last saint from the earth before He pours out His wrath. With the beast slaughtering most of them, there won't be all that many. This is a clean-up operation, the Lord making sure not a single believer is left on earth no matter where he might be hiding. He will join Him in the sky, *"in the twinkling of an eye"* (1 Cor. 15:52).

SWING YOUR SICKLE. The exact timing of the Lord's harvest of His saints is up to the Father (Mk.13:32). So a messenger, an angel, emerges from the temple with word that it is time to use the sickle. This is not a command to the Lord. Rather it is like the starting gun in a race. To Jesus, it means He can now summon what remains of His saints on the earth to join Him in the sky. They've got to be off the earth before God's wrath can be poured out, for this is "the hour" from which He promised to keep them safe (3:10). Since the bowls of wrath are signaled by the last trumpet, we have now placed the rapture of the church at the last trumpet (1 Cor. 15:52). As soon as this crop of saints, though small in number, is harvested, the way is clear for the *"fire"* angel to do his work. And here he comes.

17. Then another angel came out of the heavenly temple and he too had a sharp sickle. 18. Then from the altar came still another angel and this one had charge of the altar's fire. He shouted to the angel with the sharp sickle:

"Take your sharp sickle and gather in the earth's grape harvest for its clusters are ripe for judgment."

19. So the angel swept his sickle over the earth and gathered in its grapes and threw them into the great wine press of God's wrath. 20. The grapes were trodden in the wine press outside the city and for a distance of 180 miles blood flowed from the press, reaching as high as a horse's bridle.

ANOTHER ANGEL. This time *IT IS* an angel who takes the harvest with his sickle. Before, it was a MAN. This angel receives his instructions from an angel of the altar, the angel in charge of the fire. This second harvest is clearly one of judgment, or to use John the Baptist's figure, *"burning the chaff with fire."* The wheat harvest (saints) has been gathered into the barn and now it is time to deal with the overripe grape harvest (God's enemies). God has shown remarkable patience, giving rebellious man every chance to change his mind: 1.) He has allowed men to wreak havoc on the earth, destroying 1/4 of their fellow men. 2.) God Himself, warned them with the trumpet judgments, destroying 1/3 of the natural realm. As a further warning, He loosed demons and a demonic cavalry on them, but they wouldn't repent. Finally God has had enough. The day of His wrath has come.

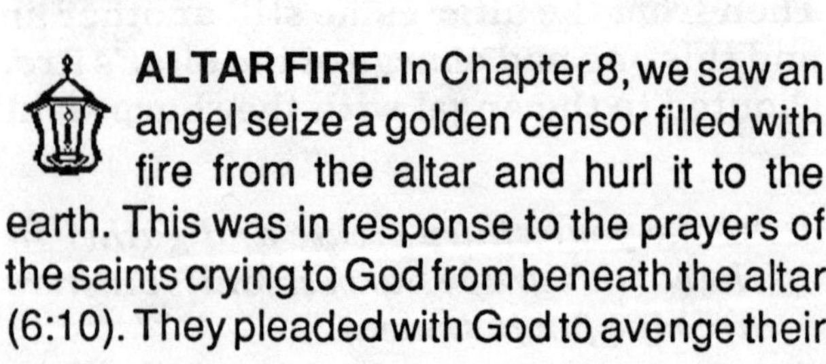

ALTAR FIRE. In Chapter 8, we saw an angel seize a golden censor filled with fire from the altar and hurl it to the earth. This was in response to the prayers of the saints crying to God from beneath the altar (6:10). They pleaded with God to avenge their blood on the unrepentant, godless world below. And now the fire is about to fall. The altar and its fire typically mean death and judgment in scripture. With these verses, the apostle John gives us a summary of what's coming, but provides very few details. Even so, it is clear he is showing us the *beginning point* of the day of wrath (the removal of the church), and the *ending point* (the battle of Armageddon). We're left with only the start and the finish, with nothing in between. We'll read the in between details in Chapter 16.

WINE PRESS. John's figure is quite clear. The overripe grapes picture a polluted, corrupted mankind that is totally hostile toward God. A world that prefers Satan's man (the beast) to God's man (Jesus). Nothing and no one can make them change their minds. So these rotten "grapes" are tossed into the huge wine press, where they are trodden into blood. We are indebted to the prophet Joel, who mixes the figures of the grain harvest and the grape harvest, for the location of the wine press. It is the Valley of Jehoshaphat, which lies between Jerusalem and the Mount of Olives (Joel 3:2). This is where the Lord will trample the grapes, that is, slaughter the nations in a blood bath that will send blood flowing for 180 miles, reaching as high as the horses' bridles. If taken literally, this river of blood would extend to the Northern end of Palestine. Is this the battle of Armageddon? Yes.

REV

14

206

REMARKABLE DRAMA: John included Chapters 12 to 14:13 to focus on the Great Tribulation. That is the heart of the book, the real message he wanted the seven churches to receive. Because of this book, Christians of every generation must ask themselves, *"Would I reject the mark of the beast? Am I prepared to die for Jesus?"* This is what John is after. Will his readers face the truth? Probably no better than those of our generation. Human nature always looks for an escape or a way out. So now we have met the satanic trinity: the dragon, the beast and the false prophet. God's purpose in bringing them and the Great Tribulation on the scene is clear. Never in history has the whole world been forced to choose between God and the devil, and life and death, *at the same time.* This is a remarkable drama, bigger than the exodus of Israel from Egypt. John didn't want his readers to miss the astonishing separation of the wheat from the tares. So now it is clearer than ever why Chapters 12, 13, and 14, are in this book.

REVELATION 15

As before, when John is about to unveil a dramatic action, He precedes it with an introduction. So here, as we come to the bowls of God's wrath, we first meet the seven angels who will pour out that wrath. Also we will hear the great multitude of tribulation martyrs sing God's praise for bringing judgment on the unbelieving world. And well they might, for God, as a righteous person, must punish sin. Righteousness cannot overlook evil or wink at sin. God laid the sins of the whole world on Jesus and since the Lord died for those sins, God's justice demands that anyone refusing to accept Jesus' death for his sins must be punished. Thus God's righteous judgment is about to be directed against a world that has rejected His mercy through Christ. But first the martyr choir will declare, in song, how right it is for God to do this.

15 **1. Then I saw in heaven another awe-inspiring scene: seven angels bearing the seven last plagues: last because with them God's wrath is completely and fully disclosed to the unrepentant world.**

ANOTHER SCENE. John has spoken to us of plagues before, but nothing like that which is before us. Mankind has never seen anything such as the seven angels are about to unleash on the world. Heaven has had it with human evil. This planet will be drinking blood instead of water, burned by a scorching sun and suffer an earthquake that will reshape the world. And that's just the beginning. It won't be over until Jesus treads the winepress of the fierce wrath of God. Translated, that means billions will die as the nations gather at Armageddon to prevent the Lord from taking over the kingdoms of this world. Will Christians endure any of this? No. They will witness it from the sky. The rapture is now behind us. Not a single Christian is left on the earth. The salvation door has been slammed shut (Matt. 25:10).

COMPLETELY. Isn't it great that God's wrath has a limit? That it can be satisfied? There is no way He could remain angry forever. That would mar His eternal joy. But satisfying His wrath doesn't mean God is through dealing with rebellious man. Though His wrath is satisfied, *His justice* has yet to be satisfied. Justice is part of God's nature and like His mercy, endures forever. Therefore certain righteous acts must follow the pouring out of the bowls of His wrath. The beast and the false prophet will be immediately cast into the lake of fire, without any trial. Satan has one final task to perform at the end of the millennium, then he too will be cast into the lake of fire where the beast and false prophet await him. Finally, all the unsaved dead will be raised and judged according to their works and sentenced to eternal torment in the lake of fire (20:13-15).

AS THE ANGELS PREPARE TO POUR OUT GOD'S WRATH, WHAT WILL THE SAINTS BE DOING?

2. Next I saw what looked like a sea of glass fused with fire. Standing beside this heavenly red sea and holding the harps God had given them, were those who had emerged victorious over the beast and his statue and the number that represents his name. 3. They were singing the song of Moses, the servant of God, and the song of the Lamb:

"Lord God almighty, everything You do is great and marvelous. Thou King of the ages, all of Your ways are just and true. 4. Lord, You alone are holy, who shall not fear Thee and do homage to Your name? All nations will come and bow down before Thee, now that Your righteous judgments have been revealed."

VICTORIOUS. This is a crowd of happy Christians. Their sufferings are over and they are enjoying their victory over the beast. They suffered greatly and lost their lives out of loyalty to Jesus. But that's behind them now, and they can sing. There seems little doubt but what these are the tribulation martyrs who are now filling heaven with their joyous music. Harps are handed to them that they might form a unique orchestra. If this can be taken literally, imagine the sound of millions of harpists pouring out their praise to God. Having experienced His faithfulness in keeping His promises, these songs come from their hearts. If this is not to be taken literally, then it speaks of something even more glorious.

SEA OF GLASS. The red sea of glass, beside which the triumphant saints are standing, would have great meaning to the apostle John. He is thinking of another Red Sea where God performed Israel's greatest deliverance when the children of Israel came out of Egypt. And just as the delivered Israelites stood on the opposite shore and witnessed the destruction of Pharaoh's chariots, so these tribulation saints are standing on the shore of the crystal sea before the throne witnessing the destruction of their enemies. Moses and the Israelites sang their songs of *deliverance* and praise to God. Similarly these sing to celebrate God's *righteous judgment* on His enemies. They are saying in effect, that God has every right to use His unlimited power in anger, even against frail men. The world has been given every opportunity to repent, so that the rightness of what God is about to do can't be questioned. All nations will come and bow before Jesus' throne, and no one will ever challenge God's right to do what He did to the world.

5. After this, I observed that the heavenly temple was wide open 6. and from it came the seven angels bearing the seven plagues. They were dressed in spotlessly white linen with golden sashes across their chests. 7. Then one of the four living creatures handed to these

seven angels, seven golden bowls filled with the wrath of God who lives forever. 8. Meanwhile, the smoke of God's glory and power filled the sanctuary to the place where no one could enter it until the plagues of the seven angels had run their course.

AFTER THIS. Music from the heavenly choir fades into the background as John's attention is drawn to the temple. From out of the temple come the seven angels with the seven last plagues. Since they are emerging from the presence of God (the real significance of the temple), it is clear theirs is a divine mission. Their clothing speaks of the sacred nature of their job, with the golden sash symbolizing royal status. When we compare their dress with that of the Lord in Chapter One, it is clear they have the authority of God and the power to execute their mission. Therefore we conclude, that as these angels pour out God's wrath, they will be demonstrating the righteous character of God. This leaves no doubt that what follows is solidly God's will, as though He Himself were doing it.

BOWLS. Actually the seven angels don't have any bowls in their hands when they emerge from the temple. But shortly, one of the four living creatures (the guardians of the throne), appears and hands each a bowl filled with God's anger. At this point, the stage is set for the earth to experience the other side of God. Until now, people felt they could get away with anything, since they had been doing it for centuries. To them, if God really existed, He was a softy who wouldn't hurt a fly. But now they are to learn that He can be as tough as He is tender. The love that took Jesus to Calvary is a righteous love. God's love is never expressed apart from His righteousness. And *judgment* is the response of His righteous character to evil. He can be as angry as He can love. In the next chapter, we'll see how God vents His anger.

SMOKE. When God's holiness comes in contact with sinful man, you get smoke. If *"Our God is a consuming fire,"* (Heb.12:29), it should be no surprise to see smoke when He is enraged. There is always smoke when anything is consumed by fire. When God's presence descended to Mount Sinai to deal with the Israelites, the mountain was covered with smoke (Ex.19:18). And now, with God's anger red hot and about to deal with sinful man, smoke is an expected by-product. Fortunately God's rage passes once the bowls of His wrath are emptied. But until then, no one dares enter the temple. In Moses' day, if even an animal came near that holy mountain while God's presence was there, it was to be killed (Heb. 12:20). And now, with God's fury at its peak and ready to explode on the world, this is no time for anyone, angel or agent, to enter into His presence. Therefore the sooner those bowls are poured out, the better. That takes place in the next chapter.

COMMENT: When John speaks of people being excluded from His presence, don't feel that applies to you. If you have taken Jesus as your Savior, you are already *in Christ,* never to be separated from Him. As high in rank as the four living creatures might be, as well as the angels assigned to this holy mission, they are not family. They cannot enter God's presence at this time. At least that's the picture John is painting for us. Symbolism aside, at this point we are already with the Lord in the sky and nothing can separate us from Him (Rom. 8:38,39). The whole family of God, i.e., believers of all ages, will be there, including those raptured off the earth at the last trumpet. The entire assembly will stay with Him in the sky until all the bowls are poured out and all human government destroyed. We will witness every bit of this from the sky. Then as Jesus descends to Mount Olivet, we'll descend with Him to begin our joint-reign over the earth (Zech. 14:4).

RIDING OUT THE WRATH

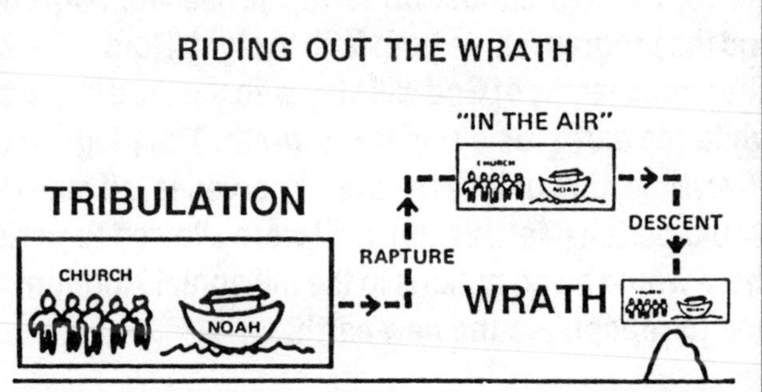

Noah's experience typifies that of the saints. God leaves His people (like Noah) on earth to endure tribulation, but when He is ready to pour out His wrath, He calls His people out. At the rapture, the remnant of the saints will join Jesus in the sky. ALL THE SAINTS will be with Him as He takes vengeance on an unbelieving world. Once His enemies are punished and the world shaken and reshaped, we will descend with Him to Mt. Olivet. The Noah story is a perfect illustration, one which Jesus meant for us to understand (Matt. 24:37-39).

REVELATION 16

We have arrived at an incredible chapter, one that will see God's wrath poured out on those who have rejected His offer of free grace. With the Christians removed from the earth, the way is now clear for God to vent His rage upon His enemies. The most terrible kinds of destruction are about to be visited upon the earth, as the 7 bowls are poured out in rapid succession. To this point, man has had every opportunity to repent, but that opportunity is now gone. The door of salvation was slammed shut when the Lord appeared in the sky. With the Lord visible to those on earth, the need for faith ends and the program shifts from faith to sight (Rom. 8:24,25). The whole family of God will stay with the Lord in the sky while the earth reels under His wrath. The plagues are so terrible, that unless the Lord intervenes, all mankind would perish (Matt. 24:22). If all were allowed to perish, there would be no nations in the millennial kingdom, no one to repopulate the new earth.

16 **1. Then I heard a mighty voice coming from the temple and it thundered to the seven angels,**

***"Go now and pour out on the earth
the seven bowls of God's wrath."***

2. So the first angel went and emptied his bowl upon the earth; and ugly and painful sores broke out on everyone who had the mark of the beast and worshipped its image.

3. The second angel poured out his bowl over

the oceans and their waters turned to blood like the blood of a dead body, and every living thing in the seas died.

MIGHTY VOICE. Since no one is allowed to enter the temple until the seven bowls of wrath run their course, we should probably understand this to be God's voice coming from the temple. When Peter, James and John were with the Lord atop the mount of transfiguration, a cloud enveloped them and they heard God speaking directly to them (Matt.17:5). So the idea of God speaking directly to men is not without precedent. His fury now at its peak, God's command to the angels likely roared like thunder. There is no mercy tempering these bowls. This is absolutely the undiluted pure wrath of God. The fire of His fury will now be felt by every man and woman on earth.

BOWL #1. If the followers of the beast wanted marks on their bodies, God has some marks for them to display. The first bowl attacks the *health* of all those on earth, producing ugly and painful sores on their bodies. Observe that this first judgment is not directed against nature, but against people. With every single Christian removed from the earth, only the beast worshippers are left. All of them bear his MARK. But now God has marked their bodies with ugly sores. During the trumpet judgments, which were warnings, men could change their minds and be saved. But with the sounding of the last trumpet and Jesus appearance in the sky, the SALVATION DOOR was closed and the opportunity to be saved is gone. When we get to the 3rd bowl, we'll see that the unsaved masses have no intention of repenting, NO MATTER HOW MUCH THEY SUFFER.

COMMENT: There are parallels between the bowls of wrath and the plagues visited on Egypt, but drawing out the comparisons doesn't really help our understanding all that much. Similarities can also be noted between the bowls, the seals and the trumpets. That's to be expected, inasmuch as the intensity of the judgments has been building with each set of plagues. The seals featured a partial judgment (1/4), the trumpets were more severe (1/3), and now the bowls of this chapter bring total destruction. I have elected to stay on track with John as he reports what he sees, rather than digress to related observations.

BOWL #2. The second angel is ordered to pour out his bowl on the sea. When he does, all ocean water quickly turns to blood. It's not fresh blood either, but the coagulated blood one finds in a dead body. As such it is highly toxic. This kind of blood won't support life, so all sea life dies. This is a serious plague for much life-giving food is drawn from the sea. Talk about pollution! Imagine the stench this creates as the carcasses of sea life, from whales to minnows, wash up on the shores. As the first bowl attacked the *health* of the beast-worshippers, this bowl lays waste to a *vital food source*. All will feel the effects of this plague, not just those who make their living from the sea. The yachts of the rich will be caked with gooey, deadly blood.

4. The third angel emptied his bowl upon the rivers and springs and they became blood.

**WOW! PEOPLE HAVE TO DRINK TO STAY ALIVE. IF ALL DRINKING WATER IS TURNED TO BLOOD, WON'T ALL MEN QUICKLY DIE?
DOES GOD REALLY MEAN FOR HIS PLAGUE TO BE THIS EXTREME?**

BOWL #3. As the sea turned to blood at the second bowl, so now all the fresh water sources turn to blood as the 3rd angel pours out his bowl. Everything in the sea dies, and death spreads everywhere as blood is delivered to the homes instead of water. With the drinking water so polluted, think of the panic created when there's nothing to drink? When people open the tap and get blood instead of water, many will think the end of the world is at hand. It's a question as to whether the population will see the connection. The beast and his followers were eager to shed the blood of Christians, now they must drink blood. Even if they don't make the connection between taking blood and drinking blood, we see the justice of it. It seems very appropriate.

WHO ELSE FEELS IT'S APPROPRIATE?

5. Then I heard the angel of the waters announce,

"You are just in bringing these judgments, You Who are and were, The Holy

One! 6. You are giving them what they deserve, for they shed the blood of Your saints and prophets and now You're giving them blood to drink."

WATER ANGEL. One might be inclined to feel God is too rough on weak and helpless men; that He need not be so extreme in His punishing judgments. But we must remember these bowls *are not* calls to repentance. That ended with the 6th trumpet judgment. This is God's wrath and it must be released. It has to come out. If "angel of the waters," refers to an angelic officer charged with managing the world's water supply, then perhaps he would be more concerned than anyone else. Yet, he says, this judgment fits the crime. We're so used to the goodness of God, we tend to forget He has another side to Him. We're seeing that other side now and it is clear that nothing in past history can begin to compare with this terrible destruction wrought by His rage. Still no positive response from the heathen world.

7. And I heard a corroborating voice from the altar saying,

"Yes, Lord God almighty, all of the judgments You pronounce are true and just."

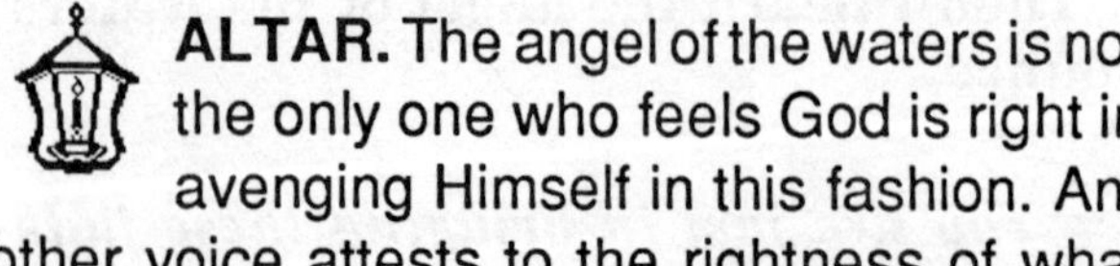

ALTAR. The angel of the waters is not the only one who feels God is right in avenging Himself in this fashion. Another voice attests to the rightness of what

God is doing, and it comes from the altar. While men often question the ways of God and doubt that He really cares about what is right, the angels of heaven have no problem with what He's doing here. They know He's just and they're proclaiming the rightness of His ways. It would appear we are to consider the altar has a voice. This is akin to what we sometimes say, "If these walls could only talk." Here John has the altar speaking. The altar, long associated with judgment and sacrifice, would know all about the evil that men do—and its price tag. So if an altar could speak, it would have a right to comment on the justice of God's judgments. The two witnesses concur that God is true and just in all His ways.

8. The fourth angel emptied his bowl on the sun and it was allowed to scorch men with burning heat. 9. All were seriously burned by the searing heat and they cursed the name of God who had the power to order such plagues, and they refused to repent and worship Him. 4

BOWL #4. Only the sun is affected by the 4th bowl. It probably remains dimmed, along with the moon and the stars, but its heat output is raised to such a level that men's bodies are scorched. Scorching heat does not require an increase in light from the sun, only a slight adjustment in the forces of nature. This normally brilliant jewel of creation, so often worshipped by men, now becomes their enemy. The sun worshippers wail in agony as blisters rise on their skin. The fact that the sun is *"allowed"* to do this, indicates God is controlling this plague. The trumpets announced that the judgments were from the hand of God. The heathen world also understands that God is behind this plague, even as Pharaoh understood God was behind the Egyptian plagues and it hardened his heart. Those suffering the bowls of wrath will have pharaoh-like hearts, with no interest in His mercy or forgiveness.

CURSED. This heat apparently doesn't kill anyone, for the pagans survive it to curse God and blaspheme His name. Repentance is out of the question for these people. If any were inclined to repent, they would have done it during the trumpet judgments. As it is, God has so structured the judgment series, that only the *spiritually unsalvageable* remain to endure His wrath. That's why the rapture had to wait until the very last minute; until just before the bowls were poured out. As part of the cleanup operation, the rapture will remove those who repent during the trumpet judgments right up to the last man to be saved. When that last man is saved, the rapture will occur in a flash *("in the twinkling of an eye")* just before God orders the bowls to be poured out.

10. The fifth angel poured out his bowl upon the throne of the beast and his kingdom was plunged into darkness. 11. His people gnawed their tongues in agony and cursed the God of heaven for their pains and sores, but they refused to repent of all their evil deeds.

BOWL #5. With the 5th angel, the kingdom of the beast is the target. The capitol of the evil empire (Jerusalem at this time), is subjected to supernatural darkness. The darkness intensifies the pain from their sores, with the heat of the sun, bringing a terror of its own. Things always seem worse at night. When you can't see the person in front of you, you're afraid to move and tend to panic. Even though there is no light from the sun, the heat continues. By now the pain is so bad, they gnaw on their tongues. In spite of their sores, their pain, the continual heat and the darkness, there's no sign of any repentance. Even though they know the plague is from God, they sink deeper into their defiance and curse Him.

12. The sixth angel poured out his bowl over the great river Euphrates and its water was dried up to prepare passage for the kings marching from the East. 13. And I saw three evil spirits, resembling frogs, coming from the mouths of the dragon, the beast and the false prophet. 14. These miracle-working demons are sent out to summon the kings of the world to assemble for battle against the Lord on the great day of Almighty God. 6

BOWL #6. The Romans regarded the Euphrates river as the Eastern boundary of the empire. This 2200 mile river, stretching from the Turkish mountains to the Persian Gulf, was the last natural barrier between the Middle East and the Orient. It provided protection against the dreaded

Parthian tribes occupying the land beyond the river. John pictured the Parthian land armies on their way to attack Jerusalem. For us, however, it pictures the removal of all barriers that would keep the oriental armies from joining the armies of other nations for the Armageddon campaign. There is a temptation to link these armies with the 200 million horsemen of the 6th seal, but that was a demonic cavalry, one that attacked people during the Great Tribulation. The context of this passage clearly speaks of *preparation for war,* the gathering of "the kings of the world" for the great battle that takes place at the end of this age.

SUMMON. In the vision, John sees three evil spirits leaping like frogs as they exit the mouths of the unholy trinity. Actually, they don't leave anyone's mouth. It's the command to go that comes from the mouth. No longer able to operate in the spirit, these demon agents must travel the same as anyone else. They are in bodies and must travel by plane. The point here is, they waste no time in responding to the command from the mouths of their masters. Scrambling like interceptors, they fly to the rulers of the nations. Since they can no longer work INSIDE PEOPLE, they are forced to rely on outward *MIRACLES* to accomplish their deceptions. These demonic deceivers, with their miraculous signs, easily persuade the "kings of the world" to send their armed forces to the staging area for the final battle.

WHAT SHOULD MODERN BELIEVERS THINK WHEN THEY READ OF THE PERSUASIVE POWER OF THESE DEMONIC MIRACLES?

15. "Behold, I am coming like a thief! Blessed is the man who keeps watch, whose clothes are at hand so that he will not have to go naked and be shamefully exposed."

THIS SOUNDS LIKE ANOTHER INTERRUPTION

A very brief pause in the narrative occurs here as the Lord sounds a caution. The readers have just observed how deceptive and persuasive demon forces can be. Even though they've been ejected from the spirit-realm and limited to the flesh, satanic agents still manage to deceive the kings of the world with miracles. Christians, of course, won't be on earth when God's wrath is poured out, but demon power will be operating during the tribulation period all the way to the 6th trumpet. Any Christians alive at that time will be exposed to it. In this verse, the Lord is warning them to check on their own spiritual preparation and be on their toes. It is quite easy to persuade people with miracles. There is a natural tendency to think all miracles are from God. That's why Satan uses them.

16. The place where the demon-spirits gather the armies of the world is called in Hebrew, Armageddon.

GATHER. After explaining how the miracle-working demons manage to lure the kings to the Mideast, John nails down the rallying point—Armageddon. Normally Armageddon is associated with the ancient city of Megiddo, which commands the pass to the Plain of Esdraelon, a historic place of slaughter. This enormous valley separates Galilee from Samaria and it is here the armies will be coordinated. The demon messengers must be extremely clever with their miracles, because their task is to get the kings of the world to believe they can prevent the Lord from taking over the world by defeating Him in battle. The final phase of this battle will be the coming of the Lord. To us it seems ridiculous that anyone thinks he can defeat the Lord, but Satan knows this is his last chance to try. From what John told us in 14:20, the range of these armies could stretch for a distance of 180 miles, the distance from Armageddon to Jerusalem. What a slaughter it is going to be!

17. The seventh angel poured out his bowl into the air; and from the throne within the temple a loud voice shouted, "It is over!" 18. Then there were flashes of lightning, followed by peals of rolling thunder and a tremendous earthquake such as has never occurred since man has been on the earth. 19. The great city was split into three parts, while the cities of the nations collapsed in ruins. In all this God did not forget Babylon the great, but made her drink the cup of the wine of His furious wrath. 20. All the islands vanished and the mountains were nowhere to be found.

21. Huge hailstones, weighing as much as one hundred pounds each, crashed down upon men from the sky and they cursed God because the plague of hail was so savage.

BOWL #7. This last bowl brings more devastation than any of the others. All are terrible, but this is the greatest catastrophe of all time. The focus is on "the great city," Jerusalem, the capitol of the beast. John is not referring to ancient Babylon, for that was destroyed before John's day. The Roman Empire was itself destroyed some centuries later. John was no doubt thinking of Rome as the city of the beast. To his mind, the destruction of Rome meant the end of all secular power in the world, which would have been true had the destruction occurred in his day. But he had no way of knowing that the destruction of Rome (Babylon) merely foreshadowed the ultimate collapse of all worldly opposition to God. With the 7th bowl poured out on the atmosphere, the effect is more deadly than what happened to the earth, sea, rivers or the sun. Once that bowl is emptied, a voice from the throne announces that the seven last plagues have run their course. In effect, we're hearing God say...*"It is over!"* The wrath now ends, but God's dealing with sinful man still has a long way to go.

EARTHQUAKE. In Chapter 15, we were told that the seven last plagues would complete the wrath of God. With the pouring out of the last bowl, that day has arrived and God Himself announces that His wrath is complete. Along with His announcement came the usual accompaniments of lightning, thunder and an earthquake. It is the earthquake that captures our attention. No one can guess how high this will read on the Richter scale, but it will be of sufficient magnitude to flatten mountains, reshape the earth and destroy the major cities of the world. In Chapter 6, an incredible earthquake moved islands and mountains from their places to announce the day of God's wrath was at hand. But here a more destructive earthquake signals the end of God's wrath. In this final quake, the mountains and islands don't just move, *they disappear!* God obviously finds earthquakes useful for reinforcing His messages.

BABYLON. The passage speaks of "the great city" that was divided into three parts. We have identified this city as Jerusalem, the capitol of the beast. "Babylon the Great" or Rome, with her religions, was clearly the center of world government BEFORE the beast destroyed her near the beginning of the Great Tribulation. In Chapters 17 & 18, John will pause in his narrative and flash back to her destruction. As a final feature of God's wrath, one hundred pound hailstones fall on men from heaven. When Joshua was battling 5 kings, God killed more people with hail in the battle than He did with Joshua's sword (Josh. 10:11). As severe as this plague is, it fails to bring the beast's followers to their knees. Instead they curse God. So for the third time, we see how all this suffering and pain served only to expose the depravity of the people's hearts.

COMMENT: While verse 19 says God remembered Babylon the Great, it is clear that "Babylon the Great" was not destroyed at the pouring out of the last bowl. The beast is in control of the whole world during the Great Tribulation and would not tolerate competition from Rome. For her to be carrying on her religious trade at the same time the beast is making his covenant with Israel, isn't thinkable. His passion to be accepted as Messiah and finally worshipped as God, would be seriously obstructed by this woman. There's no way he could allow her to remain. In the next chapter we'll flashback to her destruction at the hands of the 10 kings. They will destroy her in a single day.

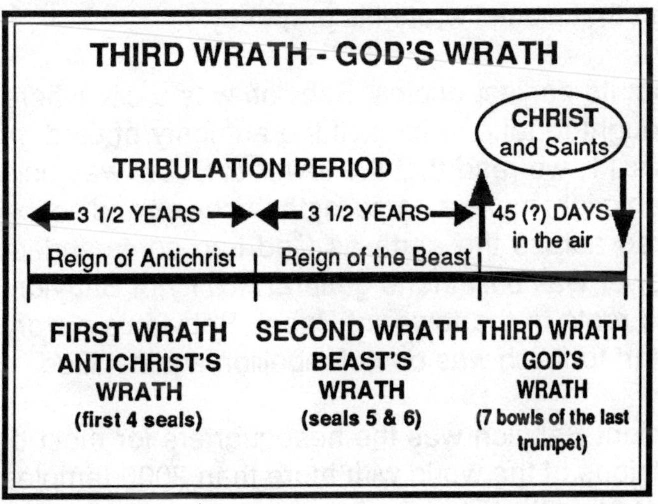

BEFORE READING REVELATION 17

Chapters 17 and 18 deal with one subject—Babylon and her fall.

Babylon is a city, a city so wicked that John portrays her as a prostitute. It was a great city that existed 6 to 7 hundred years before Jesus' time. It was built on the banks of the Euphrates River about 75 miles South of the modern city of Baghdad. In Daniel's day, it was the capitol of a major world power, a power that destroyed the Southern kingdom of Israel and carried off its finest young men, one of whom was Daniel. It was from Babylon that Daniel wrote his prophecy.

From its earliest origins, Babylon was a city where man sought to take to himself the authority of God. In Genesis 11, we read that the tower of Babel was built that men might make a name for themselves and not be scattered across the earth as God had commanded. That tower was built in the general vicinity of Babylon. With its roots in the tower of Babel, Babylon's history from start to finish was one of rebellion against God.

Ancient Babylon was the headquarters for most of the religions of the world with more than 2000 temples dedicated to different gods. Astrology, sorcery and contact with the spirit-world were all a part of the religions of this anti-God city. It stood against anything that represented the true God. From here, the religions of Babylon flowed like rivers into nearly every region of the world. Easter and the mother-child cult come from this city, along with the Christmas tree.

Hundreds of years before John wrote the Revelation, Babylon fell and faded from existence. Even so, the name *BABYLON* has remained as a buzzword for everything that is opposed to God. To the Jew, "Babylon" represented a man-made religion that was demonic in nature with a lifestyle that was abominable in the sight of God. Jews came to apply the name *"Babylon"* to any city that shook its fist in the face of God.

When John was writing the Revelation, all his mind could see was—Rome. He saw its power, he saw its evil, and all that he saw he summed up in one word—*"Babylon!"* To him, she was a religious prostitute, with the mighty power of Rome at her disposal. When early believers began to read John's Revelation, there was no way they could feel he was describing anything but the cruel power of Rome.

We can understand why 1st century Christians would think that. Since they were suffering heavy persecution, they thought they were already in the Great Tribulation and that the Roman Emperor was the antichrist. But we're not locked into that notion. Nearly 2000 years later, we know that the Great Tribulation hasn't come yet, for nothing in history even comes close to what John describes as the Great Tribulation. Many of those events are yet to occur, the most significant of which is—the return of the Lord.

REVELATION 17

By now you are aware of John's flashbacks, interludes and interruptions. Well, we've just come to another and this one is two chapters long. The bowls of God's wrath have been poured out and we're set for the Lord's coming and the battle of Armageddon, but John feels this is a good time to stop and go back and fill us in on the destruction of Babylon. So he flashes back to Chapter 14:8, to the the judgment of Babylon the Great. Chapter 17 introduces us to this woman, while Chapter 18 features her destruction. In Chapter 17 we meet the infamous lady, the most successful prostitute of all time. We'll see John's astonishment as he beholds her power and influence. An angel will do most of the talking while John listens. When he learns what is going to happen to this woman, he is even more amazed. As great and powerful as she is, she will be destroyed in a single day.

FLASHBACK to the Destruction of Babylon

17 **1. Then one of the seven angels who was holding the seven bowls came over to me and said:**

"Come with me and I will show you what is going to happen to the great harlot who sits enthroned over many waters. 2. The kings of the earth have committed adultery with her and the inhabitants of the earth have made themselves drunk on the wine of her filthiness."

COME AND SEE. The apostle John gets an unusual summons from an angel, one of the high ranking seven who carry out various missions for the Lord throughout this book. The angel takes John back to a point in time near the beginning of the Great Tribulation. He wants to show John the destruction of a prostitute. But this is no ordinary prostitute. She is in fact, the mother of all prostitutes. That's what makes her the GREAT HARLOT. John is not speaking of an actual woman, but of a city. He personalizes the city as a prostitute to better picture its degrading influence. This is a woman (city) who has dominated kings and manipulated masses of people throughout the world with her seductive practices.

FLASHBACK to the Destruction of Babylon

ADULTERY. John is not speaking of literal immorality. The word "adultery" is commonly used throughout the Bible to describe unfaithfulness to God. Whenever Israel (the wife of Jehovah) turned from God to worship other gods, she was called an adulteress (Hos. 1:2). Thus John's harlot is the world's greatest seductress who uses materialism, immorality and religion to lure men and women away from the Lord. This is not the first time a city has been described as a harlot. Nineveh was such a city, who betrayed nations with her harlotries and charms (Nahum 3:4). When John's readers come upon this passage, only one city comes to their minds. To them the harlot is Rome.

COMMENT: Now that we have identified the city as Rome, please remember this is a flashback to Chapter 13. If John hadn't stopped his narrative, we'd be reading about the Lord's descent and the battle of Armageddon. Instead, he returns to the days when the beast was rising to power; when he needed the backing of Rome; when he needed her religion to achieve his political ambitions. As prophecy unfolds in the daily news, we can expect to see Rome playing an ever increasing role in the politics of world government. When the beast has no further need of the prostitute, he'll have her destroyed. The ten kings or nations associated with him will take care of that for him. Her destruction occurs some years before the bowls of God's wrath are poured out onto the world. The *"many waters"* is a reference to Rome's pervading influence as it flowed throughout the entire world.

FLASHBACK to the Destruction of Babylon

3. Then he carried me in the Spirit to a wilderness where I saw a woman riding on a scarlet beast that had seven heads and ten horns and who had blasphemous names scribbled all over her. 4. The woman herself was clothed in purple and scarlet, and was decked out with beautiful jewelry made of glittering gold, precious stones and pearls. In her hand she held a golden goblet, full to the brim with her obscenities and the lewdness of her harlot ways. 5. Written on her forehead was a mysterious title:

> ***"Babylon the great, the mother of all prostitutes and of every abominable thing on earth."***

THE WOMAN ON THE BEAST. As the curtain goes up, John is not transported to Rome as we might expect, but to a wilderness. She is going to be dealt with on an individual basis, *with no one to help her.* A wilderness provides the perfect setting for such a judgment. Besides, there is little else to distract John's vision. All he sees is this woman. The first thing he notices about her is that she is riding on the seven-headed beast, the one we have already identified as the antichrist. The blasphemous scribbling aids further in her identification. She is riding on the beast, because, *at this point,* she is the more powerful of the two. The antichrist needs her influence to get where he's going and will curry her favor until he becomes the ruler of the world. After that, her influence will no longer be needed. When he enters into a covenant with the Jews, wanting to be proclaimed Messiah, there will be no room for Rome and her religion. It is at that point that the ten kings (ten horns) are ordered to destroy her.

DECKED OUT. Religion is big business. If you don't think so, look at the way the harlot is dressed. Her jewelry is a testimony to the tremendous wealth accumulated by religion—in any era. The style of her dress is not that of a simple Christian life, but of one who has an abundance of the finest things of this world. And she knows how to use it in seducing men and women. With her goblet full of obscenities, she knows how to attract weak men. She promises them the fulness of pleasure—as much as their evil natures desire. She is skilled in appealing to the worst in men, to their basest instincts. Then, cloaking her seductions in religion, she has no trouble leading men away from God.

The very thing that should bring men to Him (religion), she uses to lead men away from Him. That's why the Lord hates her so.

MOTHER OF PROSTITUTES. The Lord Jesus called Satan the "father of all lies" (John 8:44). Here the woman, Babylon the Great, is titled the "mother of all prostitutes." Not everyone is going to understand the meaning of "mother of prostitutes," because the title is a mystery. But when we remember the biblical use of the word "prostitution"—leading people away from worship and fellowship with the Lord—the meaning is not so vague. This woman, this city, is more than just a person famous for wealth, corruption and power. She is also one who is not content to enjoy what she has, not satisfied with what she has. She is not happy unless she can cover the earth with her harlotry and filthiness. As the Communist party originally set out to make the world communist, so this woman sought to have everyone in the world participate in her obscene practices. That's what makes her the "mother of all prostitutes."

IS THAT THE ONLY REASON GOD HATES HER?

6. I could see that the woman was drunk—drunk with the blood of the saints she had killed, the blood of all those who were martyred for Jesus, and I just stood there staring at her, totally overwhelmed by what I was seeing.

BLOOD. The most hateful thing about this harlot is not her passion to lead the world away from the Lord and into the depths of her filth, but that she is ready to kill those refusing to go along with her. This is what makes her such an ideal partner for the beast. They think alike. Both kill their opposition. It's true that believers in the Lord Jesus have always been persecuted down through the centuries, but that is nothing compared to what this evil woman is going to do when she teams up with that political giant—*the beast.* She will be responsible for the wanton slaughter of countless Christians. John was shocked to see that the killing of saints had such an intoxicating effect on the harlot; that she was actually drunk on the excitement of killing believers.

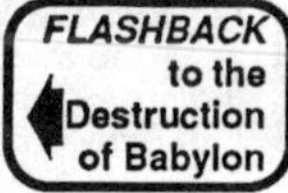

7. Noticing my astonishment the angel asked:

"Why are you so surprised? I will explain to you the mystery of the woman you saw and the seven-headed beast on which she rides and who has the ten horns. 8. The beast you saw was alive at one time, but is now dead. However, he will soon come up out of the the abyss only to be cast into eternal destruction shortly thereafter. The inhabitants on earth, that is, those whose names have not been written in the book of life since the foundation of the world, will be staggered by the resurrection of this one who was once alive, died and reappears."

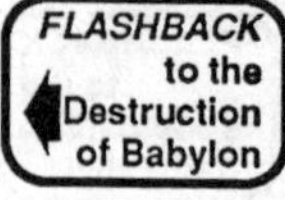

THE ANGEL EXPLAINS. No wonder John is amazed! The sight of the woman is bewildering. Now he is to have a better look at the beast, whom the angel describes in some detail. There are not two mysteries here, just one. The woman and the beast are not separate mysteries. Together they are one mystery. The remainder of this chapter will be devoted to explaining the beast, while Chapter 18 will describe the judgment of the great prostitute. Now for some details about the beast that we did not get in Chapter 13. In that chapter we learned that the beast received a fatal blow, apparently died and then recovered. We also learned that the man who recovered was quite different from the man who died. He died a charming, brilliant charismatic leader, but he was resurrected with the passions of Satan. He died as antichrist and rose as the beast, which is not surprising, inasmuch as the one indwelling him is *"out of the abyss."*

INHABITANTS STAGGERED. Those dwelling on the earth are awestruck by the resurrection of this man. They knew he died, but here he is again—and so different. They will soon find out that the resurrected leader has but a single passion—*to be worshipped as God.* That's because Satan is living inside him. As antichrist, he operated in Satan's *power*, as the beast he will operate with Satan's *passion*. The devil has hated God for centuries. Now that hatred will explode through the beast. Since he cannot lay his hands on Jesus, his fury will be vented against His people. That's what makes it the Great Tribulation. The rest of the world, those not listed in God's family register, will be dazzled by the beast. His resurrection will convince them of his incredible, unbeatable power. They'll ask, "*Who can war against the beast?*"(13:4). Jesus said only *one sign* would be given to the world, His own resurrection from the dead. But with the world ruler performing that *very same sign,* the pagan world goes crazy over him. They will believe his claim to be God.

BUT JUST WHO IS THIS BEAST?

9. "Those with discerning minds should weigh carefully my explanation. The seven heads are seven hills on which the woman sits. 10. They also represent seven kings. Five have already fallen, one now reigns and the other has yet to come on the scene. When he does, he will reign only for a little while. 11. The beast who was once alive, but now is not, will surface as the eighth king, yet he is of the seven. However his reign will end with his complete destruction."

FLASHBACK to the Destruction of Babylon

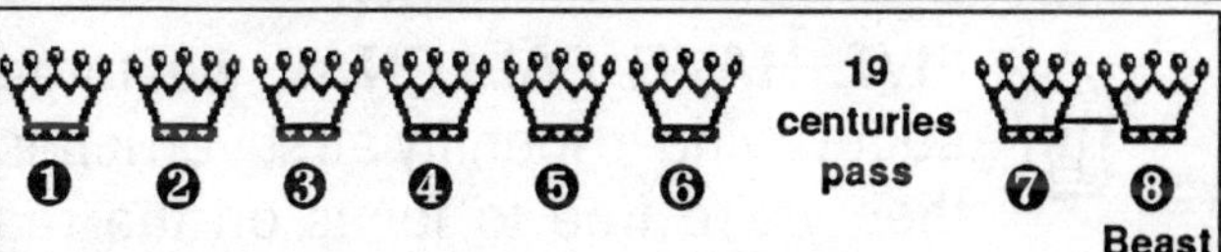

Those 8 crowns represent the eight kings to whom John is referring. As John writes, #6 is in power. But he had no way of knowing that 19 centuries would pass before #7 would appear. He does know #7's reign will be brief. We will see that the 8th king, who is of the seven, is actually #7 who dies and is resurrected as the beast.

SEVEN HILLS/SEVEN KINGS. The mention of the seven hills would be an instant clue for the early readers of this book. Since Rome was built on seven hills, that city would immediately pop into their minds. And there was no doubt in anyone's mind but that Rome was the anti-Christian center of the world. However the interpretation must go beyond that city or there is no mystery. That wouldn't take any discernment. To learn that the seven heads are also seven kings moves us beyond the city and out into the Roman Empire. But when we try to identify the seven kings, we find we can't do that from John's words. That is probably by design. It is likely that God does not want us focusing on any succession of Roman emperors, but instead see the whole of Roman domination compressed into one man—the beast. John, of course, didn't know how much time would pass before this man appeared. But he did know the final ruler would be a monster that personified the power of hell. This means we must discern the identity of the 8th king in some way other than tracing the succession of Roman emperors.

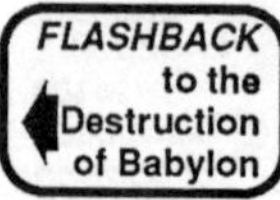

FIVE HAVE FALLEN. If we forget about trying to identify all seven kings, then we're free to focus on the real riddle—the eighth king—the beast. When John says five kings have already fallen, he may be simply observing that we are coming to the end of the line of kings. The 6th king was in power as John was writing, but he had no idea that 19 centuries would pass before #7 would arrive. The angel says #7 's reign will be brief, possibly cut short by assassination to pave the way for king #8. In saying king #8 was *"once alive, but now is not and is one of the seven,"* John wasn't peering into the future. He was reporting the angel's words.

SOLVING THE RIDDLE. Since John's time frame will not accommodate all 8 kings, the best way for us to solve this riddle is to work backwards from king #8. Centuries have already passed and these events are still future to us. The time span between king #6 and #7 is now more than 1800 years. So, working backwards from king #8, with only a *brief gap* between him and #7, we are forced to conclude that the beast was formerly king #7. That would make him the antichrist. So when the angel says... *"Once alive, but now is not,"* he is referring to the short interval between kings #7 and #8, between the death of antichrist and his resurrection as the beast. In this way, though we call him king #8, the beast is actually one of the seven. This explains why the inhabitants are so astonished. They see king #7 resurrected shortly after being fatally wounded.

FLASHBACK to the Destruction of Babylon

NOTE: If Nero were suggested as a candidate for king #7, or Antiochus Ephiphanes or Alexander the great, people wouldn't recognize them. It would be a tough selling job to convince the public a former emperor had returned from the dead. Who'd believe it? Besides, any of them would be too far removed from what is going on. No, for the people to be in

such awe of this man, as the text says, it has to be someone they'd recognize instantly. In any event, his career won't last long. Forty-two months later he ends up in the lake of fire (19:20).

COMMENT : When John was writing, the rising of the beast was centuries in the future. His arrival on the scene had to await the antichrist who would be fatally wounded. With antichrist rising to power so rapidly, he was bound to make enemies, one of whom may have arranged for his assassination. It will be his resurrection *as the beast*, that will thrust him into the position of king #8. Those who feel the seven heads refer to former empires must add two empires (Egypt and Assyria) to Daniel 4 to make the scheme work. In that case, Egypt, Assyria, Babylon, Persia and Greece would be the "five that are fallen." The one "*that is*" would be Rome. The one "yet to come," #7, would be a restored Roman Empire, and the beast would be the 8th king, growing out of the restored Roman Empire. This is a viable approach if one feels comfortable in adding the two world empires that preceded the Babylonian empire. It comes out the same anyway.

FLASHBACK to the Destruction of Babylon

12. "The ten horns which you saw are ten kings who have not yet come to power. When they do, they will be assigned their kingdoms for one hour and will share royal authority with the beast. 13. All of them are of one mind and purpose in committing their power and strength to the beast. 14. They will join the beast in waging war on the Lamb, but the Lamb, along with His called, chosen and faithful followers, will easily conquer them. For He is the Lord over all other lords and King of all kings."

TEN KINGS. The angel next explains the ten horns. They are kings of 10 nations not in existence in John's day. Therefore they are not ten former emperors of Rome, for none of them has any kingdom as yet. They arrive on the scene very late and enter into some kind of a deal with the beast whereby he ends up with their power. It is quite likely they play a role in establishing the beast as the 8th king. According to John, this confederacy lasts only a short time, *one hour*. The beast will use the 10 kings to destroy Babylon the Great as well as adding their armies to his for battling the Lord as He descends to Mount Olivet. It is a foolish move, but Satan knows it's his last chance. So the beast will be challenging the One Who made the heavens and the earth and before whom all earthly kings and lords must bow.

15. The angel continued to explain:

"The waters you saw on which the great harlot sat enthroned represent nations, populations, races and languages. 16. As for those ten horns you saw on the beast, those ten kings will all hate the harlot. They will strip her naked and leave her deserted. Beyond that, they will consume her flesh and burn what is left of her. 17. God has put it into their minds to follow a plan that will fully accomplish his purposes. In siding with the beast and committing their power to him, they are unknowingly fulfilling the word of God. 18. As for the woman you saw, she is the great city that sways the rulers of the earth."

WATERS. We needn't be in doubt as to the meaning of the waters on which the harlot sits. They are not lakes and rivers—they are the multitudes of the world. John uses the figure of lakes and rivers to emphasize the universal nature of Rome's power, a city in control of the entire Mediterranean world. When the beast is through using the harlot, he will destroy her. In graphic language, John pictures hands ripping off her royal garments and leaving her nude. The ten kings attack her with the fury of a pack of wild hyaenas leaving only her bones. What's left is devoured by flames. The city will be burned to the ground. Who is responsible for her fall? The angel says God planted the idea in the kings' minds. Again, to John, the harlot is Rome whose evil influence had permeated the world of that day.

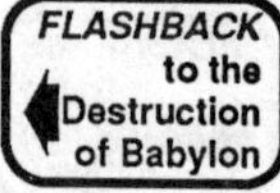

REVELATION 18

In Chapter 17, an angel invited John to come and see the great harlot who manipulated the kings of the world. The apostle was overwhelmed by her greatness and power. To think anyone so mighty and with such world-wide influence could be wiped out in a single day, was too much for him. John's astonishment is tempered when angels affirm that Babylon the great is as good as gone. Chapter 18 won't reveal the pulling down of her walls and the slaughter of her people. Instead, the angels will convince John that what he is hearing is true. In fact John won't say much at all. The angels do most of the talking. The ten kings who supported the beast in his rise to power, will destroy the harlot around the beginning of the Great Tribulation. For that reason, we won't see her participating with the beast in the battle of Armageddon. It is important to keep in mind that these two chapters are a flashback.

FLASHBACK to the Destruction of Babylon

18 1. After all this I saw another high-
ranking angel coming down from
heaven with such authority that the
earth was illuminated by the glory of his
presence. 2. With a mighty voice he shouted:

"Fallen, fallen, is Babylon the Great!
She has become a dwelling for demons,
a hangout for every evil spirit, a roost
for all birds, unclean and hateful to
man. 3. All nations have drunk the
maddening wine of her filthiness.
Aroused by her passionate immorality,
the kings of the earth have wallowed in

REV 18

intimacy with her, and the merchants of the world have grown rich off of her extravagant dissipation."

ANOTHER ANGEL. If we see special importance in the fact of two high ranking angels, it would be that the news of Babylon's fall is so shocking to John. He needed such angels to help him accept the idea. It isn't that John doubts the first angel; it is simply that the thought of such a mighty power being erased in a day is so overwhelming. Any message announcing the complete destruction of Rome would need considerable authority behind it or it just wouldn't be believed. On the other hand, John shouldn't have been too surprised. Ancient Babylon did fall in one night. The second angel apparently comes directly from the presence of God, for he reflects the radiance and glory of God, much as did Moses after meeting with God (Ex. 34:33-35). The radiance in Moses' face was so great he had to wear a veil to keep from terrorizing the people.

FLASHBACK to the Destruction of Babylon

COMMENT: John has brought us some distance. The first four seals we called "*the beginning of sorrows.*" The fifth and sixth seals mark the reign of the beast as he vents his rage against the church. We call that period, *the Great Tribulation.* Then came the trumpets. The first 6 trumpets, though they were judgments, constituted God's final warning to man. People could still repent and be saved. Then came the last trumpet which brings *the wrath of God.* With this trumpet, the door of salvation is slammed shut and no one can be saved beyond that point. We were all set for the Lord's descent and the battle of Armageddon, when it's as though someone asked, "*Hey! What about Babylon?*" John took time out to flashback to the first seal, when the beast no

longer needed the assistance of the harlot to become the ruler of the world.

NOTE: This chapter presents one main idea—the fall of Babylon and the effect it has on three groups of people: 1.) the kings of the earth, 2.) the merchants of the earth and 3.) those who make their living from the sea. And that's about it.

FALLEN. In Chapter 16, right after the bowls of God's wrath had been poured out, John announced...*"God did not forget Babylon to make her drink of the cup of His wrath"* (vs:19). Now he has flashed us back in time to catch us up on the details. The words *"fallen, fallen, is Babylon the Great,"* didn't originate with John. These are the words Isaiah cried out when word reached Israel that ancient Babylon had been destroyed (Isa. 21:9). And when he speaks of creatures inhabiting the ruins, those are also Isaiah's words (Isa. 13:20-22). Now we're about to learn that the nations involved with Babylon will also endure God's wrath for taking part in her dirty business, for the sake of money.

FLASHBACK to the Destruction of Babylon

4. Then I heard another voice from heaven saying:

> ***"Come out of her my people, lest you become involved in her sins and share in her punishment. 5. For her guilt mounts as high as heaven and God has a complete record of all her crimes. 6. Deal with her as she has dealt with you.***

Pay her back double for all she's done. In her cup, which she mixed for others, mix a portion twice as strong for her. 7. For all the glory and luxury she gave herself, give her an equal amount of torment and grief. 'I sit as a queen on my throne,' she boasts, 'I am not some helpless widow without a man. There is no sorrow coming my way.' 8. Therefore in a single day all her plagues shall come upon her: death, sorrow and famine, and she will be burned to the ground. For such is the power of the Lord God who pronounces this judgment upon her."

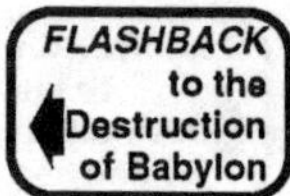

COME OUT OF HER. Suddenly John hears another voice from heaven. This time it is a command from God to His people. Don't forget this occurs back when God's people ARE STILL HERE. The command ascribed to God's voice comes cloaked in Jeremiah's words. It orders believers to separate themselves from Babylon and flee the harlot's web. Obviously, Christians are involved with her, otherwise what would be the point of such an order? It is always tempting for Christians, when caught in a dangerous situation, to compromise with worldly programs so as to make make life safer and easier for themselves and their families. All across the scriptures God bids His people to separate themselves from the world. The voice John hears is telling believers to run from any organization or fellowship not locked into the historic doctrines of salvation and godly living.

COMMENT: While the destruction of the city holds no big lesson for us *(unless the reader is living in the time of the announcement)*, the voice from heaven does. In saying, *"Come out of her my people,"* God is not telling us to turn our backs on people, but to reject the thinking of the world. God's ways and man's ways go in different directions. We all have Babylons that confront us daily and we must choose between loving the world and loving Jesus. In his epistle, John commands: *"Do not set your heart on the world or what's in it. Anyone who loves the world does not love the Father. Everything in the world, all that panders to the appetites or entices the eyes, all the arrogance based on wealth, these spring not from the Father, but from the world. That world, with all its allurements is passing away, but those who do God's will remain forever"* (1 John 2:15-17 REB).

SHARE IN HER PUNISHMENT. The angel offers two reasons for fleeing the city: 1.) not to be a partner with Babylon in her crimes, 2.) to escape the plagues coming upon her. Her punishment is guaranteed, for her sins are said to have reached heaven. That is probably a word play on the "tower of Babel" (Gen 11:4). Her sins are piled as high as the tower rebellious man sought to build in defiance of God's command, and now it is pay back time. In spite of what people might think, nobody really gets away with anything. The harlot made the nations drink of the cup of her filthiness, now God will make her drink of the cup of His wrath. As if speaking to the angels of His vengeance, God orders the mix in her cup doubled, which probably means: *"Make sure every sin is accounted for. Don't allow the law of the harvest to fall short by a single sin."*

FLASHBACK to the Destruction of Babylon

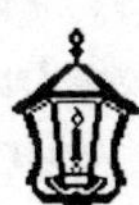

"I SIT AS A QUEEN." The agents are ordered to see that the misery she suffers is in the same proportion as the luxurious lifestyle she chose for herself. In other words, her punishment is to fit the crime. Like many unbelievers today, the harlot doesn't believe she'll suffer any consequences for her self-indulgence. She feels she can live any way she wants. In her arrogance, she sees herself as the mistress of the world with the kings of the earth as her lovers. How can anything happen to her? Her real sin, however, is that she places all her faith in her own powerful resources—not in the Lord. She is blind to her spiritual deadness and content to glorify herself and indulge herself in sensuous living. Because of her arrogance and self-confidence, her plagues will come on her suddenly. Using the ten nation confederacy allied with the beast, the Lord will bring death, famine and fire to the city. In ancient times, ascending smoke was a signal to all that the city had collapsed. Once those fires got going, nothing could stop them.

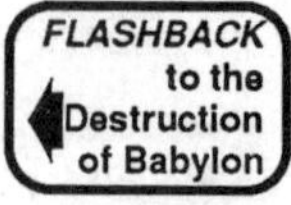

WHAT EFFECT WILL BABYLON'S DESTRUCTION HAVE ON THOSE WHO PROSPERED FROM DEALING WITH HER?

9. "The kings of the earth, who took their pleasures with her and wallowed in her extravagance, will weep and wail as they see the smoke rising from her smoldering ruins. 10. Standing at a distance for fear of becoming involved in her torment, they will cry, 'Alas, O great city, alas, O mighty Babylon. In one quick hour you have gone to your doom!'"

DOOM. The destruction of Babylon is explained in an unusual way. Instead of disclosing what the armies of the ten kings did to her, the angel is going to reveal the effect of her destruction on three groups of people, 1.) the kings of the earth, 2.) the merchants of the world, 3.) the maritime industry. All three are stunned by the almost instant death of the city. Although the kings hated this woman, they are sorry to see her go, for much of their own luxury vanishes with her. Beyond that, the handwriting on the wall is clear...God can play rough and the day of His wrath is approaching. Note that the kings are not about to rush in and help Babylon, but stand off at a safe distance. Later these same kings will join the beast in the battle of Armageddon. For the moment, however, they are dumbfounded that such a powerful city could be reduced to ashes in such a short time.

FLASHBACK to the Destruction of Babylon

11. "The merchants of the world will weep and mourn for her, for now who will buy their cargoes? 12. She bought huge shipments of gold and silver, precious stones and pearls, fine linens, purple, silk and scarlet cloth; all sorts of scented wood, every kind of object fashioned of ivory, bronze, iron and marble; 13. cargoes of cinnamon and spice, perfumes and myrrh and incense; wine, oil, flour and wheat, cattle and sheep, horses and chariots, slaves and the very souls of men. 14. 'All that you longed for so desperately is now gone,' they will say. 'All your glory and glam-

our have vanished, never to be seen
again.' 15. Those who traded in all these
things and who grew rich by selling
them to her, will stand off at a distance
for fear of exposing themselves to her
terror and punishment. 16. Weeping and
mourning, they will cry out, 'Alas, Alas,
O great city, you who went about clothed
in the finest purple and scarlet linens,
and decked out with gold and precious
stones and pearls! 17a. In one brief hour
all that great wealth has vanished!'"

SO MUCH FOR THE KINGS, HOW ABOUT THE MERCHANTS?

MERCHANTS. Next it's the merchants turn to lament the destruction of Babylon. They grew rich off of the extravagances of Rome. One commentator writes that Nero spent $100,000 to import roses from Egypt for a single banquet. Another emperor spent 20 million dollars on food alone in a single year. From this broad list of things supplied by the merchants, it appears the excesses of the prostitute were boundless. Huge cargoes flowed into Rome from all over the world and now those same merchants are stuck with big inventories. Our attention is drawn to the human cargo. Among the items on the shopping list are the bodies and souls of men, with people traded as merchandise. It is estimated that there were as many as 60 million slaves in the Roman Empire. Given the means to buy, it seems the fools of this world will spare no expense in satisfying their cravings. This created a huge market for the merchants who now moan and groan over the demise of the woman who made them so prosperous.

WHAT ABOUT THE SEA TRADERS?

17b. "The sea captains, and all who sail with them, as well as all who make their living from the sea, watched the smoke of her burning from a distance 18. and they cried out, 'What city can compare with this great city?' 19. They even threw dust on their heads as they wept and wailed, crying aloud, 'Alas, alas for that great city! She made all of us who sail the seas rich through her prosperity! And now in the space of a single hour, all that magnificence is gone!' "

FLASHBACK to the Destruction of Babylon

SEA CAPTAINS. The third group to suffer profit shock is the shipping industry. The maritime moguls are amazed to see so many fortunes go down the drain. Almost everything on Rome's wish list had to be imported, generating a tremendous flow of goods through Ostia, her seaport. So great was this flow, that all those in the maritime industry benefitted, right down to sailors, fishermen and pearl divers. Like the kings and merchants, they stand off and watch the smoke rise from burning ruins, overwhelmed that it happened so fast. With Rome the hub of all this shipping, she was probably the home base for most people involved in the business—a double reason to mourn.

HOW DOES HEAVEN REACT TO THIS?

20. "'Let all of heaven rejoice over her fall. Let all of God's saints and apostles and prophets rejoice, for God has dealt with her as she dealt with you!'"

REJOICE. Not everyone is wailing. Heaven and all the saints with the Lord are urged to rejoice over this. Some might feel that believers are being told to rejoice over the suffering of the unsaved people involved with the harlot. But God is not like that. It is the destruction of the city with its satanic way of life that calls for rejoicing. It is akin to hating the sin, but not the sinner. This city symbolizes the rise of evil in the world from the time of Cain. Sin bursts into full bloom in this city with its defiance of God and fiendish delight in the slaughter of His people. The blood of His saints have cried out for justice, from righteous Abel to the tribulation martyrs. And now God has dealt with her as she has dealt with His people. The destruction of the city is therefore an act of righteous judgment and heaven is exhorted to rejoice over it.

HOW WILL GOD DRAMATIZE THE ANNOUNCEMENT OF ROME'S DESTRUCTION?

21. Then a mighty angel picked up a boulder as big as a millstone and threw it into the sea, shouting as he did:

"In this way shall Babylon, that great city, be brought down, never to be seen

again! 22. Never again will the sound of harpists and musicians, flute players and trumpeters be heard in you; never again will crafts and business activity of any kind be found in you; 23. never again will your homes or streets be lighted, nor will the happy sounds of weddings be heard in you again! At one time, the tycoons of the earth were your business associates, for you bewitched the world with your sorceries! 24. The blood of all martyred prophets and saints was found in her and she was responsible for the deaths of all who had been slain on the earth."

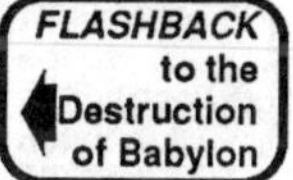

NEVER AGAIN. How better to picture the sudden and violent end of the prostitute than with a boulder cast into the sea. It sinks quickly to the bottom and then there is silence. No music is heard, no industry noise, no more weddings. Silence reigns in the city and the place is dark. No longer do lights burn in the shops with the craftsmen furiously trying to fill orders. Centuries before, when ancient Babylon was destroyed, the prophet Jeremiah was ordered to tie a stone to the book he was reading and cast it into the Euphrates River. With that, he was prophesying that Babylon would never rise again (Jeremiah 51:63,64). And now that prophecy has its parallel with the destruction of "Babylon the Great," the tribulation Babylon. She is to vanish from the face of the earth with a single swat from the hand of God!

BEWITCHED. Verses 9 to 19 told us how the destruction of the city affected her business and political associates, now we're seeing what happened *within* the city. All commerce comes to an abrupt halt and the city is permanently silenced. We learn also that the nations serving as her trading partners were bewitched into thinking nothing could ever go wrong. Businessmen don't normally put all their eggs in one basket, but she deceived them into thinking she was indestructible. This led them into a false sense of security and they believed their fortunes were guaranteed forever. Her most wicked crime against God was using the governments of the world to eliminate His children. Because she ruled the world, the responsibility for all who died in the world is laid at her doorstep.

No, this is not the end of the flashback.

REVELATION 19

Our flashback is not over yet, there are four more verses to go. In 18:20, heaven was told to rejoice over the destruction of Babylon, but we have yet to hear any such rejoicing. Now we will. With the next 4 verses their responses reach our ears and then the flashback will be over. Ever since Chapter 16 we've been waiting for an announcement concerning the return of the Lord and His reign over the earth. That announcement is just a few verses away. In the last chapter we heard the woeful laments of the kings, merchants and seamen who lost everything when Babylon fell. Now the host of heaven is going to give us the opposite of a lament, a "Hallelujah Chorus." This will surpass anything heard on earth and it comes in obedience to the command in 18:20. When that is done, we will hear a new command from the throne ordering heaven to break forth with an even greater chorus. This chorus will follow the announcement concerning Jesus' return.

FLASHBACK to the Destruction of Babylon

19 **1. After this I heard what sounded like the roar of countless voices in heaven shouting:**

"Hallelujah! Salvation, glory and power belong to our God alone, 2. for His judgments are true and just! He has passed sentence on the great prostitute who poisoned the earth with her adulterous ways, and He has avenged Himself on her for the murder of His servants."

REV 19

3. Then they shouted a second time:

"Hallelujah! The smoke of her burning will continue to rise throughout all ages to come!"

VOICES. When heaven is commanded to rejoice, whose voices should we expect to hear? Who else but those saints who died at the hand of the harlot. The reason for their praise, as stated in verse two, is that God has punished the prostitute. With their deaths avenged, they eagerly praise God. We are placing the destruction of the city about the time the beast comes to power, when the woman no longer rides on him. The woman killed these saints, but many more are due to die under the beast. Bear in mind, this praise is part of the flashback dealing with the fall of Babylon. The first word from their lips is "Hallelujah!" which means, "Praise the Lord!" This is the only passage in the New Testament where it is found, and it is derived from two Hebrew words..."Halal," which means praise and "Jah" which means God. The second shout affirms that the destruction of the wicked city is forever.

FLASHBACK ENDS

4. The twenty-four elders and the four living creatures fell down and worshipped God who was sitting upon the throne, and they cried out:

"Amen! Hallelujah!"

AMEN! We have now reached the end of the flashback. The twenty-four elders and the four living creatures affirm this is so. They shout "Amen!" (So be it!) in response to the praise of the martyred host. Since the chief task of the elders seems to be that of falling down before the throne and worshipping God, it is not surprising that they would exclaim: "HALLELUJAH!" What is interesting is that praise from the lips of the martyred believers also brings the four living creatures to their knees. Is it because God is thrilled to see His children emerge as successful overcomers? This is apparently what God longs to see—His sons and daughters triumphant over death in their desire to please Him. Anything that brings God great joy is bound to trigger praise in heaven.

FLASHBACK ENDS

COMMENT: In Chapter 16 all 7 bowls of God's wrath were poured out. The earth was reeling, convulsing and reshaping itself under the flexing forces of the world's greatest earthquake. The next event should be the coming of the Lord, but suddenly a statement concerning Babylon appeared in verse 19 of that chapter. It's as though someone had asked John, "*What about Babylon the great? Did God forget about her?*" John says no, and then paused in the narrative to give us a two chapter flashback depicting the destruction of that wicked city. The flashback ends with verse 4 of Chapter 19. The reader must be careful not to include verse 5 as part of the praise over Babylon's destruction. Verse 5 presents an entirely *new command,* one totally separate from 18:20. Verse 5 asks for praise to God for a very different reason—*the wedding banquet of the Lamb.* A gap of seven years exists between verses 4 and 5. This forthcoming praise will be more thunderous, involving the entire host of God. With verse 6, John picks up the story from where he left off at the end of Chapter 16.

(Flashback over—we're back on track.)

5. Then a voice came from the throne saying:

> ***"Praise our God, all you who serve Him, all you who fear Him, both small and great!"***

6. And then I heard what sounded like a huge crowd, whose shouts equalled the roar of a mighty waterfall mingled with the crash of rolling thunder, and they were yelling:

> ***"Hallelujah! The Lord our God, the Almighty, has begun to reign over His kingdom. 7. Let us rejoice! Let us express our ecstasy with great gladness as we praise the Lord, for the wedding day of the Lamb has come and His bride has made herself ready. 8. She clothed herself in fine linen, bright and clean, that was provided for her to wear." (The fine linen represents the righteousness of the saints).***

VOICE. This 4th Hallelujah is given in response to the voice from the throne. Verses 1-4 *looked back* to the destruction of the prostitute, whereas the verses before us now *look forward* to the marriage of the Lamb. The voice John hears is not the voice of God, but of someone speaking for the throne, someone so close to God that John is moved to fall at his feet to worship him. This voice from the throne commands the whole family to praise God, as indicated by the words *"small and great."* Consequently we are at a point where all of the redeemed are with Him. The whole family is caught up in the excitement of being with Jesus and is ordered to express its joy in unison. Thus heaven itself reverberates with the thunder of their "Hallelujahs!" Note the absence of confusion in heaven, for even the praises of the saints are orchestrated so that they sound as one mighty voice.

WEDDING. The reason for this great Hallelujah is clear, it's time for the wedding banquet or feast of the Lamb. The rapture has already occurred. That took place at the last trumpet (1 Cor. 15:52). This feast occurs <u>after</u> the believers have appeared before the judgment seat of Christ. They have already been rewarded or penalized for the place they gave the Lord Jesus in their earthly lives. Our judgment probably occurred while the 7 bowls of God's wrath were being poured out. It would be hard to imagine a happy banquet with that final exam hanging over the heads of the saints. But with that exam out of the way, the believers can relax and enjoy themselves at the banquet. One result of this final exam is that each Christian will be able to take his place at the "table" consistent with his earned rank. His seat at the "table" will be representative of his job assignment in Jesus' kingdom.

MADE HERSELF READY. There is little anyone must do to be clothed with the righteousness of God. But even that "little" has to be done (John 6:29). In a specific act, one must RECEIVE the "gift of eternal life" (Rom. 6:23). God offers people His righteousness as a free gift, but just hearing about the offer doesn't make anyone righteous automatically. The gift has to be received. And doing so is as simple as putting on a wedding dress. But again, the dress has to be put on. When it is, the believer is instantly a child of God and clothed with His righteousness (2 Cor. 5:21). To be ready for the wedding, one need only put on the dress which is provided. This readiness for the wedding should not be confused with being ready to reign with Jesus. The jobs and ranks believers receive for the kingdom are NOT provided. They must be earned. Those jobs are awarded at the judgment seat of Christ and are based on WORKS. The wedding dress, on the other hand, is a free gift.

COMMENT: The judgment seat of Christ (2 Cor. 5:10), should not be confused with the great white throne judgment of Rev. 20:11-12. These two judgments are separated by Jesus' 1000 year reign over the earth. The former judgment deals with the *believer's* works, whereas the latter judgment deals with the *unbeliever's* works. The Christian's judgment determines his position in eternity with God. The unbeliever's judgment determines his position in eternity with Satan. There will be ranks and assigned places in hell, just as there will also be in heaven. Our rewards are clearly related to our future jobs with Jesus, jobs we'll hold forever. That is why it is so urgent to live for Jesus and not ourselves. From God's perspective, our earthly life is a qualifying run to see what place we'll give Him in our lives. The place we give Him in this life determines the place He gives us in the next life. What a shame to neglect this great opportunity, when a little sacrifice *now* can make such a big difference *then!*

9. And the voice said to me:

"Write this down: Blessed are those who are invited to the wedding feast of the Lamb." Then he added, "These are the very words of God!"

FEAST. As the heavenly roar fades into silence, John is ordered to write about a special blessing, an invitation to the feast. When he speaks of the wedding feast, one might ask, *"Is this a literal feast of the Lord with His people sitting down to a meal, or does the term 'feast' merely symbolize that the church has reached its ultimate fulfillment in this face to face meeting with Jesus?"* It's true the Lord spoke of eating and drinking with His disciples in the kingdom and that will no doubt happen. However, even though the believer's resurrection body may handle food, we must remember it is a spiritual body (1 Cor. 15:44). It no longer derives energy from food, but runs on spirit. The resurrection body is not limited to space and time, but will also operate in the realm of thought. That is, think to yourself, *"I want to be in Brazil,"*—and you're there that same second!

COMMENT: Remember the wealthy man who came to Jesus wanting to be saved, but went away sad because he put his wealth ahead of Jesus (Luke 18:23)? Then it was the Lord who commented, *"There is no one who has given up home, or wife, brothers, parents, or children for the sake of the kingdom of God, who will not be repaid many times over IN THIS AGE, and in the age to come have eternal life."* People seek happiness in money and possessions, but happiness

does not satisfy the soul. It merely satisfies emotional, physical and psychological needs. The deepest need of the soul is *BLESSING.* Only blessing satisfies the cravings of the spirit. Made in the image of an infinite Creator, man has *infinite needs* that can only be satisfied by the *infinite One* Himself. When we give Jesus first place in our lives, He meets those deep needs in our souls IN THIS LIFE, something money could never do for us. Then, when we meet Him face to face at the wedding feast, we'll discover what it's like to have those needs satisfied on a CONTINUAL BASIS. Then we'll know the *real meaning* of eternal life.

INVITED. Those not invited to this feast are people who have rejected Jesus, who refuse to have Him as Savior and Lord. This wedding feast is a gathering of God's own family and no one who is not wearing the right clothes will be admitted (Matt. 22: 11-14). God's family can be entered only by birth, for that is the only way family traits can be acquired (John 3:3). The family trait of God's family is *righteousness* and is passed on by birth. However, FAMILY is but one image used to picture the relationship between Jesus and His church. The church is also described as a body, building, bride and a city. All these images represent an invisible reality, but they help us picture our relationship with Jesus. At the feast, however, we will experience the reality. Even so, it will still be a family event.

10. When he said that, I fell at his feet to worship him, but he said to me:

"Stop! You must not do that! Address your worship to God alone. I am nothing more than a servant of God, the

same as you and your brothers who hold to the testimony of Jesus. As you know, the testimony of Jesus is the spirit underlying all prophecy."

SPIRIT OF PROPHECY. Did John mistakenly assume the speaker to be the Lord? After all, the voice came from the throne saying, *"These are the true words of God."* Apparently some angel or being stepped forward to address John and the apostle immediately fell at his feet. We might have done the same, for this is an *overpowering situation.* But the agent, whoever he is, quickly corrects the situation. He explains that he is a fellow servant of God and redirects John's worship. At the same time he reminds John of his high call to the prophetic ministry. We have now reached the moment of the Lord's appearance where all the roads of prophecy converge. Behind all prophecy there is but one spirit—the testimony of Jesus! But what is that? The drum beat of Jesus' message... *"If I go, I will come again!"* <u>And now He is about to do it</u>.

COMMENT: At one point the Pharisees demanded Jesus tell them when the kingdom of God would come (Luke 17:20). He replied, saying in effect, *"You can't see it by looking here or there, because the kingdom of God is within you!"* In other words, the kingdom is invisible. And it is still invisible today. With the King living in our hearts, the kingdom is indeed within us. This has led some to conclude that the kingdom is wholly spirit and will never be seen on earth; that it is foolish to look for a visible reign of the Lord on earth. But the scriptures cannot be broken. Biblical prophecy insists that Jesus will return as He said and fulfill the promises made to

Israel, as well as to His disciples. At this point in God's plan, only the souls of believers have been redeemed. Our bodies belong to the unredeemed creation. That's why they are ravaged by sickness, disease and Satan. But in the day when we are revealed as the sons of God, our bodies will be redeemed along with the rest of creation (Rom. 8:19-23). So for now, the kingdom is invisible, but when Jesus returns, the kingdom will no longer be invisible. It will be visible. Every eye shall see Him.

AFTER ALL THE ANNOUNCEMENTS AND SHOUTING, WILL THE LORD FINALLY APPEAR IN THE SKY?

11. Then I saw heaven opened and a white horse appeared before my eyes. The One sitting on the horse was called Faithful and True and because of that, He is always right when He judges and makes war. 12. His eyes blazed like fire and on His head were many crowns. A name was written on Him, the meaning of which was known only to Himself. 13. He was wearing a garment dyed in blood and the name by which He is known is the Word of God.

WHITE HORSE. We have reached the climax of the book of Revelation—the return of the Lord Jesus. Suddenly a white horse appears in heaven and the appearance of this horse and its rider spell the end of this world as we know it. It marks the beginning of a new world. Chapter 1 promised He would return and every eye would see Him. That moment has now arrived. When Jesus made His triumphal entry into Jerusalem, He rode on a donkey to symbolize His coming in peace (Zech 9:9). But here He is mounted on a white horse, symbolizing His return as a conquering king. Jesus is no longer the "suffering servant" Who came to die at the hands of men. Here He is the WARRIOR KING bent on crushing every vestige of worldly power and wiping out His enemies. Since God is just *by nature,* He is just even when He makes war.

NAME. The words "faithful and true," identify the rider as Jesus, for He was described in those terms earlier (3:14). But the name written on Him is a mystery—*for the moment.* At this point no one has a clue as to what Jesus is like when He is filled with fight. We all know Him as the "gentle Jesus," but He has another side to Him. The fire in His eyes tells us He is on a mission that will shortly reveal His other side. Back in Chapter14, He was pictured as a man seated on a cloud reaping the harvest of the earth, because the harvest was ripe. But here He's about to jump into the wine press of God's wrath and stomp the grapes of wrath. In the process His clothing will become blood red. Of course all this is symbolism, which we're used to by now. There'll be no actual horse and no wine press, but the reality won't be far away. The Lord is ready to slaughter millions of people, whole nations even, to set up His kingdom the way He wants it. Here His blood soaked garment symbolizes His victory in the upcoming battle of Armageddon—which is the wine press of God's wrath.

THE PRE-WRATH RAPTURE

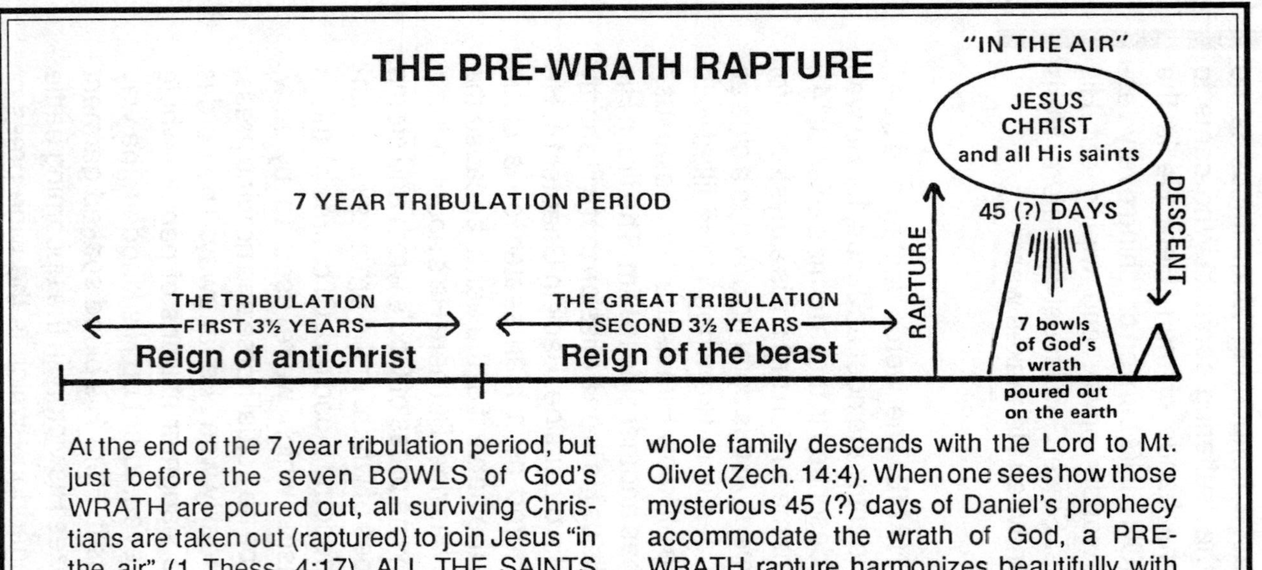

At the end of the 7 year tribulation period, but just before the seven BOWLS of God's WRATH are poured out, all surviving Christians are taken out (raptured) to join Jesus "in the air" (1 Thess. 4:17). ALL THE SAINTS remain with Him throughout the 45 (?) days until the wrath of God is finished. Then the whole family descends with the Lord to Mt. Olivet (Zech. 14:4). When one sees how those mysterious 45 (?) days of Daniel's prophecy accommodate the wrath of God, a PRE-WRATH rapture harmonizes beautifully with the rest of Scripture (Dan. 12:11, 12).

MANY CROWNS. The crowns on Jesus' head are the crowns of majesty, making them quite different from the crowns believers receive for faithful service. His crowns are not earned, but are His by virtue of being the Son of God. He inherits His kingship, as do most sons of kings. Beyond that, He is "the Word of God," which links Him with John's gospel and identifies Him as the Creator of the world. As the Creator of the world and everything in it, He has the power, the right and authority to destroy it and establish a new world, as He pleases. His many crowns are in contrast with the 7 crowns of the dragon and the 10 crowns of the beast, and proclaim His unlimited sovereignty. When someone with that kind of power comes to deal with His enemies *in anger*, the battle can't last very long.

SURELY HE'S NOT COMING BY HIMSELF?

14. The armies of heaven which were right behind Him were dressed in fine linen, white and clean and also riding on white horses. 15. Out of His mouth came a sharp sword all set to strike down the nations whom He is scheduled to rule with a rod of iron. What's more, He also treads the winepress of the fierce wrath of Almighty God. 16. The following title is written on His cloak where it crosses over His thigh:

King of kings and Lord of lords!

ARMIES. The Lord is not coming alone. He made it clear in Matt. 25 that all the holy angels would be with Him (vs.31). What's more, the apostle Paul teaches that once His disciples join Him in the sky, they'll never be separated from Him again... *"and so shall we ever be with the Lord!"* (1Thess. 4:17). That means: wherever He goes, we go too. Normally His army would consist entirely of angels, but since we're with Him, we'll be part of His army, too. There's nothing fearful about being in this army since it doesn't appear we'll be doing any of the actual killing. There's no blood on our garments, as on His. At the same time those white clothes indicate it is a righteous thing for us to be there with Him in the battle.

SWORD. The sword represents the deadly power of His Word. After all, God said, *"Let there be light and there was light!"* That kind of power is irresistible. All the Lord has to do is *speak* and any judgment He cares to visit on people is executed immediately. That makes the word of God the sword of the Lord. When Jesus speaks, that sword flashes! It is very probable that when the Lord speaks, confusion will sweep through the ranks of the armies of the beast and the false prophet and they will turn their swords on each other. That would produce a tremendous slaughter in a very short time. This is likely the way Jesus will tread the winepress of God's wrath. Where His sword would normally hang, His rank is written in plain letters...*King of kings and Lord of lords.* There's no higher rank than that.

ROD OF IRON. Adorned with all this rank, He's coming to rule the nations with a rod of iron. Even if all of the beast's soldiers are killed in the battle, there'll still be survivors from the nations. Otherwise there'd be no people for Jesus to shepherd, none to populate His kingdom. There must be survivors to enter the kingdom. With the curse removed from the earth, the population will mushroom. There'll be no pain in childbirth, plenty of wealth and great health, generating a population explosion. The survivors, however, will be UNREDEEMED PEOPLE. Their children will also be unredeemed, for there is no way for anyone to acquire a new nature. The opportunity to be born again ends with the last trumpet. This means Jesus' kingdom is going to be populated with unregenerate men and women. That's why it will be necessary for Him to keep an iron grip on the nations. The saints who reign with Him, will have their hands full trying to run a righteous government made up of unrighteous people. But it'll be a great experience.

COMMENT: Among the reasons for a 1000 year reign of Christ on the earth, and there are several, is providing the saints with schooling and practice in handling ruling authority on a world wide scale. In this way, the millennium serves as transition-school for eternity. In the kingdom, the populace with their fallen natures will yearn to sin, but they'll be restrained. Some Christians will undoubtedly serve as "kingdom cops," policing *the thoughts* of the people. Believers ministering in this capacity will monitor the thinking of the

unsaved and confront them before they can do any evil. Regarding evil in the kingdom, scripture insists, *"None shall hurt in all my holy mountain"* (Isa. 11:9). Consider the police work needed to keep evil people from doing evil in a righteous kingdom. Jesus' rod of iron will largely consist of Christians with administrative assignments enforcing the laws of the kingdom world-wide. In time, the unsaved citizens will come to hate righteousness, even though their lives in the kingdom will be easy, pleasant and bountiful.

17. Then I saw an angel standing in the sun, who cried aloud to all the birds that soar in midair:

> ***"Come! Gather together for God's great feast. 18. Come and you shall eat the flesh of kings, commanders, and warriors, the flesh of horses and those who ride them, the flesh of all mankind, free men and slaves, small and great!"***

19. Then I saw the beast mustering the kings of the earth and their armies to go into battle against the One sitting on the white horse and His army. 20. But the beast was taken prisoner and along with him, the false prophet who had performed miracles on behalf of the beast, by which he deceived those who had received the mark of the beast and had worshipped his image. Both of them were thrown alive into the lake of fire that burns with sulphur.

EAT FLESH. The battle is drawn. The forces of the beast are lined up ready to prevent the Lord from taking over Jerusalem (the beast's headquarters) and the kingdoms of this world. The Lord and His army are descending to claim the creation He has redeemed with His blood. But this shouldn't happen without some fanfare. So an angel appears in the sun to call the birds circling in the mid-heaven. He invites them to come to a feast prepared for them by God, a feast that stands in gruesome contrast to the marriage feast of the Lamb. The two armies meet and the battle of Armageddon gets under way. It would seem the battle is not to be taken symbolically, though it is described in symbolic language. It is an actual event that utterly destroys the forces of evil in this world and ushers in the long awaited time of peace on earth. The end of human history as we know it, is just arriving.

COMMENT: There is another important battle involving Israel and that has a similar scene where the birds of heaven are invited to devour the flesh of slain enemies. John doesn't mention that battle, because it takes place before the beast comes to power, before the tribulation begins. The earlier battle is found in Ezekiel 38 and 39, where the king of the North attempts to invade Israel. It is called the battle of Gog and Magog and ends in similar fashion as the battle of Armageddon. God intervenes to protect Israel and the invaders are slaughtered. The birds of heaven are invited to feast on the carcasses of slain warriors. Thus we have two similar events occurring in the last days of human history. The battle before us will be over quickly and the mess cleaned up in short order. But that's not true in the case of the Ezekiel battle. That will take months, possibly years to clear away the wreckage.

TAKEN PRISONER. You wouldn't think anyone would be stupid enough to take on the Lord and His army, yet the kings of the earth have gathered at Armageddon to fight God Almighty. Perhaps they didn't realize at the beginning they'd be taking on the power behind all creation, but when an army descends from the sky, that truth should hit them in a flash. But they have come to fight and fight they will. However, some fight is bound to go out of them when their leaders are seized right at the start. The seizure of the beast, who is the most powerful man in the world, politically and militarily, will undoubtedly chill their spirits. Then to see the false prophet, who led them into this mess with his great wonders, also snatched from their midst, should leave them dazed and confused. The seizure of these two is certainly literal, while the lake of fire into which they are cast has to be symbolic.

The beast is blinded and clothes are ripped from his body, as he is consumed by the radiance of the Lord's coming!

WHAT HAPPENS TO THE BEAST'S ARMIES WITH THE LEADERS GONE?

21. All the rest were slain by the sword that issued from the mouth of the rider and all the birds swooped down to gorge themselves on their flesh.

SWORD. The Lord speaks and His Word does the work, performing better than millions of swords. If it is correct to assume the Lord sends confusion into the minds of the beast's soldiers, so that they destroy each other, then it is proper to say they were all slain by the sword from His mouth. The seizure of the beast and the false prophet would be the starting point for the confusion. So with the battlefield one huge mass of dead bodies, the vultures swoop down to gorge themselves on the mountains of flesh. The confusion coming at the Lord's command would also explain why His garments are covered with blood and ours are not. He alone treads the winepress of God's fury, as the difference in the garments indicates.

COMMENT: We probably shouldn't suppose the vultures will do the whole cleanup job by themselves. Vast amounts of hardware left on the fields will have to be disposed of and the vultures could have no part in that. In all probability there will be some kind of a *supernatural* "cleanup" of the area to make way for the New Jerusalem. Zech. 14:4, speaks of the Lord touching down on Mount Olivet, which is just East of Jerusalem. It also speaks of the mountain dividing with an immense new valley being created. Perhaps, as we use "cut and fill" methods to build our modern freeways, the Lord in similar fashion may create an instant graveyard for the abandoned weapons of war. Jerusalem, the capitol of the beast, will undoubtedly be shaken, levelled and the ground reshaped in preparation for Jesus' capitol. Even as this is happening, His capitol, the New Jerusalem, is descending from heaven. A good earthquake could probably do the whole job in a few minutes.

NOTE: There can be no argument as to whom the recipients of this letter are—*the seven churches of Asia.* We've already seen how they represent the entire church moving through the centuries. With the return of the Lord Jesus now behind us, we can make a significant observation. Strange as it may seem, John has NOT been putting the emphasis on the return of the Lord, as we might have expected. Instead he has put it on Satan, the beast and the false prophet and the religious prostitute, Babylon. Three chapters (12-14) are devoted to the unholy trinity and two chapters (17-18) are devoted to Babylon. Why? Because that's where the most serious threat to the church lies. This is where the church faces its biggest temptation and trial. There is no threat in meeting Jesus in the sky, nor is there any threat in descending with Him to Olivet. Looking back, we see clearly the real purpose behind John's letter—*preparing the church for the Great Tribulation!* John's concern is that his readers stand firm through the tribulation and win the martyr's crown.

REVELATION 20

We have come to the millennium, that period of time following the return of the Lord, when the entire world becomes a garden paradise once again. Millennium is a Latin word meaning one thousand years. During this period, the curse that was placed on the earth at Adam's fall is removed, and the world is restored to what it was when God first put man on the earth. Life will be easy, free from danger and the ground will explode with food. Under the personal reign of Christ, the earth will be filled with the knowledge of the Lord (Isa. 11:9). Death will come only by accident, so that should a 100 year old man die, he will be regarded as still a child (Isa. 65:20). The animal kingdom will go vegetarian, so that the lion and the ox graze together and no animal will be killed for any reason. Children will safely play with pet cobras for nothing will be allowed to hurt in all the kingdom (Isa. 11:8,9). Now that the Lord has returned, let's see what the apostle feels should be unveiled next.

20 **1. I also saw an angel coming down from heaven with the key to the abyss and a great chain in his hand. 2. And he seized the dragon, that ancient serpent who is the devil, or Satan, and chained him up for 1000 years. 3. He then shoved him down into the abyss, locking and sealing him in there so that he might not be able to deceive the nations anymore until the thousand years had gone by. After that, he would be set free for a little while.**

SATAN. We saw the beast and the false prophet cast into the lake of fire, but nothing was said about Satan. Even though the millennium is before us, very little is going to be said about it—or the Lord. It is the devil who gets the attention in this chapter. It is not enough to destroy the agents of Satan, the evil prince must himself be destroyed. You can't run a righteous kingdom with Satan on the loose, so he has to be put out of business—for a time. God needs him for a final test at the end of the 1000 years, and that's why he was not cast into the lake of fire along with the beast and the false prophet. Instead, he is locked up and sealed in the abyss to keep him from deceiving the nations. From this it is clear that nations will exist in the kingdom (See Zech. 14:16).

1000 YEARS. The millennium is an ingenious part of God's plan. Before it is over, the wonder of God's wisdom will be obvious. Yet, it's strange from the start. We'll see a mix of immortal believers

(1 Cor. 15:53) mingling on the earth with mortal humans and they'll communicate well. The believer's resurrection body, though a spiritual body (a body subject to the spirit), will have two arms and legs and won't be too different from the bodies of the unsaved survivors who enter the kingdom—*and their children.* Something else is interesting: the nation of Israel will turn to Jesus when He returns and the entire nation will enjoy *national salvation* (Rom. 11:26). This is NOT individual salvation whereby one becomes a child of God. Rather it is the nation Israel acknowledging Jesus is her Messiah and receiving the *physical promises* God made through the patriarchs and the prophets. As far as nations go, she will be the empress of the world. As far as individual Jews are concerned, there is nothing spiritual for them to inherit, no *personal salvation.* They forfeited that by rejecting Jesus and are therefore as unsaved as the rest of the unregenerates in the kingdom.

SET FREE. God has been using Satan from the beginning to test man, and while we have come to the millennium, the testing is not over. He is still needed for one final test before he is cast into the lake of fire (Matt. 25:41). One would think there would be no place for Satan in God's plan once the Lord Jesus assumed control of the world. But the question comes, "What about all those born during the millennium when the earth is filled with the "knowledge of the Lord" (Isa. 11:9)? After mankind has lived under the righteous reign of Jesus for 1000 years, we need to see what effect that environment has had on them. Will they love the Lord? Is it possible that someone with just an old nature could love righteousness and hate evil? That's why Satan is set free for a little while. He is fully expert in bringing out the evil buried deep in human hearts. So when he is released to do his dirty work once again, it will be a perfect test for all the inhabitants of Jesus' kingdom, including the Jews. Not us, of course. We're part of the government.

COMMENT: To understand the nature of the test, it is vital to realize the Holy Spirit will not be operating during the millennium; He will NOT be drawing people to Jesus as He did during the age of the Holy Spirit (the church age). And yet, on one occasion Jesus said no one could come to Him unless he was drawn by the Father (John 6:44). Beyond that, the Lord also made it clear the Holy Spirit could not come as long as Jesus was on the earth in a body (John 16:7). When Jesus is present in glory, He is the drawing card. In the kingdom, therefore, people will have to respond to Jesus' literal presence on earth as King of kings, with the earth filled with His teachings. The nations will come to the mountain of the Lord and learn of His ways (Isa. 2:2-4). And the Jews will play a part in educating the nations about the Lord (Zech. 8:23). But can this knowledge plus the presence of the Lord really change their evil hearts? Can mere knowledge of the Lord make a man godly? That's why Satan is turned loose. We'll get the answer in a moment.

4. Then I saw thrones set up for those who were appointed to be judges. And I saw the souls of those who had been beheaded for their testimony about Jesus and for proclaiming God's Word—those who had not wor-

**shipped the beast or his statue, who had not
accepted his mark upon their foreheads nor
their hands. They came to life again and
reigned with Christ for a thousand years, 5.
This is the first resurrection. (As for the rest
of the dead, they did not come to life again
until the thousand years had passed). 6.
Blessed and holy are those who share in this
first resurrection! They are immune to the
second death, for they will be priests of God
and of Christ and will reign with him for a
thousand years.**

THREE GROUPS OF PEOPLE IN THE MILLENNIUM

❶	❷	❸
SURVIVING GENTILES (UNSAVED NATIONS)	JEWS (UNSAVED NATIONAL) ISRAEL)	CHRISTIANS FROM ALL AGES
Those who DID NOT partake in First Resurrection	Those who DID NOT partake in First Resurrection	Those who DID partake in First Resurrection
RESTORED bodies	RESTORED bodies	GLORIFIED bodies
Servants of "bride" of Christ and Israel	Enjoy favored nation status, inherit promises made to Abraham	Reign with Christ over Jews and Gentiles (Rev. 5:10, 20:6)

THRONES AND SOULS. John interrupts himself momentarily to speak of thrones and souls. Remember those souls under the altar who cried out for God to avenge Himself on those dwelling on the earth (6:9-11)? That was the fifth seal. God told them to wait until their fellow servants had been killed as they had been. Now that has happened and here they all are resurrected together, ready to take up their jobs in the kingdom. Those thrones represent jobs. Many attempts have been made to identify these people in some special way, but it seems best to understand this group as representing all the redeemed of the earth, the whole family of God. All believers take part in the first resurrection, therefore the second death, the lake of fire, has nothing to do with them. Another group is mentioned, "the rest of the dead." This is the entire population outside of the family of God, and the lake of fire awaits them all.

SECOND DEATH. There are two births and two deaths in God's word. When we're born to our mothers, that is our *physical* birth, and as is true of all living creatures, we die *physically*. Even if raptured, our bodies would be changed as surely as if they had died. So that is one birth and one death. When a person receives the Lord, he is born again. That is his second birth, a *spiritual* birth. That birth ushers him into eternal life which has no death. There is no death for the believer. The person who is not born again, obviously has no spiritual birth, therefore no eternal life. He not only dies *physically*, which is the first death, he also dies spiritually, which is the second death. This is the source of the often quoted line, *"Born once, die twice. Born twice, die once."*

WHEN IS SATAN FINALLY DISPOSED OF?

7. Then when the thousand years have passed, Satan will be released from his prison, 8. and will once more set out to deceive the nations in the four quarters of the earth—Gog and Magog. With their number as countless as the sands of the sea, he will lead them into battle. 9. They marched across the whole breadth of the earth and encircled the camp of God's people, the city He loves. But fire came down from heaven and consumed them. 10. The devil who deceived them was thrown into the lake of fire and brimstone to join the beast and the false prophet. There they will be tormented day and night forever!

RELEASED. 1000 years in prison has no effect on the devil. Confinement can't change anyone's nature and God didn't expect any change in Satan. He plans to use him and his deceitful ways to test the massive population of the earthly kingdom. With no death, easy births and great health, the population will be huge at the end of the 1000 years. However, these people have not been able to sin, though their fallen natures yearn for evil. They've heard nothing but God, God, God, for 1000 years and they're sick of it. By this time, they'll hate righteousness so much, they'll be ripe for any evil Satan offers. Under these conditions, Satan needs only a "little time" to rally the nations as a battle force. The *"four quarters of the earth,"* refers to the universality of Satan's success. He manages to get every citizen to join his assault on Jesus' headquarters, the beloved city, the New Jerusalem.

GOG AND MAGOG. It would be easy to confuse the "Gog and Magog" of Ezekiel 38, with the Gog and Magog of this passage. They are not the same. The Ezekiel passage refers to a specific country and prince from a territory in the *"North parts"* who launches an invasion against Israel some time *before the tribulation.* Here the term "Gog and Magog," is symbolic of the nations (worldwide) that Satan gathers for an assault on the camp of God's people. The *"breadth of the earth"* phrase gives us a clue of what the world will be like with the mountains and the oceans gone. Satan's armies swarm like ants across the broad plain of the earth to encompass the camp of believers. Actually it is an enormous city, but John uses the word "camp" to reminds us that even though we are in the New Jerusalem, we're still pilgrims in a foreign place. This world is not our home, no matter what kind of a city is built for us. We seek a city that is eternal in the heavens (Heb. 11:16).

JOIN THE BEAST. Satan has finished his final task. He has led the masses to war against God for the last time. No further judgment is needed in his case, so he is cast directly into the lake of fire to join the beast and false prophet. However, those he led into this war are consumed by fire from heaven. That means their bodies are evaporated and their souls are all set to line up before the great white throne. The devil is not judged, for the lake of fire was prepared for him from long ago (Matt. 25:41). He will preside over the place and the beast and the false prophet will no doubt serve him there. The devil will never again be able to harass the Lord or His people. It was fun for him perhaps, for a time, but now he must content himself with taking out his torment and frustrations on the billions sent directly to him from the great white throne. Since they are neither sons of God nor "heirs of salvation," they remain under the authority of the devil (Heb. 1:14). Imagine living in that evil kingdom—forever!

WHAT HAPPENS TO THE "REST OF THE DEAD?"

11. And now I saw a great white throne and the One who was seated on it. Earth and sky fled from His presence, because there was no longer any need for them.

EARTH AND SKY. We have come to the very last event in the human story, the judgment of the "rest of the dead," the unsaved. And the whole matter is dealt with in just five verses. Once this is taken care of, there will no longer be any need for the earth or sky and in Peter's words..."*the heavens will disappear with a loud bang and the elements will vanish in tremendous heat*" (2 Pet. 3:10). With the human experiment concluded, there is no longer any place for physical things. The physical world is gone! Since it was all held together by the "word of His power" (Heb. 1:3), He only had to speak and it all went back to energy. Of course, that is what an atom bomb is, releasing the energy holding atoms together. Hence the big bang! Dealing with those who have rejected Him, is Jesus' very last job as "The Son of Man." With that done, and the physical universe dissolved, His role as GOD'S SON will be over and He will *surrender up Himself* and His kingdom to God. Time and space will be finished and God will be all in all (1 Cor. 15:24-28).

WHITE THRONE. Believers were judged *before the millennium*, so they could take their places in Jesus' government. There'd be no way to run the kingdom smoothly unless each saint knew his job in advance. But now the earthly kingdom itself has come to an end. What's left is the final act of human history, judging the unbelievers who have appeared on the earth from Cain to the last person born into the kingdom. But who is this awesome person on the throne, before whom the unrighteous dead appear? It is Jesus (Acts 10:42). At first glance one might think it is the Father, but it is not He. The Father has already committed "all judgments unto the Son" (John 5:22). He did so for two reasons: 1.) *"That all men may honor the Son even as they honor the Father"* (vs.23). Those who said they loved God, but considered the Son to be less than God, will be in this crowd. 2.) "Because He is the Son of Man" (vs. 27). Only a man can judge other men fairly. The Father has never walked in man's shoes, only the Son has lived on earth as a man. That's why the judging will be fair.

**12. Then I saw the dead, great and small,
standing before the throne; and the books
were opened. Another book was there, the
book of life and it was also opened. The dead
were judged for their deeds, as recorded in
the books. 13. The sea gave up the dead that
were in it, and death and hades gave up the
dead they were holding. And each person was
judged according to his deeds.**

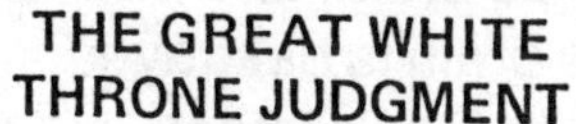

THE GREAT WHITE THRONE JUDGMENT

FOR ALL UNSAVED DEAD
(those who did NOT partake in First Resurrection)

great white throne and One who sat upon it (Rev. 20:11a)

SALVATION

book of life

ALL UNSAVED DEAD JUDGED ACCORDING TO THEIR WORKS
(Rev. 20:12,13)

WORKS

book of works

whose names were not found in the "book of life" were flung into the lake of fire (second death) (Rev. 20:14,15)

death and hell flung into lake of fire (Rev. 20:14)

LAKE OF FIRE
(SECOND DEATH – Rev. 20:6,14; 21:8)

BOOKS. When John speaks of the dead as great and small, he is saying no one is too important not to be judged and no one too unimportant to be judged. This judgment is for every unsaved person born into human life. Each will be judged for his works or deeds as recorded in the books. What books? Does God have a library? No, no need for that. Each man's mind *(not his brain)* is a marvelous recorder. Even if the brain is destroyed, nothing is ever lost. Made in God's image, man's capabilities range far beyond the body. Besides, if heaven and earth flee from Jesus' presence, no bodies would be there. This judgment takes place in the spirit, not in the flesh. If a shark eats a person's body, he will still appear in the spirit. Besides, all bodies and brains decay, but minds do not. What could be more fair than flashing before a man the record of his deeds *from his own mind?* In this way, God's justice can never be questioned or challenged.

DEEDS. Observe how this judgment is for works—only. Sins are not in the picture. The unsaved man dies in his sins (John 8:24). That means he takes his sinful nature with him into the lake of fire. The judgment determines his place in Satan's fiery kingdom, the same as the believer's judgment determines his place in Jesus' heavenly kingdom. If saints and sinners alike are judged for their works, what is it that sends the unsaved to the lake of fire? Their names are not in the book of life. That's the only thing that

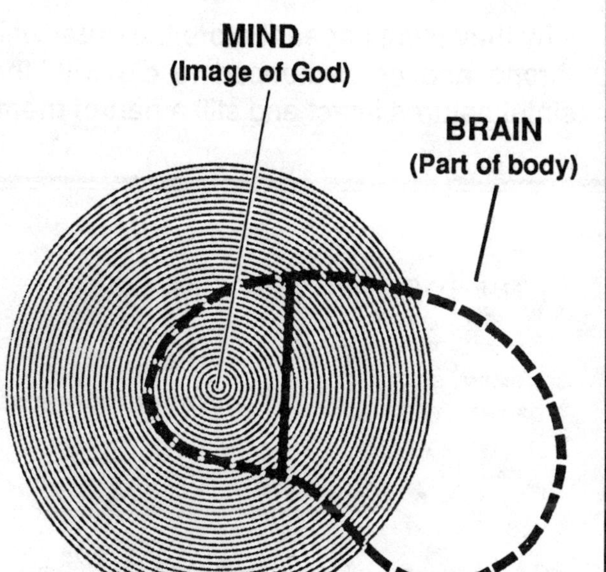

A person's mind and his brain are two different things: The brain is a part of the physical body, the mind is the image of God, which is spirit. It is in the mind that our complete history is recorded. Every thought that has passed through our heads, every emotion we've ever felt and every experience we've ever had, is all there. Nothing is lost. That's why scripture is silent on body disposal methods. All the Bible has to say is that the human body came from dust and to dust it will return. Whether bodies are buried, burned or eaten by sharks, makes no difference as far as this judgment is concerned.

sends them there. It is not their works, not their sins...except the one unpardonable sin—rejecting Jesus (1 John 5:16). That's what they've done. That's why their names are not in the book of life. Their sins were paid for at Calvary, where Jesus took on Himself the sins of the whole world, but they refused to accept Jesus' atoning death on their behalf. That's why they must appear before the great white throne and be sentenced to die with their sinful natures intact and still a part of them.

THE TWO THRONES OF JUDGMENT

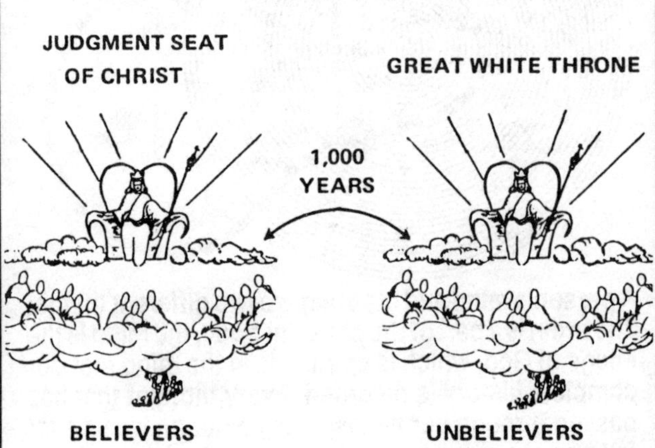

Those two thrones are for judging the WORKS of men. There is NO throne for judging sin. Sin was judged at Calvary. If a man trusts Christ, all of his sin is removed. If a man refuses Christ, he is guilty of ALL sin (Ja. 2:10). But there are DEGREES of heaven and hell. And the future job or status of a person in either place is determined at the thrones of judgment. Believers are judged for their works at the judgment seat of Christ. Sinners are judged at the great white throne. The rewards of which the Bible speaks have to do with one's future rank or status in either place and it is based on his works performed during his lifetime on earth. In this way each man gives an account of himself to God and the law of the harvest stands (Gal. 6:7).

14. Then Death and Hades were themselves thrown into the lake of fire. The lake of fire is the second death. 15. If anyone's name was not found entered in the book of life, he was thrown into the lake of fire.

DEATH AND HADES. It is quite clear now that the human program is over and eternity is beginning. God is all through with Death and Hades, the awful accessories of the sin program. Death followed sin and Hades was the holding tank for those who died as a result of sin. But death is only useful when there are sinners left to die. The holding tank was emptied when God summoned the dead before the great white throne. With no further use for Death or Hades, both are thrown into the lake of fire. This is God's dumping ground, His final disposal for creatures that were made to exist forever. We also have solid confirmation as to why these people are sent to Satan's eternal kingdom—*their names are not in the book of life.* That book is present and open at the great white throne. Why? It shows that God knew from the beginning those who were His (2 Tim. 2:19).

THE END OF THE PROGRAM

John has taken us to the very end of the earthly story. To proceed from this point would launch us into the eternal realm and there is no way to discuss eternal things in terms of space and time. So apart from some closing words about Jesus' return and a warning about adding or taking away from His words, this is the end. Actually we should go to verse 6 of Chapter 22. But you'll say, *"Hey, there are two more chapters."* Yes, but that's not because there is more to the narrative. There isn't. However, John didn't tell us anything about the millennial capitol, the headquarters of Jesus' world government and what life will be like in the New Jerusalem. He skipped that.

1154 — REVELATION 22:12

The Dead Are Judged

11Then I saw a great white throne and him who was seated on it. Earth and sky fled from his presence, and there was no place for them. 12And I saw the dead, great and small, standing before the throne, and books were opened. Another book was opened, which is the book of life. The dead were judged according to what they had done as recorded in the books. 13The sea gave up the dead that were in it, and death and Hades gave up the dead that were in them, and each person was judged according to what he had done. 14Then death and Hades were thrown into the lake of fire. The lake of fire is the second death. 15If anyone's name was not found written in the book of life, he was thrown into the lake of fire.

The New Jerusalem

21 Then I saw a new heaven and a new earth, for the first heaven and the first earth had passed away, and there was no longer any sea. 2I saw the Holy City, the new Jerusalem, coming down out of heaven from God, prepared as a bride beautifully dressed for her husband. 3And I heard a loud voice from the throne saying, "Now the dwelling of God is with men, and he will live with them. They will be his people, and God himself will be with them and be their God. 4He will wipe every tear from their eyes. There will be no more death or mourning or crying or pain, for the old order of things has passed away."

5He who was seated on the throne said, "I am making everything new!" Then he said, "Write this down, for these words are trustworthy and true."

6He said to me: "It is done. I am the Alpha and the Omega, the Beginning and the End. To him who is thirsty I will give to drink without cost from the spring of

ing impure will ever enter it, nor will anyone who does what is shameful or deceitful, but only those whose names are written in the Lamb's book of life.

The River of Life

22 Then the angel showed me the river of the water of life, as clear as crystal, flowing from the throne of God and of the Lamb 2down the middle of the great street of the city. On each side of the river stood the tree of life, bearing twelve crops of fruit, yielding its fruit every month. And the leaves of the tree are for the healing of the nations. 3No longer will there be any curse. The throne of God and of the Lamb will be in the city, and his servants will serve him. 4They will see his face, and his name will be on their foreheads. 5There will be no more night. They will not need the light of a lamp or the light of the sun, for the Lord God will give them light. And they will reign for ever and ever.

6The angel said to me, "These words are trustworthy and true. The Lord, the God of the spirits of the prophets, sent his angel to show his servants the things that must soon take place."

Jesus Is Coming

7"Behold, I am coming soon! Blessed is he who keeps the words of the prophecy in this book."

8I, John, am the one who heard and saw these things. And when I had heard and seen them, I fell down to worship at the feet of the angel who had been showing them to me. 9But he said to me, "Do not do it! I am a fellow servant with you and with your brothers the prophets and of all who keep the words of this book. Worship God!"

Note how the line skips from the end of Chapter 20 to verse 6 of Chapter 22 as we go directly to John's closing words. I did this to feature the apostle's final flashback. So, as you read Chapter 21, bear in mind it is but another flashback and not a continuation of the narrative.

So that's what we'll get in Chapter 21. It will be his final flashback in which he'll describe for us how the New Jerusalem comes down from heaven to replace the old Jerusalem, the ruined headquarters of the beast. The earthquake probably buried it. We'll learn who's going to be in the New Jerusalem and who won't. While the chapter is loaded with symbolism, one can't help but feel that it will be a great place to live and serve the Lord.

THE 5 FLASHBACKS OR INTERRUPTIONS IN THE NARRATIVE

#1. Ch. 7 is the first break in the narrative—144,000 Jews sealed—tribulation multitude saved.

#2. Ch.10—11:14, announcing that God is fed up, declares there is going to be no more delay. God's wrath, the third woe, is all set to be poured out on the world. The order to pour out the 7 bowls is expected momentarily.

#3. Chs.12—14:13 flashback to the Great Tribulation and provide details on the satanic trinity, the fate of the beast and of those who follow him.

#4. Chs.17 and 18, flashback to the beginning of the Great Tribulation and show the destruction of Babylon the Great (Rome). God uses the 10 kings of the beast to destroy this city.

#5. Chs. 21—22:6, flashback to Jesus' descent with His people, pictured as the city of the New Jerusalem coming down from heaven.

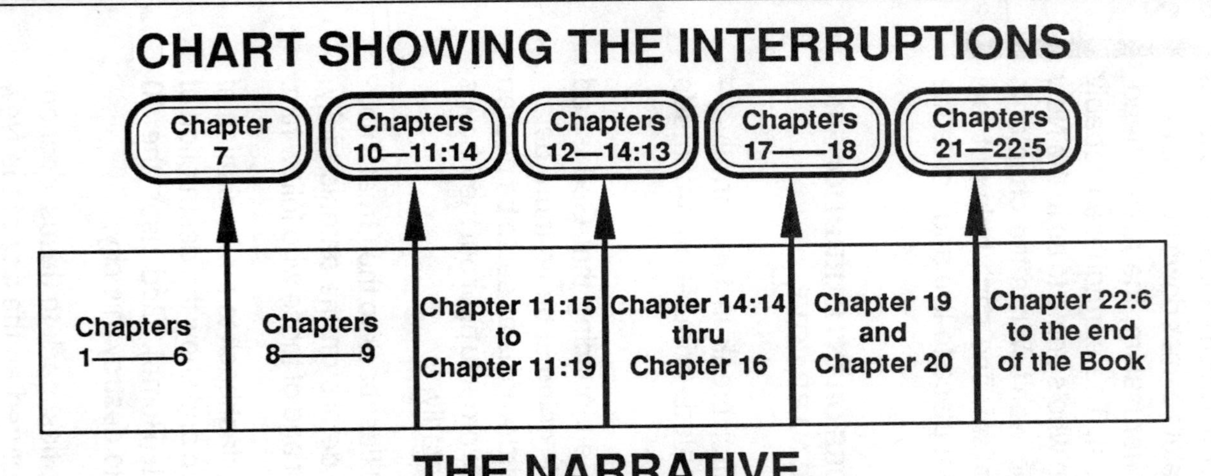

This simple chart may be the most important chart in the book. It goes a long way toward demystifying the Revelation. Make yourself aware of the 5 interruptions and the flow of the book becomes quite clear.

REVELATION 21

We have come to John's final flashback. Chapter 20 was the end of the story, closing with the great white throne judgment. That was the end of history. But now we're going to go back to where John left off—with the battle of Armageddon. The Lord was descending with His armies when suddenly the battle was over and the beast and the false prophet were cast into the lake of fire. As John flashes back, he pictures the descent of Jesus and His family in a much different way. Here is the 5th picture of the church in scripture—a city. We've listed them before; body, bride, building, family and city. The city is called the New Jerusalem and it is descending to a very different earth, with a very different sky overhead. The earth has endured massive earthquakes that utterly changed the landscape. There are no mountains. The oceans have given up their water to form a new heaven, one we might describe as a water mantle, much perhaps, as it was in Adam's day. There is no longer any danger from cosmic rays, for the water mantle makes the world a veritable greenhouse. It is to this kind of an earth that the Lord is bringing His bride. This chapter will give us some details concerning the New Jerusalem, the millennial capitol of the Lord.

FLASHBACK to the new Jerusalem —Jesus' Capitol city

21 **1. Then I saw a new heaven and a new**
earth, for the old heaven and the old
earth had disappeared and there was
no more sea. 2. And I, John, saw the Holy City,
the New Jerusalem, descending out of heaven
from God. She was beautifully prepared as a

bride, ready for her husband. 3. Then I heard a loud voice from the throne proclaim:

> ***"Behold! God is making Himself at home in the midst of men! He will dwell among them and they shall be His people. Yes, it's true! Their own God will be among them 4. and will wipe away every tear from their eyes. There will be no more death or mourning, crying or pain, for all of those things are now gone forever!"***

NEW HEAVEN. With Satan chained, we're breathing different air! So great is the new environment, you may think to yourself... *"We're in eternity!"* But then ask yourself, "What is eternity doing with a new heaven, *or an earth!"* An earth is physical, and the heavens are physical as well. The only thing eternal about this city is the people in it. They are eternal souls. We're looking at the same creation as it was before, BUT WITH THE CURSE REMOVED—and restored to look like new. This is a *redeemed* heaven and earth, with things probably much as they were before Adam sinned. The apostle Paul says the creation has been waiting for this moment, waiting to be delivered from the bondage of corruption. However, it had to wait for the *"manifestation of the sons of God"* (Rom. 8: 19-22). When the believer is set free, the whole creation is also set free. The two things happen together.

COMMENT: The entire physical creation is redeemed and the curse removed when the Lord descends to take over the kingdom of this world (11:15). However, *until the Lord returns,* all that is redeemed is the souls of men. Believers are redeemed souls living in unredeemed bodies. That's why we get sick. Our bodies are part of the unredeemed creation. But when the Lord removes the curse, our bodies are redeemed along with the rest of the physical world, says Paul (Rom. 8:23). Even the unsaved will have redeemed bodies, even though their souls remain unredeemed. The earth will still be *an earth.* And that earth will still have a *heaven.* What descends is the Lord and His people and their city, NOT a new heaven and a new earth. John simply saw them in his vision. It is the removing of the curse that restores the physical creation. Again, it is a redeemed creation.

FLASHBACK **to the new Jerusalem —Jesus' Capitol city**

NEW JERUSALEM. With the descent of the New Jerusalem, a voice from the throne announces that the dwelling of God is with men. Were this taking place in *eternity,* the voice would have said... *"Now the dwelling of man is with God and they shall live with Him!"* But no, we have the reverse of that. We have the Lord descending to be with man. That is certainly not eternal. What's more, Jesus is returning to receive His inheritance. He is returning as the *HEIR*, as the Son of Man. *"When the Son of Man shall come in His glory, and all the holy angels with Him, then shall He sit on the throne of His glory"* (Matt. 25:31). This city belongs to Jesus by right of succession (Luke 1:32). He is heir to the throne of David and we are "joint heirs" with Him (Rom. 8:17). The whole millennial kingdom is Jesus' reward for faithful service to His Father...AS A MAN!

COMMENT: Living with two natures results in a real struggle for believers (Gal. 5:19; Rom. 7:14-24). But God needs that struggle to shape us into His likeness...*as best He can.* Without something to overcome, growth is impossible, which explains why we still have the old nature after salvation. However, at death (or the rapture) that old nature, which has already been circumcised off the heart (Rom. 2:29; Col. 2:11), drops off with the flesh. And then all that's left is the *new man,* who is as righteous as Christ (2 Cor. 5:21). Like the sculptor who keeps his work under canvas until it is finished, God keeps His creations under a veil of flesh until He is ready to display them. In the day when Christ appears, we will appear with Him—minus the old nature. We'll then be revealed as we really are (Col. 3:4). How we have developed in His likeness will also be apparent. Even in glory not all will be alike, for some submit more willingly to His chisel and hammer than others. Even so, the finished products will be startling, even gorgeous. Every member of God's family will have been brought to His best. Even the worst Christian who ever lived will be pleasantly surprised by what God has made of him.

FLASHBACK to the new Jerusalem —Jesus' Capitol city

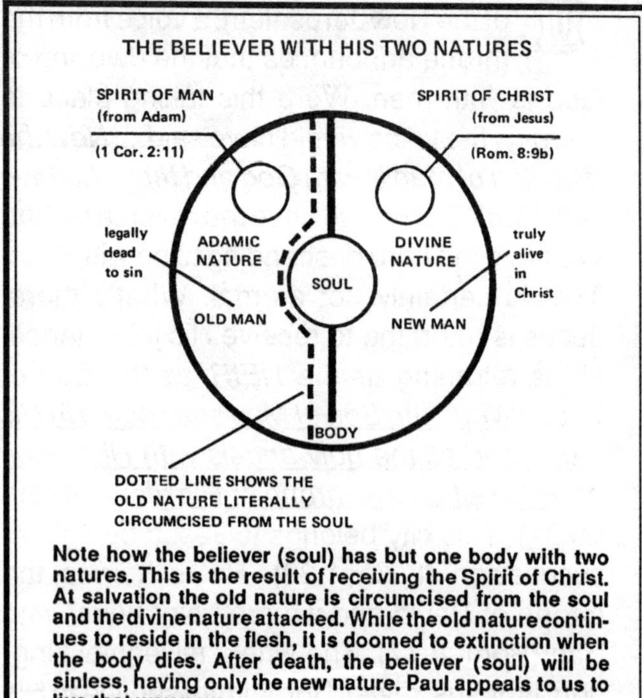

Note how the believer (soul) has but one body with two natures. This is the result of receiving the Spirit of Christ. At salvation the old nature is circumcised from the soul and the divine nature attached. While the old nature continues to reside in the flesh, it is doomed to extinction when the body dies. After death, the believer (soul) will be sinless, having only the new nature. Paul appeals to us to live that way now.

NO MORE TEARS! The believers in the 7 churches were all too familiar with death and pain, sorrow and tears. They had been hunted down and slain just because they were Christians. They were thrown to the lions simply to see how long it would take the lions to tear them apart. With their lives so full of tears, to hear of a city with no tears, pain or sorrow of any kind, sounded like heaven to them. These may have been the most comforting words in the whole book to the earliest readers. They don't sound bad to us either, for we have all experienced pain in some form. We lose loved ones, which is painful. Many more are enslaved in the fear of death (Heb. 2:15). What a thrill to find ourselves living on the other side of death. Those really close to Jesus in this life, find they can live now as though they were already in the celestial city. Their faith in God's promises is so strong they live now as though they already had them.

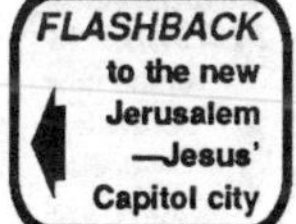

5. The One Who was sitting on the throne said to me,

> ***"Behold I am restoring all things like new."***

And then he said:

> ***"Put all this down, for these words are absolutely trustworthy and true: 6. It's over! I am the Alpha and the Omega, the Beginning and the End. The thirsty shall drink freely of the water of the spring of life as a free gift from Me. 7. And the***

person who overcomes will certainly have his share in all this and I will be his God and he shall be My son. 8. But not the cowardly, not those who refuse to believe in Me, not those living vile lives, not the murderers, fornicators, sorcerers, idolators or liars of any kind. The lake of fire and brimstone awaits them all, and that is the second death."

THINGS LIKE NEW. Jesus now speaks to John from His millennial throne, affirming that all the changes seen in the creation are His doing. After all, in the beginning He spoke and it all sprang into being. Then, when Adam sinned, the curse was pronounced and the creation fell into decay. Now that God has removed the curse, He has only to speak and the earth again becomes a garden paradise. From this John understands that whatever God says is absolutely true and dependable. Therefore, he is instructed to write down what God has said about being in the midst of His people and that it will be a painless, tearless world. The business of judging the earth is over. The bowls of wrath have been poured out. Now it is time for the millennial kingdom to get under way. The citizens of the kingdom (the redeemed believers) are in for a blessed time, living in the millennial capitol.

FLASHBACK to the new Jerusalem —Jesus' Capitol city

COMMENT: We identify the voice from the throne as that of the Lord Jesus. The Lord has now assumed *"the throne of His Father David"* (Luke 1:32). And as if to remind us that He has returned to earth as a MAN, the Lord Jesus repeats the

earlier identification of Himself as the *Alpha and Omega, the beginning and the end* (1:8). These are time/space concepts, finite terms. Only TIME has a beginning and ending, *eternity does not.* Beyond that, the Lord Jesus is still functioning in the role of THE SON. THAT IS NOT ETERNAL. He has NOT returned as God, but as a MAN. The throne is His inheritance as the "*Son of David.*" As the King of kings, (a human title) he has the right to say who will be allowed in His city and who will not. If this were taking place in eternity, words such as these would be totally unnecessary. Those 8 kinds of people wouldn't even be mentioned. They'd already be in the lake of fire.

THIRSTY PEOPLE IN THE CITY? Because we are the image of the infinite God, we have *infinite appetites.* God's appetite for us is infinite and so is ours for Him. We were made for Him and designed to be satisfied by Him alone. Therefore the deepest longing of the human heart is to be satisfied by Jesus—whether we know it or not. Men of this world, unaware that they were created for Jesus, try to satisfy their hearts with *the pleasures of this world.* But it doesn't work. With their infinite appetites, they always want *more.* The soul of man is ever hungry and thirsty. So when the voice from the throne speaks of drinking freely from the spring of life, it is referring to our need to be satisfied by Jesus Himself. Therefore, believers, *with their infinite appetite for Jesus,* are invited to come and drink all they want of Him, because they're going to be with Him from then on. The New Jerusalem will be a city of deep satisfaction for us. It will be almost as good as heaven, but not quite. Perfect satisfaction won't come until we're spirit to Spirit

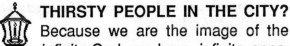

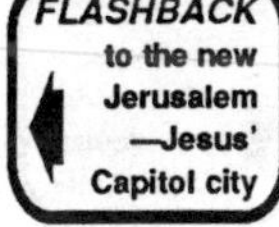

with Jesus in eternity. Mutual indwelling reaches its climax in the spirit, not in bodies (John 14:20).

WILL WE GET A CLOSER LOOK AT THE NEW JERUSALEM ?

9. Then one of the seven angels who had poured out the seven bowls filled with the seven last plagues came to me and said:

> ***"Come and I will show you the bride, the wife of the Lamb."***

BRIDE/WIFE. John is about to describe a fabulous city, but before we see this city we should understand the apostle is not concerned so much with a place as he is with the people. God's passion is for us, not for any city, no matter how spectacular it might be. He died for His family, not for any heaven or earth. That being the case, we now watch as the angel approaches John with an invitation to witness the descent of God's family to the earth. Don't let it bother you that the church is referred to as both a bride and a wife. The bride symbol refers to her beauty and purity, while the wife image refers to her intimacy with the Lord. The marriage has already taken place, but that isn't stressed here. Earlier John was invited, probably by the same angel, to see the harlot in the wilderness, to behold the worst in man. Now he is invited to behold "the wife," the best God can produce in man.

**10. Then he took me in the spirit high atop a
towering mountain and there showed me
Jerusalem. It was the Holy City, descending
out of heaven, sent by God. 11. The whole city
glowed with the glory of God and its brilliance radiated with the sparkle of a priceless
jewel, like a crystal clear jasper. 12. All around
the city was a great high wall that had twelve
gates in it and stationed at the gates were
twelve angels. The names of the twelve tribes
of Israel were written over the gates. 13. There
were three gates to the East, three to the
North, three to the South and three to the
West. 14. The city wall, too, had twelve foundation stones and on them were engraved the
names of the twelve apostles of the Lamb.**

HE TOOK ME. The devil took Jesus *in the spirit* to a high mountain and showed Him all the kingdoms of the world *in a moment of time* (Luke 4:5). You can do things like that in the spirit, for then you are outside of time and see things that haven't happened yet. The angel does the same thing with John. In similar fashion, he is carried *in the spirit* to a high mountain for a commanding view of the church's descent from the sky. Of course, this is not an actual mountain. The mountains are gone. Rather this is a *spiritual* observation point. From this point, John watches the Lord make His entrance into the world of men. With Him are all the redeemed from both the Old Testament and the New Testament. Collectively they are one family, though pictured here as a city. There is a real city, of course.

THE HOLY CITY. John caught a glimpse of the city earlier, but now gets a more detailed look and is awed by what he sees. And well he should be. This city *glows with the glory of God.* This is the shekinah glory that filled the Holy of Holies in the wilderness tabernacle. Only there it was veiled, concealed. Here God's unrestrained glory causes the whole city to glow with the radiance of the most precious jewel imaginable. Absolutely stunned, John likens the glow to crystal clear jasper, which suggests it may have had a greenish tint. It's hard today to identify ancient stones of the Bible, but that doesn't matter. It is enough to see that God's glory lights up the whole city in living color. See how this city is *"not made by human hands."* It's as Stephen said, "The *Most High does not live in houses made by men" (Acts 7:48).* That's why it descends from the sky. God makes His own dwelling among men. Consider again the 5 different ways the church is pictured in the New Testament and then realize John doesn't hesitate to mix his metaphors. It's important to get used to this.

GATES/WALL/FOUNDATION. Regarding the structure of the city, John focuses on three of its features: the wall, the gates and the foundation. The wall is so high that if you're not invited through the gate, you can't get in. Verse 17 tells us it is also several hundred feet thick. The wall also has twelve gates, which are named after the twelve tribes of Israel. The gates are distributed so that there are 3 on each side of the city, 3 opening to each point of the compass. The foundation of the wall consists of 12 *separate layers,* with each layer a massive gem. Each layer bears the name of an apostle. It's the APOSTLESHIP that is in view, not the individual apostles. With the gates identified by the 12 tribes and the foundation stones by the 12 apostles, there is pictured the oneness of believers in both Testaments, Old and New.

**15. In the hand of the angel speaking to me,
was a golden measuring rod with which to
measure the city, its gates and its walls. 16.
When measured, the city was found to be
foursquare, as long as it was wide. Yet, when
the height was measured, it turned out to be
a cube, for all three of its dimensions were the
same, roughly 1400 miles. 17. When he measured the wall he found it to be a little over 200
feet thick by human standards, even though
an angel was doing the measuring.**

MEASURE. Want to know how big this city is? An angel with a 10 foot golden rod is going to measure it. The city is laid out in a square, roughly 1400 miles long and 1400 miles wide. And we find that it also rises 1400 miles into the sky. That, of course, would make it a cube. If the wall around the city rose to that height, you wonder what purpose it would serve. If such measurements are taken literally, the gates are reduced to pinholes. So we're forced to seek a symbolic meaning. One thing is clear, John is having a tough time expressing the vastness as well as the beauty of the city. But there is something striking about the *CUBE* that Jewish readers would appreciate right away. The inner sanctuary of the wilderness tabernacle, the "Holy of Holies" was also a cube, 15 feet in each direction. It was here that the high priest would go on the day of atonement to stand in the veiled presence of God. But John sees the entire New Jerusalem as the "Holy of Holies" OF THE WORLD, the place of God's presence on earth. Describing it as a 1400 mile cube would be one way to *magnify* the majesty of such a truth!

THE WALL. The great high wall, a little over 200 feet thick, is a formidable barrier. But what are walls for? To protect from outsiders. This tells us that beyond those walls are people who are not welcome in the city. It's the only reason for a wall. Verse 8 gave us a list of 8 classes of people who were barred from the city. What's more, the last verse of this chapter tells us that nothing impure, no deceivers nor those who do shameful things, as well as those whose names are not in the book of life, will enter this city. This is why guardian angels are stationed at each of the city gates. Here we have another reason for believing this city is not our eternal home, but is instead, Jesus' millennial capitol. He will rule from this city and we will operate from here as well. What place would walls have in heaven? It is quite clear now that we are discussing a flashback, John's last flashback.

**18. The wall was made of crystal-like jasper,
while the city itself was made of pure gold, as
clear as glass. 19. The foundations of the city
wall consisted of 12 layers of stone with each
layer made of a separate gem. The first course
was made of jasper, the second of sapphire,
the third of chalcedony, the fourth of emerald, the fifth of sardonyx, 20. the sixth of
sardius, the seventh of chrysolite, the eighth
of beryl, the ninth of topaz, the tenth of chry-
soprase, the eleventh of jacinth, the twelfth
of amethyst. 21. The twelve gates were twelve
pearls, with each gate a single pearl. The
broad main street of the city was made of pure
gold, like transparent glass.**

PEARLY GATES/STREETS OF GOLD. The value of precious stones is determined by their beauty and scarcity. Men sell their souls for gold, they kill for it. Yet this enormous city is made of gold so pure the light of God's glory passes through it. What's more, this gold is used instead of concrete, bricks and asphalt, which renders worldly treasure worthless. Thus we see that what men regard as precious, God regards as dust. The apostle Peter views all these as "perishable" (1 Pet. 1:18). This is hardly an eternal city if it is made of perishable things. Even so, it is a magnificent sight to the mind's eye. Imagine a golden city encased in a jasper wall 200 feet thick and so clear the golden glow of the city can be seen through it. In addition to all this, the wall sits atop a foundation made of layers of solid gems of every color and hue.

FLASHBACK
to the new
Jerusalem
—Jesus'
Capitol city

COMMENT: Who could calculate the worth of such a city! John witnessed something impossible to describe, yet was ordered to write down what he saw. So he tries, taking what is valuable to men and using it to communicate something beyond description. As an added touch, he says the gates of the city are made of a single pearl. If we can conceive of a pearl big enough to serve as a city gate, then it is reasonable to consider the foundations of the wall as being layers of pure gems. One is no more improbable than the other. When the apostle Paul was caught up to the third heaven, a situation not unlike that of the apostle John, he was NOT commanded to write what he saw. In fact, he refused even to try, saying it couldn't be done (2 Cor. 12:4). But poor John had no choice. He had orders to write.

22. There was no temple for me to see in the city, for the Lord God Almighty and the Lamb are there in person. They are its temple.
23. The city has no need for light from the sun or the moon, for the glory of God is the light source and the Lamb is the lamp that radiates it.

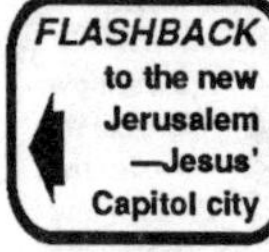

TEMPLE. Temples are for worshipping gods you cannot see. And so it is with the Lord Jesus. Right now, He is out of sight, and people meet in specific locations to worship Him by faith. But once we meet Him face to face in the sky and descend with Him, temples are reduced to museum pieces. With God's presence permeating the whole city of Jerusalem, those dwelling there will be living in the "Holy of Holies!" The Lord Jesus told the woman at the well a day was coming when God's presence would no longer be restricted to physical locations. Still, there is a sense in which that day is yet future. In the New Jerusalem, God's presence, while manifested *through a body*, will still be concealed.

Even the New Jerusalem is a specific place where His presence is circumscribed. However, it symbolizes the final state in eternity where we will be with Him and enjoy Him *spirit to Spirit!*

LAMP. Here is a light bulb. You flip a switch and suddenly light radiates in all directions. Are the light and the bulb the same? No, one is the source, the other the radiance or manifestation of the energy. But the two are close to being one, as close as a lamp and its burning wick are one. In the New Jerusalem, God the Father is the source, whereas the Son is the radiance or manifestation of the Father's glory. As the Son, the Lord Jesus will be in a body, a glorified body to be sure, but still a body. And so will we... *"We know that when He appears, we shall be like Him, for we shall see Him* (with physical eyes) *as He is"* (1st John 3:2). The Lord made it clear that He was coming *"in the glory of His Father"* (Matt. 16:27). That is the glory that will illuminate the New Jerusalem.

FLASHBACK to the new Jerusalem —Jesus' Capitol city

COMMENT: After the millennium is over and all the unsaved have been sentenced, Jesus' role as the Son, will end. *"Then comes the end when He hands over the kingdom (that's us) to God the Father...then the Son Himself will be made subject to Him Who put everything under Him, so that God may be all in all!"* (1 Cor. 15:24-28). For the purpose of the human experiment, the omnipresent God manifested Himself as a man. A real man, born of a woman. And as a man, appeared on the earth to do two things: 1.) reveal what God is like as a person, 2.) redeem us by the blood of His cross. But once the millennium (His inheritance and our transition school) is over, Jesus' role as the Son is finished. Thus, when we get to

heaven, we will not see 3 Gods, nor even the Father and the Son. We will see only One God and that God will be just like Jesus. In point of fact, is not Jesus Christ the only God we know?

24. And the nations shall go about their business by the light of the city and the kings of the earth will bring their glory into it. 25. At no time will the gates ever be closed, for there will be no night there. 26. The splendor and honor of the nations shall be brought into it. 27. But nothing unclean will be permitted in the city, nor anyone who deals in filth and lies—but only those whose names are written in the Lamb's book of life.

NATIONS AND KINGS. The nations and their kings seen here, must certainly baffle those who believe this city is our eternal home and not Jesus' millennial headquarters. If this were an eternal scene, there would be no nations here. They'd all be gone. But who are these kings who bring their glory into the Holy City? Verse 27 says only those whose names are in the book of life will be allowed in the city. Clearly no unsaved can enter the city. So who are these people? John spoke earlier of believers as being *kings and priests and reigning* with Christ (5:10). Undoubtedly these are Christians who have earned the right to SERVE AS KINGS over the nations. Since there is no night here, the gates will always be open. But that presents no risk, the guardian angels will see that nothing unclean nor any unsaved enter the city.

COMMENT: We have now come to the end of Chapter 21, but we have not come to the end of John's flashback. That continues through verse 5 in the next chapter. The nations outside the city are those the Lord Jesus rules with a "rod of iron." Chief among those nations will be the nation of Israel. The Lord made *physical* promises to Abraham that must be kept. And while the Jewish nation has rejected Him, He remains faithful to His word. The Old Testament prophecies concerning the future glories of Israel will be fulfilled in the millennium. The Lord Jesus will reign over Israel and she will be supreme among the other nations. The status of the other nations will be determined on the basis of their treatment of Israel (Matt. 25:31-32). After the 1000 years are over and the people of the nations appear before the great white throne, Israel's role as God's chosen nation will end. She will have received the promises and enjoyed them. But *physical promises* end when the *physical program* is over. There are *NO* physical promises that extend into eternity. The church inherited the spiritual promises that the nation of Israel rejected.

THE CITIZENS OF THE KINGDOM

JERUSALEM

The Lord and His "bride" will reign from the golden city. Only those whose names are in the book of life, will be allowed to come and go as they please. No outsiders will be allowed inside the walls.

The New Jerusalem, possibly rising many stories above the earth, will have no elevators. The believers, with their *spiritual bodies*, will move about (up, down or sideways) by command. A good number will have tasks that will take them outside the city. Inasmuch as the outsiders still have sinful natures and Jesus means to IMPOSE righteousness on His kingdom, certain Christians will be charged with policing the population. Operating with spiritual powers, the "kingdom cops" will move in a flash to confront anyone contemplating evil in his heart. In this way, they will help Jesus execute His righteous reign. The Jews having favored nation status, will enjoy privileges not extended to the Gentile nations. However, neither Jews nor Gentiles will be allowed in the city. It is the exclusive domain of the saints.

REVELATION 22

The flashback continues. Don't let the fact that we are entering a new chapter blur the truth that John is still describing the New Jerusalem. He will continue to do so through verse five. Keep in mind that the New Jerusalem is also a symbol for God and His people. As has been mentioned, it is but one of the five pictures of the church in the New Testament. Remember too, that the apostle is not picturing a city in some distant heaven. This city is on earth, a restored earth. John is showing us the splendor of the church as she appears with Jesus in His millennial kingdom. This New Jerusalem is not some far away home of the saints, but the family of God on earth, enjoying the presence of the Lord in her midst. Having previously exposed us to the radiant structure of the descended Jerusalem, John now turns our thoughts to the blessedness of life within the city. This will be our home on earth for 1000 years.

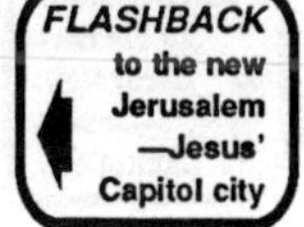

22 1. Then the angel directed my attention to the river of the water of life, glistening like crystal as it flowed from the throne of God and the Lamb 2. down the center of the main street. On either side of the river a tree of life was growing, bearing twelve kinds of fruit and yielding a fresh crop each month. The leaves were for the healing of the nations.

RIVER. The garden of Eden had a flowing river and its tree of life. Similarly the New Jerusalem also has a river and life sustaining trees. The angel is evidently escorting John and pointing out the outstanding features of the city. The first feature is the crystal river that issues from the throne and flows down the middle of the main street. Next the tree of life is pointed out with its 12 different kinds of fruits and its medicinal leaves. Some scholars insist this is not one tree, but two rows of trees lining either bank of the river. That may be so, but it doesn't change the symbolism in any way. We're dealing with three things: the water, the fruits and the leaves.

WATER. In verse 6 of Chapter 21, the One on the throne said to John, *"The thirsty shall drink freely of the water of the spring of life, as a gift from Me!"* With all the inhabitants of the city believers, how could anyone be thirsty? Made in the image of the *infinite God,* you and I have INFINITE APPETITES. Thus we are always thirsty. Men of the world have this thirst too, but they don't know it is a thirst for Jesus. So they try to satisfy it with the pleasures of the world. The voice from the throne is addressing the Christian's need to be satisfied by Jesus. Actually, it is an invitation for God's children to come and *be filled with Him.* The endlessly flowing river speaks of the abundant satisfaction that will be ours when we're face to face with Jesus. The key thought here is <u>abundance</u>.

FRUITS. In the same way, the 12 crops of fruit bespeak the abundance of everything needed to sustain us in the kingdom. While our resurrection bodies can eat food (Luke 22:30), there is no reason to suppose we'll NEED food of any kind. Our carnal bodies require food for energy, but our new bodies, *being spiritual*, will derive their energy from the spirit realm (1 Cor. 15:44). The 12 crops may symbolize the limitless source of our energy. It appears the millennial kingdom still has *months*, which relate to the cycle of the moon. Surely there'll be no months in eternity for there is no time there. But apparently months will be reckoned in the millennial city, which argues strongly against the idea this city is our eternal home. Months have to do with the moon's rotation about the earth.

FLASHBACK to the new Jerusalem —Jesus' Capitol city

LEAVES. The medicinal leaves may possibly be exported to the nations, which would make the city a source of blessing to those outside the city. In that case, it would symbolize God's abundant care for all the inhabitants during the kingdom years. The believers, with their *spiritual* bodies, would be immune to any kind of sickness or injury, but that's not true of those outside the city. The text seems to be saying there will be times when healing is needed. On the other hand, healing would have no place in eternity. Eternity is not physical. It is unseen, therefore eternal (2 Cor. 4:18).

3. There will no longer be any curse. The throne of God and of the Lamb will be there and so will his servants. They will worship Him 4. and see Him face to face with His name written on their foreheads.

CURSE. When Adam sinned, God immediately placed a curse on the earth, and from that time man has had to make his living by the sweat of his brow and women have had to bear children in pain (Gen. 3:16-19). Weeds and insects came along with flesh eating animals. The curse reached even the weather with its storms and floods, and the world became a place without peace. The suffering and evil in the world today are a direct result of that curse. But now the angel tells John the curse has been lifted. Such a thing could never be said of heaven, for it has no curse to lift. With Satan bound throughout the kingdom age, life will be abundant for everyone on the restored earth. Man will not have to work for a living, though he will have to reap the bounty of the earth. There will be plenty of time for family life and to contribute to the population explosion.

FACE TO FACE. One of the greatest privileges we'll have in the kingdom will be seeing Jesus "face to face." That means we'll be able to sit close to Him, touch Him and ask all the questions we want. We can put our arms around Him and hug Him, something we can only do by faith at the present time. With the old nature gone, and clothed only in His righteousness, His name can then be written on our foreheads. This suggests we will be able to *think as He thinks,* even understanding, perhaps, the mystery of God (Col. 2:2). But do not look on this "face to face" fellowship as the ultimate Christian joy. There is more to come. The millennium is but the final phase of God's earthly program. It is the last 1000 years of the 7000 years set aside for dealing with man on the earth. When it is over, we'll arrive at our final destination, the eternity of God.

THRONE. Wonder how God and the Lamb might occupy the same throne? Not too difficult when you consider the Lord Jesus is the only one in a body. The Father is present in the same sense as when Jesus said, *"I am not alone, because the Father is with Me"* (John 16:32). In the first chapter of his gospel, the apostle quotes Jesus as saying, *"No man has seen God at any time; the only begotten Son Who is in the bosom of the Father, has made Him known"* (John 1:18). That helps. As the Eternal Spirit, God remains invisible to physical eyes. No one will SEE God until the kingdom age ends and His family is gathered to Him in eternity. The only way God can be seen as He really is, is for us to be "absent from the body" (2 Cor. 5:6). The Lord Jesus is God in a body, operating inside space and time. God the Father, an omnipresent Spirit, is *present to* the incarnate Christ. The Father is IN the Son and the Son is IN the Father (John 14:20).

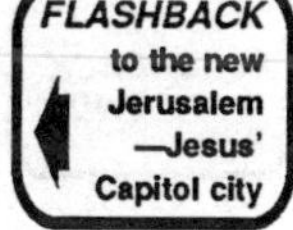

Therefore it is proper to speak of the throne as belonging to both God and the Lamb.

COMMENT: The kingdom experience is temporary, a transition period. When it is over, we'll be ready for eternity. We're not ready now, but we will be then. We have much to learn about omniscience, omnipresence and handling omnipotence. We'll get training in those things in the millennium. In eternity we'll get more. Then we will behold God, SPIRIT TO SPIRIT, an experience far deeper and more intimate than anything we could know or enjoy in a body, even a glorified body. Though we are in the kingdom, God remains a SPIRIT, whom no one has seen at any time, except the Son. (John 1:18; 1 John 4:12). We will see Jesus—*in a body*—but the Father will remain unseen. When the kingdom ends, and Jesus' role as *the Son* is over, He will deliver the kingdom up to the Father and eternity will begin (1 Cor. 15:24). In that day we will see God as He is and we will be like Him.

FLASHBACK ENDS

5. There will be no more night, eliminating all need for lamps or the sun, for the Lord God will give them light; and they shall reign forever and ever.

LIGHT. The believers serving the Lord in His illuminated city won't need any rest. Their bodies, fueled by *spirit,* will be tireless. As God *"neither slumbers nor sleeps,"* neither will we (Psa.121:3). Resting at night is for mortal bodies, those fueled by food. So, in the kingdom, like our heavenly Father, we'll work around the clock. And there'll be plenty to do ruling over an exploding population of unsaved people. Every Christian will have a job. Some will be of high rank and some very low, depending on the place they have given the Lord Jesus in this life. Made in the image of a busy Creator, we'll all work. Then, when the kingdom has ended, we'll take our places in eternity. Once we're in eternity with God, we will indeed *"reign forever and ever!"* But we must wait until then to find out the exciting opportunities we will have. What a fantastic future awaits us!

THE END OF THE FLASHBACK

COMMENT: John has finished his detailed description of the New Jerusalem and now adds an epilogue to the book. He wants his readers to understand that his words are directly from heaven, and he uses testimonies from the Lord and the angel to reinforce his words. This, he feels, will help his readers take his words more seriously. John has given us a glimpse of the Holy City. And from this we gather something of *"the riches of His glorious inheritance among His people"* (Eph. 1:18). Granted it's a faint view, but it should stir us to give Jesus an ever increasing place in our lives. The glory we see in the New Jerusalem is but a faint outline of the eternal age *that lies beyond* the kingdom. When that age dawns, we will behold the full manifestation of God's glory—*SPIRIT TO SPIRIT!*

6. Then the angel said to me:

"These words are trustworthy and true. The Lord, the God Who speaks through the spirits of the prophets, has sent His angel to show His servants what must soon take place."

THESE WORDS. The apostle has faithfully put down in black and white all that he heard and saw, as he was instructed at the beginning. Now he wants to make sure the churches realize his words are authentic and directly from heaven. So he writes an epilogue that will include a certification by the angel who has been instructing him, as well as a statement by the Lord Himself. This is akin to the way marketing people use testimonies to convince the buying public of the value of a product. Only in this case, John wants his readers to understand his revelation is from heaven itself. His first testimony is a quote from the angel, who affirms that John's words are true. The angel also affirms that the events recorded in the book are due to occur soon. Since 2000 years have now gone by, "soon" should be understood as soon in *sequence*, but not soon *in time.* That is, these things will mark God's *NEXT* intervention into the affairs of men.

7. "Behold I am coming soon! Blessed is he who takes to heart the words of prophecy this book presents."

8. I, John am the one who heard and saw these things, and upon hearing them and seeing them, I fell down at the feet of the angel who had been showing them to me and was about to worship him. 9. But once again he said to me:

"Stop! You must not do that! I too am a servant of God the same as you and your brothers the prophets and with all who take to heart the words of this book. Direct your worship to God alone!"

STOP. Someone reading the Revelation might suspect John was having a pipe dream, that the aged apostle was off his rocker. So first, John insists he has seen and heard all these things. And then he does a strange thing. He falls at the feet of the angel and is about to worship him when the angel stops him. What's strange is that this is the second time John has tried to do this (19:10). There must have been something in John's background that would prompt him to do this. The Jews held angels in high esteem, and that coupled with the awesome things he has been hearing and seeing, probably triggered this response instinctively. But the angel, insisting that angels are co-workers with the saints, redirects John's worship to God.

10. Then he ordered me:

"Do not seal up the words of prophecy contained in this book, for the time of their fulfillment is at hand. 11. In the meantime, let those who do wrong persist in their wrong, and those who are filthy persist in their filthiness, and let those who do good persevere in their good deeds and the holy ones persevere in their holy living."

DO NOT SEAL. Roughly 600 years before John wrote these words, the Lord had spoken to the prophet Daniel concerning end-time events. At that time the Lord instructed Daniel to *"Shut up the words and seal the book until the time of the end"*

(Dan. 12:4). But now we hear the angel instructing John to do just the opposite. *Do not seal the book, he says, for the time is at hand.* Consequently John understands the churches need his message of the coming tribulation and the ultimate triumph of righteousness over evil. But now that 2000 years have gone by, the words...*"at hand"* must take on a different meaning. Apparently God, in His genius, has wanted every generation to regard it's own struggle with tyranny and persecution a prelude to the return of Christ. There has always been the sense that the end is at hand, and each generation feels it will be the one to experience the return of Christ. This is healthy. It keeps believers watching and preparing for Jesus' appearance. There is plenty in Jesus' words to suggest this is a deliberate strategy to keep believers on their toes (Matt. 24:44; Luke 12:40).

PERSIST—PERSEVERE. To the mind of John, who viewed these things as *"at hand,"* there was little time left for one to change his life. People seem to grow more slowly than trees. So to John's mind, his readers were stuck with their characters and habits. They are certain to reap the consequences of the kinds of lives they have lived, with no way to change. You see, we enter heaven just as we are at the point of death and never change. Succeeding generations haven't felt that way. They have become casual about changing into the likeness of Christ. As a result, years go by with no change. They finally reach the point where a lifetime of habit patterns gives Satan such a hold on them that change is impossible. Then when the end of their life arrives, they enter heaven as they are and *never change.* Why? The conditions for change do not exist in eternity. Eternity is a changeless state. That's why God is changeless (Mal. 3:6).

WILL THE LORD HIMSELF BACK UP WHAT JOHN HAS WRITTEN?

12. "Behold, I am coming soon and I am bringing with Me My reward to compensate everyone according to what he has done. 13. I am the Alpha and Omega, the First and the Last, the Beginning and the End. 14 Blessed are those who wash their robes so that they may have the right to enter the city by the gates and eat from the tree of life. 15. Outside the city and barred from entering, are the dogs, that is, the sorcerers, the fornicators, the murderers and idolators, and all who love and practice lying. 16. I, Jesus, have sent My angel to you with this message for the churches. I am the root of David as well as his offspring, and the bright morning star that ushers in the day!"

I HAVE SENT. The Lord puts His seal on John's words, saying that He Himself sent the angel to John. He also makes it plain that the message given to John about the tribulation is for the churches. He asserted His right to speak about the end-time judgment of man, since He Himself IS A MAN. He presents His credentials in *time and space language:* only space matters can be *"first and last."* Only time has a *"beginning and end."* As a MAN, Jesus is David's offspring, which gives Him legal right to the throne of Israel. His favorite title for Himself was,"the Son of Man." As the morning star, He is the "light at the end of the tunnel" of the dark night of the tribulation. Those who come to Him for salvation and cleansing can enter His city and enjoy access to the tree of life, which symbolizes immortality. But those refusing to come to Him for salvation are barred from the city. Having only the carnal nature which is deceitful, vicious and murderous, He considers them *"dogs."*

COMMENT: Note how the Lord insists that He sent the angel with the message for the churches. It is the Lord's message. Those who reshape His message to make it say that believers will not go through the tribulation, do the church a great disservice. The Revelation was written to prepare the churches for suffering and was meant to be a comfort and blessing to those who would be called upon to give up their lives rather than deny the Lord. The tribulation message is for today and it cries out...*prepare yourself to die for Jesus!* To insist the church will be taken out before the tribulation, is to fly in the face of Jesus' clear testimony. Besides, it creates an artificial group of believers who are said to be more worthy than those choosing death rather than accept the mark of the beast. This view not only causes divisions among believers, but is a fairly new idea. No one ever heard of it before 1830. But, who can blame people for wanting to escape suffering?

MY REWARD. Jesus' return will be like lightning flashing across the sky (Matt. 24:27). His first task will be to judge His people and distribute His rewards among them. The rewards are positions in Jesus' government, which will be assigned on the basis of each man's works. The believer will be judged on the basis of what he has done as compared with what *he could have done*—therefore competing *only* against himself. In this way, every one has an equal opportunity when it comes to winning a good job near Jesus. This judgment and the assignment of jobs, will be cared for *before* Jesus descends to earth. His government will then be in place and ready to function when the New Jerusalem descends to the earth. This should challenge every Christian to put Jesus ahead of fame, fortune, family and fun—and think seriously about his future job in the kingdom. The modern church has failed to keep this truth before the people.

THE REPEATED INVITATION AND THE WARNING

17. The Spirit and the bride say, "Come!" And let him who hears this invitation repeat it to anyone who is thirsty. Tell him to "come," if he is willing, and accept the water of life as a free gift. 18. And now I give this warning to everyone listening to the words of prophecy contained in this book; if anyone adds anything to them, God will add to him the plagues described in this book; 19. if anyone takes away any part of these prophecies, God will

take away from him his share in the tree of life and the Holy City, which are described in this book.

INVITATION. As John comes to the end of the book, his mind goes to his readers and all those who will be reading his words. So an invitation to come and be saved is in order. The Holy Spirit, working through the church (that's us), gives an open invitation to anyone who has a genuine spiritual thirst to come and drink freely of the water of life. These words place a responsibility on all believers to see that the invitation goes out. It doesn't take much. If people have a real "thirst" or desire to spend eternity with God, all they need is to know they are welcome in God's family, and can obtain their salvation by putting their trust in Jesus Christ. What people do about the invitation is their own business, but getting the invitation to them is the business of every believer. The Spirit will work with any Christian willing to help get out the word of welcome.

WARNING. John feels obliged to close his book with a severe warning. The prophetic truths of the book are from God, and woe to the person who dares add or take away from them. This is not a warning to those honestly trying to set forth its veiled meanings or interpret its mysterious symbols. Rather this warning is directed to those who would willfully pervert and distort the great truths John's book contains. Regardless how one interprets the taking away of shares of the tree of life, or adding the plagues described in this book, a clear truth rings out—it is a dangerous thing to tamper with the word of God.

A FINAL WORD FROM THE LORD JESUS

20. He Who has initiated all these things declares: "Yes, I am coming soon!"

So be it, come Lord Jesus!

21. The grace of the Lord Jesus be with you all. Amen.

COMING SOON. With His statement, "I AM COMING SOON," it's as though the Lord Jesus, who commanded John to write these things, is responding to the cry of all Christians who long for His glorious appearing. He wants to comfort His saints. Who knows better than the Lord, the suffering that lies ahead for His little ones? He knows of the slaughter that will occur under the reign of the beast. God's purpose in having John write the book was to encourage the saints to be patient no matter what persecution comes upon them, assuring them they won't be sorry. Their sufferings are not to be compared with the glory that awaits them. They are to maintain their loyalty to Jesus in the days of trial and tribulation, even unto death. The apostle Paul displayed this same spirit when he exhorted the new believers at Lystra, Iconium and Antioch to continue in the faith, saying... *"We must through much tribulation enter into the kingdom of God"* (Acts 14:22). That same *TRIBULATION* applied to the churches of Asia, who were the first to receive this book. The words... *"I am coming soon,"* must have been music to their ears. The response..."So be it, come Lord Jesus!" is likely theirs. *"Come Lord Jesus"* is the equivalent of the Aramaic word...*Maranatha!* The coming of Jesus is the only thing that can interrupt the downward course of this world. So we join our dear brothers with the same cry—MARANATHA!

JOHN PRONOUNCES A BENEDICTION ON ALL WHO HAVE HAD THIS BOOK READ TO THEM OR HAVE READ IT THEMSELVES.

Amen means: "SO BE IT!"

APPENDIX

WHY THE NEW JERUSALEM IS NOT OUR ETERNAL HOME

The millennium is an essential part of God's plan for man on the earth. It is the last chapter of human history, *but not the final goal.* It is a time when God gathers up all the loose ends and winds down the human program. It is also used to prepare us for eternity. Things are accomplished in the millennium that couldn't possibly be done earlier. And when those things are done, God will close out the human story and eternity will begin for us.

John spoke of a new heaven and a new earth, but as might be expected, it is nothing other than the same old world with the curse removed. The removing of the curse makes it all *seem like new.* With the water mantle restored to the skies, the heavens will certainly appear new. The entire globe will be a veritable greenhouse. With the oceans and mountains gone, and the earth exploding with food, the change will be astounding. And when there are no floods or flies, and the animals are at peace with man, and when man is at peace with his neighbor, it will indeed seem like a new earth.

The last chapter of the human story is so incredible, some Bible students look on the New Jerusalem as our eternal home, a sort of heaven on earth. But in describing the New Jerusalem, John points out things that overrule that idea:

1. *"There is no more curse"* (22:3). Clearly the curse has been removed. However, it can't be removed from eternity—eternity has no curse to remove. The curse can only be removed from the earth. The earth alone was cursed.

2. The New Jerusalem has WALLS to keep out the undesirables. The Lord Himself called them *dogs* (22:15). This could hardly be said of eternity, for all the unsaved are judged and cast into the lake of fire, *before eternity begins* (20:15). What's more, the New Jerusalem has guardian angels at each of its 12 gates to prevent unwanted intrusions (21:12). In 22:15, Jesus lists those outside the city who are forbidden to enter. Such a remark would be pointless if this city were in heaven.

3. Were such the case, one could rightly ask, "*What is eternity doing with a heaven?"* A heaven or an earth is inconsistent with the spirit-world.

4. There is *time* in the New Jerusalem for it has *months* (22:2). Months are determined by the moon. Eternity has no moon. Months are a measurement of time. So this city is in TIME, not eternity.

5. We observe that Jesus' kingdom is made up of *"the kingdoms OF THIS WORLD,"* not the

kingdoms of some other world, nor yet kingdoms from some eternal world (11:15).

6. In Chapter 5, the twenty-four elders and the 4 living creatures affirm that you and I have been made... *"unto our God kings and priests: and we shall reign on the earth"* (5:10). It may look like a new earth, but it will still be the earth.

7. The millennial kingdom is FINITE, in that it has a beginning and an ending. *"Then comes the END when he delivers up the kingdom to God the Father...and when all things are subject to Him, then the Son Himself will also be made subject to God who made all things subject to Him, and thus God will be all in all"* (1Cor. 15:24,28). Eternity cannot begin as long as Jesus remains in the SON role. He will not be the SON in eternity, there He'll be God Himself.

OTHER FEATURES OF THE MILLENNIUM

The Lord Jesus returns to earth to inherit His kingdom. As God, He would have no need to inherit anything. But as A MAN (in the role of God's Son), He is heir to the throne and kingdom of David (Luke 1:32). Paul's statement about our being *"heirs of God and joint-heirs with Christ,"* refers to our sharing in Jesus' *EARTHLY KINGDOM* (Rom. 8:17).

In the New Jerusalem, the Lord Jesus will have a BODY. We will too, and our bodies will be like His, *"for we shall see Him as He is"* (1 John 3:2). Our bodies, like His—will be glorified bodies. In these *spiritual bodies,* we will move about in the kingdom, performing various jobs that will prepare us for eternity. However, the very fact of bodies indicates this is not an *eternal situation.* Bodies veil the spirit. Even Jesus' millennial body will conceal His real glory. Not until we see Him in heaven spirit to spirit without a body, will we behold the full glory of God.

For us, the millennium will be a *transition period* during which we will learn about such things as omnipresence, omniscience, and omnipotence...or some aspects of it, surely. We will have a lot to learn before we're ready for eternity. Right now we are in an infantile stage, knowing very little. We don't even know what will happen tomorrow.

How about the nations?

The unsaved nations living in the kingdom will enjoy the good life. They will be exposed to the truth of the Lord, that is, the kind of a person He is. They will experience first hand His kindness and generosity. The earth will be filled with the knowledge of the Lord and little ones born into the kingdom will be instructed in His ways all their lives.

But will they like it? Remember they have but one nature, the old nature. They have no way to be born again and acquire the new nature. No, they won't like it. Hearing about holiness day in and day out will get old, and they'll come to hate it. Then, when Satan is loosed at the end of the 1000 years, they'll flock to him...every last one of them. There is no way environment can change a man's nature. This answers those who say, *"If I had been living in Adam's day, I wouldn't have made his mistake."* Well, even with the Lord living in their midst, and knowing more than Adam did...they rush to make the same mistake.

God was right in closing the salvation door.

When you first read that the opportunity to be saved ends when the Lord appears in the sky, did that sound unfair to you? Did God seem unjust in closing the salvation door because the program shifted from faith to sight? Now we see that after 1000 years under the personal reign of Jesus, the rest of mankind doesn't want Him. God makes no mistakes. He knows those who are His. The return of the Lord Jesus is so timed, that when He appears in the sky, the last person with a heart for God, says... *"Yes, Lord Jesus, I want you for my Savior!"* No one can be saved after Jesus is revealed in person.

While the wisdom and ways of God are past finding out, what He is pleased to reveal to us, thrills our hearts. The millennium itself is an ingenious apparatus for preparing us for eternity and proving that God is right in all His ways!

THE JEWISH DREAM

"And so all Israel will be saved: as it is written, there shall come out of Zion a deliverer who will turn godlessness away from Jacob; and this is My covenant with them, when I take away their sins" (Rom.11: 26).

The Jews of Jesus' day were very disappointed when it became obvious that the Lord came to die for men's sins and not to restore Israel to her former glory. They didn't want a dying Savior, they wanted a conquering king who would kick out the Romans and fulfill the Old Testament prophecies concerning Israel's role as the EMPRESS OF THE WORLD. That's why they rejected Him. Most Bible students are familiar with the many prophecies that speak of Israel's future greatness.

THE JEWISH DREAM SPRINGS FROM GOD'S PROMISES

Around 2000 B.C., when the world was truly dark, spiritually, God found a man among the earth's masses who had a heart that wanted to know Him and love Him. This man was Abraham. God asked this man to leave his home behind him and journey to a strange land. Abraham obeyed so completely, that God was thrilled with him. As a result, he and God became close, personal friends.

This man was the first Jew. Technically, no one was referred to as a Jew in those days, that came much later. However, within the context of this article it is proper to think of Abraham as the father of the Jewish race. And in that sense, the first Jew.

Because of His love for this man, God appeared to Abraham and promised him three things—backing His promise with an oath (Heb. 6:13-17). Though Abraham was old and incapable of having children, and married to a barren woman, God vowed He would make a NATION out of him. The nation to come from his loins would inherit the very land on which the patriarch was standing (Palestine). What's more, God declared all nations would be blessed through His seed, which, of course, was Jesus, the Messiah. So the promises had to do with three things: THE LAND, A NATION, AND THE MESSIAH. *

ISRAEL'S REBELLIOUS HISTORY

By 1000 B.C., King David had subdued the land and all their enemies were bringing tribute into the Jewish coffers. The country was rich, reaching its zenith of glory when Solomon became king. However, Solomon was a king who squandered his nation's wealth. He had 1000 women (300 wives and 700 concubines) and his women were worshippers of false gods. His wives corrupted his heart. While it's true that a nation

*** Historically it took 400 years to build the nation in Egypt. 400 more years passed before the inhabitants occupying the promised land were driven out that the Jews might possess it. 1000 years after that the promised Messiah arrived.**

goes as its leader goes, Israel fell into Idolatry and God was furious with her.

They lost the land. In 722 B.C. the Northern kingdom of Israel was taken into captivity by the Assyrians and in 586 B.C. the Southern kingdom went into captivity in Babylon. Even so, God kept His promise to Abraham and centuries later regathered the Jews in their own land. In 1948, when Israel was declared a Jewish state and was immediately recognized by the U.S., it was the result of God keeping His promise to Abraham.

It should be noted that Israel has fought God every step of the way. She was a stubborn and stiff-necked nation. Those are God's words, not mine (Deut.9:6). Forty days after God had made them His own nation on earth, they made a golden calf and worshipped it saying... *"This is the god that brought us out of Egypt"* (Ex. 32:4) God was ready to wipe out the entire nation, but Moses reminded Him of His promise to Abraham. So God continued to keep a watchful eye on the Jews and would keep His promises. However, from the days of Moses to this very day, they have rebelled against God, insisting on doing things their own way.

Here is a nation to whom God appeared personally at Mount Sinai; whom He took to Himself and commissioned to represent Him in the world. But alas, she became a Jewish club which no one could join unless they played by Jewish rules. As a servant of God, the nation was a dismal failure. Even so, God was faithful to His word and the people became a nation. They acquired the promised land and in time brought forth the Messiah. But it was all due to God's promise to Abraham, not the merits of the nation. God keeps His word.

HOW DOES GOD REGARD THE JEWS TODAY?

One might now ask: *"How does God feel about the Jews right now?"* The answer is: He doesn't particularly like them (as a nation), but He does love them. However, His love for them is not based on their merits as a people. The apostle Paul explains the basis of God's love for Israel :

"As far as the gospel is concerned, they are ENEMIES on your account (because we're the ones bringing the gospel to them); *but as far as election is concerned, they are LOVED on account of the patriarchs, for God's gifts and His call are irrevocable"* (Rom. 11:28,29).

Note that Paul is speaking of the Jewish NATION, NOT INDIVIDUALS. See how they are not loved for their own sake, but for the sake of the patriarchs, to whom God made the promises *on an oath.* Those promises are irrevocable and constitute the election of Israel, i.e., the land, nation and the Messiah. Israel will be the PRE-EMINENT NATION in the millennial kingdom because God keeps His promises, not because she deserves the honor.

DID GOD KNOW THE JEWS WOULD FAIL?

The failure of Israel was no surprise to God. Through the prophet Jeremiah, He predicted the failure of the deal He had made with the Jews at Sinai. At the same time, He announced a new deal would be made with them in the future. Here is Jeremiah's word concerning the new deal:

> ***"The time is coming," declares the Lord, "when I will make a new covenant (deal) with the house of Israel and with the house of Judah."*** **(Jer. 31:31).**

Here's how the writer to the Hebrews acknowledges the failure of the old covenant:

> ***"If there had been nothing wrong with that first covenant, there would have been no need for another"*** **(Heb. 8:7).**

On that score God said:

> ***"They did not remain faithful to my covenant, and I TURNED AWAY FROM THEM"*** **(Heb. 8:9b).**

The new covenant is spelled out in these words:

> ***"I will put my laws in their minds and write them on their hearts"*** **(Heb. 8: 10).**

See the difference between the two covenants? The Old Testament agreement was physical, outward and national, whereas the new one was spiritual and inward. One was written on stone tablets, the other written on human hearts. The old required animal sacrifices for sin, the new one, the single sacrifice of God's Lamb, Jesus.

The new covenant WOULD NOT BE NATIONAL, as was the original one. It would be PERSONAL AND INDIVIDUAL. That is, each Jew would be responsible to enter into this covenant personally, on his own. Israel was made a nation in a day, but the new covenant, which offers righteousness, is based on receiving Christ. Can we be sure? Yes. The verse quoted at the top of this article says they'll be saved... "*When I take away their sins.*" Sin can only be removed one way and that is through faith in the Lord Jesus. Nations cannot be made righteous, only individuals.

The NEW COVENANT was originally intended for Israel (Heb. 8:10). But they forfeited their place under this covenant when they rejected Jesus. There is NO new covenant for Christians. We come into the Jewish covenant through Christ. *"If ye be Christ's, then ye are Abraham's seed and heirs of the covenant"* (Gal. 3:29).

WHAT THE JEWS FORFEITED

The Jews haven't the faintest idea what it has cost them to reject Jesus. The *physical* promises, i.e., the nation, the land and the Messiah, still hold good for the Jews. And there are many other prophecies in the Old Testament concerning Israel's glory in the latter days which will all be fulfilled when the *nation* takes her place in the kingdom as the *"empress of the world."*

In rejecting Jesus, however, the Jews forfeited the *spiritual* promises, including salvation, eternal life, righteousness and the new birth as sons of God. What a terrible price for a people

THE TWO KINDS OF JEWS
TWO KINDS OF PROMISES

See the FEW in Israel? These are true Israelites, Jews who believe God's Word and are saved. They are God-lovers, chosen by Him in eternity. But the REST of the Jews, the unbelieving mass, are hardened by the Lord. Isaiah said a "narcotic spirit" was upon them. He is referring to the anesthetic effect of unbelief upon a person. If a man turns his back on the Light, he then faces in the direction of darkness. When an unbeliever does this, he becomes "anesthetized" against the truth. No Jew is born with spiritual blindness upon him. Anyone who wants to receive Christ may. But the one who DOESN'T want to, who prefers to walk in the way of his fathers (blindly following the Jewish tradition), will remain in that blindness which God has visited upon Israel for the last 3500 years.

Old Testament promises of blessing—were outward, physical and national.

New testament promises of blessing—were inward, spiritual and individual.

with so many opportunities. Even though Israel will hold the place of honor among the nations, she will be barred from entering New Jerusalem. Only the righteous will be allowed through the gates. Unless a person's name is written in the Lamb's book of life, he will not be permitted to enter the holy city (Rev. 21:27).

BUT JEWS CAN BE SAVED

As of this moment, any Jew who wants to can open his heart to Jesus and be saved. The new covenant offer is to Jew and Gentile alike, but as soon as the Lord appears, the salvation DOOR IS SHUT. In that same instant the opportunity to be saved is forever gone (Matt. 25:10). Neither Jew nor Gentile can be saved after that. It's fair, for no one is excluded. If a Jew is going to do something about his salvation, now is the time to act. The same holds true for Gentiles. Terrible times are just ahead and there is no way a person can get ready for them overnight.

OBSERVE: When the Old Testament speaks of Israel's blessings as enduring forever, it should be noted that NOTHING PHYSICAL endures forever (2 Cor. 4:18). The only eternal kingdom is that of the eternal King, the Lord Jesus. Only that which is IN HIM stands forever. The blessings promised to Jews that *appear* to be forever, are only available in Christ (2 Sam. 7:16). To receive them, one must be in Christ. The very word *"forever"* indicates those benefits have to do with ETERNITY, not with TIME.

WHAT ABOUT YOU?

Having read this exposition of the coming tribulation, can you picture yourself boldly facing the *TERRORS* of the beast? Will your trust in Christ see you through the trials no matter what it might cost you to stand up for Him? Are you satisfied that you're ready to die for Him? Be sure now, for there'll be no room for doubt in that day.

If you have the *slightest doubt* about your safety in Christ, you'll cave in before you've gone very far. There is no way to resist the beast's demands defiantly unless you know beyond a shadow of a doubt that you are secure in the Lord. Don't fool yourself about this. If you feel even the tiniest doubt about your spiritual security, take a moment to make sure. If you're too proud to check up on your salvation, that could be fatal.

TO CHECK UP ASK YOURSELF THE FOLLOWING:

❶ Do I know the difference between: *believe and receive?*

This is not a frivolous question, especially as it applies to your safety in Christ. The average person thinks he's saved if he BELIEVES IN CHRIST. And that can be tricky. In our day the word "*believe*" doesn't mean what it did to the early Christians. In fact, in our day, the word "*believe*" is often used to express doubt.

For example: Ask a housewife when her husband will be home and *if she isn't sure*, she'll say..."I *BELIEVE* he'll be home around noon." Were she sure, she'd say, "He'll be home at twelve." The point is, a person could easily think he's saved if he relies on the word BELIEVE, when He may not be saved at all. When it comes to your salvation, apply the word..."RECEIVE." A person knows whether he has received something or not. That way no room is left for doubt.

The apostle John lays great stress on the word—RECEIVE:

> ***"To as many as received Him, to them gave He the power to become the sons of God"* (John 1:12).**

To see the difference between believing and receiving, let's say I present you with a new Bible as a free gift. I hold it up where you can see it and then ask...*"Do you believe I am going to give this Bible to you?"* You have no reason to think I won't, so you say, "*Yes.*"

"Ah, but do you have it yet?"

"No, I don't have it yet," is your reply.

"You BELIEVE it's yours, but you still don't have it, right?"

"*Yes, that's true.*"

"Okay, reach out your hand and take it from me. Now you have it. It's in your hand and you know you've got it. But as long as it was in my hand—like this, you could believe and believe, and you still wouldn't have it. It's not yours until you take it into your own hands."

"And so it is with salvation. You can believe all you want to *about* Christ, but that won't save you. You must actually receive Jesus into your heart (or spirit) to be saved. You see, eternal life is IN Christ and if you don't have Him, you don't have eternal life."

The apostle John confirms that truth with these words:

> ***"Here is the documented word: God offers us eternal life and this life is in His Son. He that has the Son has life, and he that has not the Son of God, has not life"* (1 John 5:12).**

It all boils down to whether a person has Christ or not?

❷ The next step is to know for sure *how* to HAVE Jesus.

It's as simple as receiving a gift. The Lord offers us Himself as a free gift. All that is necessary is to accept the gift, talking to the Lord either silently or aloud. . .something like this:

"Lord Jesus, thank You for Your offer to save me from the lake of fire and give me eternal life. I now ask You to come into my heart and make

Yourself real to me. I've decided I'd rather die for You than suffer the lake of fire forever."

This can be done in the privacy of your pillow. You don't need a preacher or anyone else to help you. You know whether you mean business or not. Only you and God know what goes on inside your heart. The transaction is between you and Him—and no one else.

❸ If you have already done this and know for sure that Jesus resides in you, the third step is to get used to His voice as He speaks to your spirit. You'll need that kind of closeness when you face the threats of the beast. The Lord's voice can be very reassuring when your life is on the line.

The only way you can get used to the Lord's voice is by spending time talking to Him in prayer and listening for His voice as you read the Bible. The gospel of John is great for this. It contains long passages with nothing but the Lord's words and these are fabulous for getting used to hearing Him speak within your spirit. In time, you get to know Him so well, you have no trouble turning a deaf ear to the whispers of Satan.

❹ If you have never actually invited the Lord into your heart or are not sure where you stand with the Lord, you can get it settled quickly by following the same steps outlined above. You can do this in a jail cell, a concentration camp or before a firing squad. But you must do it, or you'll end up in the lake of fire. You want to avoid that at all costs, for the term "lake of fire," translates into indescribable agony forever.

❺ All right, you're safe and secure in Christ and you feel you're ready to die rather than deny the Lord. What about your children? Your friends and relatives? Knowing what is coming, how will you prepare them? It would probably be a good idea to see that they read this book. Or if your family is used to doing things together, you could discuss portions of the book at the dinner table. It would be cruel to say nothing and let them go blindly into the tribulation with no preparation.

"He who stands firm to the end will be saved."

Have you read those words before? Of course. They're from Matthew 24, where the Lord discusses His return and the awful things that will happen to Christians before He appears in the sky.

> ***"Then you will be handed over to be persecuted and put to death, and you will be hated by all nations because of Me. At that time, many will turn away from the faith and will betray and hate each other...because of the increase of wickedness, the love of most will grow cold, BUT HE WHO STANDS FIRM TO THE END WILL BE SAVED."***

After reading through this book, you know those words apply TO YOU—if you're alive at the coming of the Lord. You and your loved ones will be terribly pressured to deny Jesus and accept the mark of the beast. The false prophets will cleverly see to it that *"a man's enemies will be those of his own household,"* for *"brother will betray brother to death, and a father his child; children will rebel against their parents and have them put to death"* (Matt. 10:21).

You know this is coming.

A few verses later the Lord instructs us not to fear those who can kill the body but cannot kill the soul (Matt.10:28). So when the death squads aim their guns at you and your children, have no fear. All they can do is kill the body; besides you'll all be getting new bodies before long. So die with His praise on your lips! Inspire your children to do the same!

Here again are the words of the 3rd angel in Chapter 14:

> ***"If anyone worships the beast and his image and receives his mark on the forehead or on the hand, he too will drink the wine of God's fury which has been poured full strength into the cup of His wrath!"*** **(vs. 10).**

And the angel followed that, saying:

> ***"This calls for patient endurance on the part of the saints who obey God's commandments and remain faithful to Jesus"*** **(vs. 12).**

Now you know what "stand firm to the end" means. It means hang in there and don't deny Jesus no matter what it might cost you, even death. The "END" that Jesus is referring to, is the end of your life. In the final days the choice will be:

choose Christ and live forever, choose the beast and die forever. That's why Jesus stated the matter as He did...

"HE WHO STANDS FIRM TO THE END WILL BE SAVED."

CAUTION:

DON'T PUT THIS BOOK IN YOUR BOOKCASE.

It won't do anyone any good there. Pass it around, share it, make your investment in it pay off. Warn your family and friends, because it takes time for people to reach the place where they're ready to die for Jesus. Decide for yourself to shift from living for the pleasures and comforts of the world, to living for Jesus. Give Him first place in your life...ahead of family and earthly security. You won't be sorry.

ACKNOWLEDGMENTS

When I began working on this commentary, certain views were sharply defined in my mind. But as I proceeded through the chapters, I found the Holy Spirit reshaping my views on point after point. So the book came out far differently from what I expected when I started. Therefore I must first acknowledge the help of the Holy Spirit, before I give credit to others. The finished product is truly the work of the Spirit.

Humanly speaking, a work such as this requires more than one pair of hands. So I further acknowledge the wonderful help of some dear friends and family around me, people I appreciate deeply:

Warren Belknap
Evelyn Broadley
Susie Gallegos
Jack Kerr
Linda Lovett
Marjorie Lovett
Marc Ugarte

I am indeed thankful for the encouragements of many friends across the country, some of whom recognized the need for this work before I did. I'm sure the Lord used their letters and prayers to get me going and keep me on track. Most of all I thank God for His kindness in letting me enjoy His witness all the way. Isn't He wonderful!

LOVETT'S LIGHTS BOOKS

#526—LOVETT'S LIGHTS ON JOHN with Rephrased Text—By C. S. Lovett • 588 Lights, illustrated with paintings, 336 pages.

#530—LOVETT'S LIGHTS ON GALATIANS, EPHESIANS, PHILIPPIANS, COLOSSIANS, 1 & 2 THESSALONIANS with Rephrased Text—By C. S. Lovett • 370 Lights, 240 pages.

#536—LOVETT'S LIGHTS ON ACTS with Rephrased Text—By C. S. Lovett • 687 Lights, illustrated with drawings, paintings, graphs and over 20 maps showing Paul's journeys, 448 pages.

#538—LOVETT'S LIGHTS ON ROMANS with Rephrased Text—By C. S. Lovett • 468 Lights, illustrated with drawings and paintings, 432 pages.

#541—LOVETT'S LIGHTS ON HEBREWS with Rephrased Text—By C. S. Lovett • 279 Lights, illustrated with drawings, paintings, graphs, 352 pages.

#558—LOVETT'S LIGHTS ON THE SERMON ON THE MOUNT with Rephrased Text—By C. S. Lovett • illustrated with drawings, 176 pages.

LOVETT'S LIGHTS BOOKLETS

#209—LOVETT'S LIGHTS ON FIRST JOHN
with Rephrased Text—By C. S. Lovett • 24 pages

#511—LOVETT' LIGHTS ON PHILIPPIANS
with Rephrased Text—By C. S. Lovett • 32 pages

#505—LOVETT'S LIGHTS ON JAMES
with Rephrased Text—By C. S. Lovett • 32 pages

WRITE FOR FREE CATALOG— **All of Dr. Lovett's works** are available from:

PERSONAL CHRISTIANITY

Box 549

Baldwin Park, CA 91706

HELPING CHRISTIANS "PREPARE FOR HIS APPEARING" SINCE 1951.

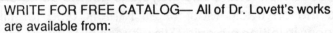

THE CHART

Spread across the next two pages you will find a chart picturing the entire book of Revelation. Observe that the central feature is the scroll. Particularly note how the 7th seal contains the 7 trumpets, the last of which covers not only the 7 bowls of God's wrath, but the rest of the human story. See how the rapture occurs at the last trumpet, but before the bowls are poured out. The final event of the Revelation is the great white throne judgment of the dead.

The chart is available in a larger size for teaching classes. You may order them from Personal Christianity or your Christian bookstore.

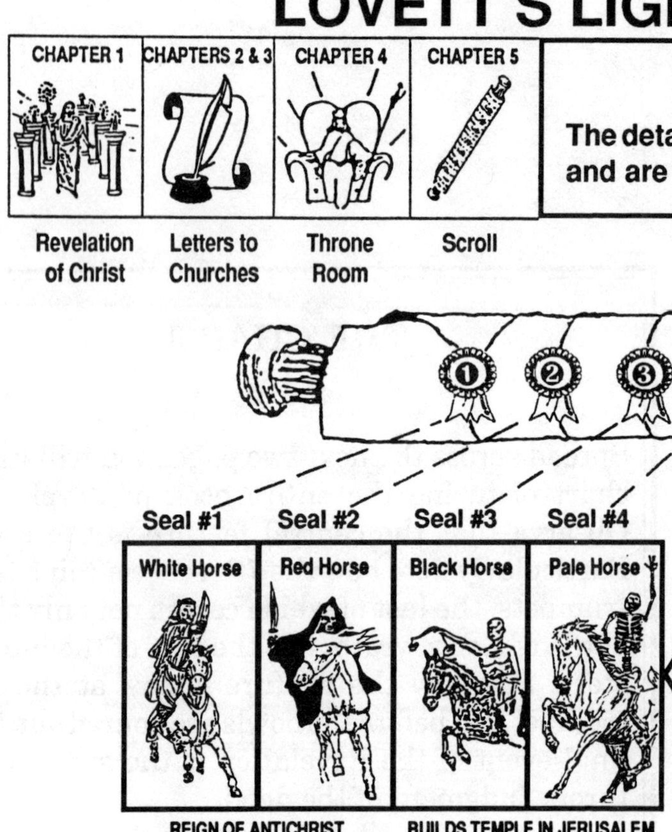

REIGN OF ANTICHRIST

BUILDS TEMPLE IN JERUSALEM

MAKES COVENANT WITH THE JEWS

"THE BEGINNING OF SORROWS" 42 MONTHS

SP

RAPTURE & RESURRECTION of the Saints

Bowl #1	Bowl #2	Bowl #3	Bowl #4	Bowl #5	Bowl
<u>Land</u> sores on men	<u>Sea</u> turns to blood all life dies	<u>Rivers</u> all blood	<u>Sun</u> scorching heat	<u>Beast's throne</u> kingdom darkened	<u>3 fro demo</u> summ the kin the ea ARM

THE WRATH OF GOD

ON REVELATION

CHAPTERS 6—to—22

ters 6—to—22 are all contained in the scroll below
was instructed to send to the churches.

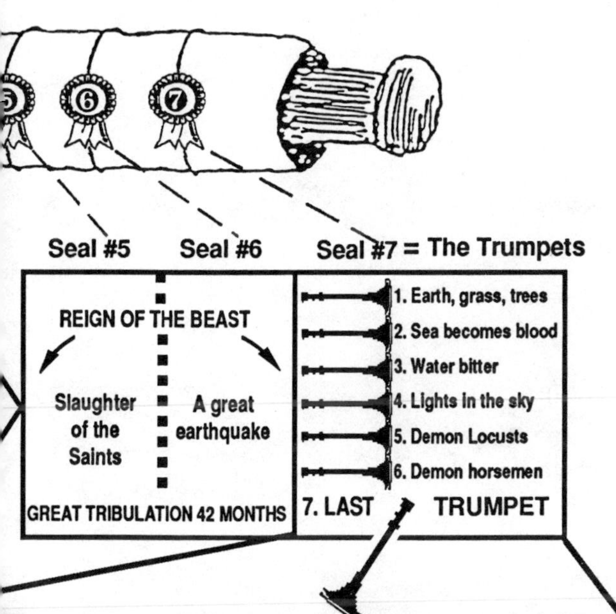

OF THE LAST TRUMPET

Saints judged in the sky

wl #7

stones	Christ's decent to Olivet with Saints	Jesus' Kingdom	Nations	1000 years	Great White Throne
thquake OON		set up on earth Saints assigned their jobs	are judged and assigned their places in the kingdom	Jesus reigns from New Jerusalem Satan loosed	final judgment of the dead

EARTHLY REIGN OF CHRIST

ETERNITY BEGINS

Notes: